Ken Russell: Interviews

Conversations with Filmmakers Series
Gerald Peary, General Editor

KEN
RUSSELL

I N T E R V I E W S

Edited by Barry Keith Grant

University Press of Mississippi / Jackson

The University Press of Mississippi is the scholarly publishing agency of
the Mississippi Institutions of Higher Learning: Alcorn State University,
Delta State University, Jackson State University, Mississippi State University,
Mississippi University for Women, Mississippi Valley State University,
University of Mississippi, and University of Southern Mississippi.

www.upress.state.ms.us

The University Press of Mississippi is a member
of the Association of University Presses.

Library of Congress Cataloging-in-Publication Data

Names: Grant, Barry Keith, 1947– editor.
Title: Ken Russell : interviews / Barry Keith Grant.
Other titles: Conversations with filmmakers series.
Description: Jackson : University Press of Mississippi, 2024. | Series: Conversations
    with filmmakers series | Includes bibliographical references and index.
Identifiers: LCCN 2024009336 (print) | LCCN 2024009337 (ebook) |
    ISBN 9781496851840 (hardback) | ISBN 9781496851833 (trade paperback) |
    ISBN 9781496851826 (epub) | ISBN 9781496851819 (epub) | ISBN 9781496851802 (pdf) |
    ISBN 9781496851796 (pdf)
Subjects: LCSH: Russell, Ken, 1927–2011—Interviews. | Motion picture producers
    and directors—Interviews.
Classification: LCC PR6118.U864 Z46 2024 (print) | LCC PR6118.U864 (ebook) |
    DDC 791.4302/33092—dc23/eng/20240506
LC record available at https://lccn.loc.gov/2024009336
LC ebook record available at https://lccn.loc.gov/2024009337

British Library Cataloging-in-Publication Data available

Contents

Introduction

In the 1970s filmmaker Ken Russell gained a reputation as the enfant terrible of British cinema. His oeuvre, like the man himself, was considered to be unrestrained, excessive, in bad taste. In his impolitic work, which featured a dialectic clash of realism and high-voltage fantasy, any conception of a responsibly moral British national cinema crumbled and collapsed.

Russell first drew notice between 1959 and 1962 for a series of unorthodox biographical films made for the BBC's *Monitor* series on such artists as Béla Bartók, Claude Debussy, and Isadora Duncan. In more than one interview, Russell explained how an intense aesthetic appreciation of music was a transformative experience for him as a young man and that his typical working method was to listen to music while writing. In these early works, Russell was already exhibiting an unconventional approach to biography that combined a loosening of historical fact, a highly aesthetic interpretation, and an acute personal vision. He went so far as to claim in his interview with George Hickenlooper that "there is no such thing as historical accuracy."

After his extraordinarily successful television film on British composer Edward Elgar in 1962, Russell was given the opportunity to move into feature filmmaking. His first two theatrical features, the offbeat comedy *French Dressing* (1964) and his adaptation of a Len Deighton thriller, *Billion Dollar Brain* (1967), starring Michael Caine, were commercial flops. However, Russell's career changed dramatically with his adaptation of D. H. Lawrence's *Women in Love* (1969). A commercial and critical success, the film garnered an Oscar for actress Glenda Jackson, establishing her as a major star of the 1970s. Its bold erotic sensibility, manifested in the famous nude wrestling scene between Alan Bates and Oliver Reed (another actor made famous by Russell), encouraged Russell to continue exploring the related themes of art and sexuality, especially, although not exclusively, in relation to music.

Russell saw artists, himself included, as visionaries who are deeply misunderstood by society. He told Lola Borg that he identified with D. H. Lawrence. Like Lawrence's alter ego in *Women in Love*, Rupert Birkin, Russell was a committed romantic who sought to liberate repressed desire through his sexually charged cinema. Birkin is related to China Blue (Kathleen Turner), the prostitute of

Crimes of Passion (1984), in her ability to act out for her male clients a variety of sexual fantasies. She is a performance artist who, like so many of Russell's characters, seeks to artfully transcend social and sexual constraints and taboos through her body.

Russell's films return again and again to themes of sexuality, often issues involving the burdens of masculine identity and the way of all flesh. His examination of Tchaikovsky in *The Music Lovers* (1971) concentrates on the composer's conflict between homoerotic desire and the dominant ideology of heterosexuality. Similarly, his film *Valentino* (1977) depicts the eponymous silent movie star as a man destroyed by his very popularity, since his sexual appeal for women is seen as a threat to the power of the American male. In the interview with Ric Gentry, Russell insists that he has no "theory of sexuality" but nevertheless goes on to discuss the relationship between sex and death that characterizes, for him, the modern condition. It's a relationship that is central to the imagery of Russell's cinema, as psychiatrist Anthony Clare points out in his short interview with the filmmaker.

The television film *Dance of the Seven Veils* (1970), about German composer Richard Strauss and his relationship to Nazism, elicited many complaints from viewers and a parliamentary motion condemning it. Russell's response? He said to Gene Phillips, "The television audience are all asleep in their armchairs. It's a good thing to shake them up, even if it's only as far as the phone." Russell maintained his particular interest in the erotics and sexual politics of music with the feature films *The Music Lovers*, *The Boy Friend* (1971), *Mahler* (1973), *Tommy* (1975), and *Lisztomania* (1975). Many viewers thought *The Music Lovers* was inappropriate, as they were disturbed by Russell's description of the film as "the story of a love affair between a homosexual and a nymphomaniac." *Lisztomania's* unrestrained use of Nazi and pop-culture iconography, climaxing with Franz Liszt (Roger Daltrey) riding a huge phallus, demonstrated to many Russell's complete loss of aesthetic control. With the exception of *Tommy*, virtually guaranteed success because of the Who's hit rock opera on which it is based, none of these films achieved a popularity comparable to *Women in Love*.

After the commercial failure of *Valentino*, Russell's career foundered. His later work had him searching for a form to contain his themes, just as the protagonist of *Altered States* (1980) almost loses his body in pursuit of his mystic vision. Of the six feature films he made in the 1980s, only *Gothic* (1986) and *Salome's Last Dance* (1988) fit comfortably within his distinctive approach to biographies about artists. *The Lair of the White Worm* (1988), adapted from a novel by Bram Stoker, showed Russell once again employing the imagery of sexual excess, although now as self-parody. He found it increasingly difficult to get funding, and in the end was restricted to making movies with his own equipment, using family and friends as actors, and with virtually no budget.

Throughout the ups and downs, Russell alternately embraced and resented being characterized as an enfant terrible. More than one interview began by referring to Russell's harsh reputation only to have it denied when actually meeting the filmmaker. Herb Lightman: "Having been conditioned by his incredibly flamboyant public relations, I almost expected some sort of foaming-at-the-mouth mad scene, but Russell acknowledges the introduction with polite restraint." Ric Gentry imagined the director as "flamboyant, primal, laconic, mad," only to find him "quite the opposite . . . even cherubic." Asked about his experience with interviewers, Russell told Patrick McGilligan and Janet Maslin, "Well, they always start off with, 'Now you're called a controversial director. . . .' You can fit in the rest from there." But in truth Russell never played it straight for long: he confided to McGilligan and Maslin that when not making films he liked to "sit on a mountaintop and look at the sun." In his 1989 made-for-television autobiography, *A British Picture*, subtitled *Portrait of an Enfant Terrible*, the Russell figure (portrayed by his son Rupert) also played up his eccentricity, sporting a rainbow-colored shock of hair.

In the earliest interview included in this book, with Gordon Gow in 1970, Russell already had decided, "I deliberately want to shock people into awareness," because viewers "gain a fresh perspective." In the later interviews, there is a sense that Russell was saying things for the sake of their shock value, fulfilling what was expected by journalists. By the time of his interview with Anthony Clare in 1988, he admitted, "When I do slightly ridiculous things at times," it was for garnering publicity.

He told Marjorie Bilbow in 1976 that his imagery came from his subconscious, particularly evoked when listening to classical music. He similarly explained to Ric Gentry, "Nothing in my work is conscious, hardly anything"—although he qualified this by declaring that the techniques by which he brought his imagery to the screen were "very precise." Russell could be extremely articulate about his directorial work, as when he explained to Gentry the reasoning behind the imagery in the hallucination sequences of *Altered States*. But he really came alive and was most engaged, as one might expect, when discussing music, composers, and his approach to biography, whether it was talking about Tchaikovsky and *The Music Lovers* with Gordon Gow, Elgar with John C. Tibbetts, or *Tommy* with McGilligan and Maslin. In the interview on *Valentino*, as author Herb Lightman observed, Russell even uses musical terms—"staccato," "legato"—to describe his use of camera movement, language he repeated when talking with Gentry five years later.

Beyond controversy, how does Russell rank as a filmmaker? He has had his staunch defenders. Gene D. Phillips, Joseph Gomez, and Michael Dempsey were among the first critics willing to look favorably at his films. But often critics have not been kind to Russell's work, as exemplified by Robin Wood's dismissal of it as hysterical self-loathing. Reviewing *The Devils* (1971), British critic Alexander Walker wrote that the film was "monstrously indecent"; and when the two met on television, Russell hit Walker on the head with a rolled-up copy of the *Evening Standard* containing the critic's negative review. Russell never mellowed in his disdain for Walker, and he remained unapologetic for physically attacking the critic. In the interview with Stuart Jeffries in this volume, one of his last, Russell said, "I wish it had been an iron bar."

In 2011 Todd McCarthy wrote of the director in the *Hollywood Reporter*, "Personally, Russell's obstreperousness could always be relied upon. Never did an interview with him fail to produce some personal or professional insult or an assault on whosoever might provide an obstacle for the director's unfettered creativity. For film critics Russell reserved a special level of hell all their own" (November 28, 2011). The interviews collected in this book are ample evidence of Russell's orneriness—read, for example, what he tells Lynn Barber about *Godfather III* and Sophia Coppola—and it's on display whether he is criticizing critics, filmmakers, and producers, or even, very occasionally, railing against his own work.

The editor gratefully acknowledges the contributions of the following friends and colleagues without whom this volume would not have been possible: Gerald Peary, Dan Barnowski, Kevin Flanagan, Graham Fuller, Claudia Gorbman, Max Tessier, and Ian Gordon and Tanya Sicoli, Brock University library. At the University of Mississippi Press, Emily Snyder Bandy, Corley Longmire, and copyeditor Lisa Williams worked diligently on the manuscript and guided it to publication.

BKG

Chronology

1927   Born Henry Kenneth Alfred Russell July 3 in Southampton, to Ethel and Henry Russell.

1941   Becomes a cadet at the Royal Naval College at Pangbourne. Later joins the Merchant Navy.

1945   Released from naval service after a nervous breakdown.

1948   Studies ballet but eventually turns to photography.

1953   Enrolls at the South West Essex Technical College and School of Art (Walthamstow Tech) to study photography.

1955   Russell's series of "Teddy Girl" photos published in *Picture Post* magazine.

1956   Makes his first important short, *Peepshow*. Converts to Roman Catholicism.

1957   Marries Shirley Ann Kingdon (div. 1978). Makes *Amelia and the Angel*.

1959   Russell is hired at the BBC, where he makes a series of short documentary films for the BBC arts program *Monitor* and then *Omnibus*, beginning with his first professional 35mm film, *John Betjeman, a Poet in London*.

1962   *Elgar* broadcast on *Monitor* (November 11), marking the first time that the BBC devotes a feature-length film to one artistic figure and the first time that reenactments are used.

1964   Russell's first feature, *French Dressing*, is released.

1965   *The Debussy Film*, starring Oliver Reed, telecast on May 18.

1966   *Isadora Duncan: The Biggest Dancer in the World*, Russell's first important film for the *Omnibus* TV series, is telecast on September 22.

1967   *Dante's Inferno* telecast on December 22. Russell's second theatrical feature, *Billion Dollar Brain*, the third Harry Palmer film, starring Michael Caine, is released.

1968   *Song of Summer* telecast on September 15.

1969   *Women in Love* released to critical and commercial success, including Russell's only Academy Award nomination for Best Director.

1970   Russell's last film for the BBC, *Dance of the Seven Veils: A Comic Strip in Seven Episodes on the Life of Richard Strauss*, is telecast to great controversy, prompting Russell to move into feature filmmaking.

1971   *The Music Lovers*, *The Devils*, and *The Boy Friend* all released.

1972   *Savage Messiah* released.

1975   *Tommy*, Russell's biggest commercial success, is released, followed by *Lisztomania*.

1978   Returns to television for *Clouds of Glory*, a two-part film about Lake Poets William Wordsworth and Samuel Taylor Coleridge, telecast on July 9 and 16.

1980   Russell makes *Altered States* in Hollywood, one of his biggest commercial successes.

1983   Marries second wife, Vivian Jolly (div. 1991).

1984   *Crimes of Passion* with Anthony Perkins and Kathleen Turner released.

1985   Establishes Sitting Duck, a production company to make video clips and music videos.

1986   Makes *Gothic*, the first of four films for Vestron.

1989   *A British Picture* (also published as a book) telecast. *The Rainbow* is released, uniting Russell with Glenda Jackson.

1992   Marries third wife, Hetty Baynes (div. 1999).

2001   Marries fourth wife, Lisi Tribble.

2006   Russell's home in East Boldre, New Forest District, is destroyed by a fire that consumes much of his memorabilia and record collection (April 3).

2011   Russell dies in London on November 27.

Filmography

Note: cast members appear as themselves unless otherwise noted.

PEEPSHOW (1956)
Director: **Ken Russell**
Writer: **Ken Russell**
Cinematography: M. C. Plomer (**Ken Russell**)
Editor: **Ken Russell**
Cast: Norman Dewhurst (magician), Shirley Russell (doll), Tom Laden, Philip Evans, Terry Rhodes, Mike Shaw
Black & white, 22 minutes

AMELIA AND THE ANGEL (1957)
Producer: **Ken Russell**, Anthony G. Evans
Director: **Ken Russell**
Writer: **Ken Russell**, Anthony G. Evans
Cinematography: **Ken Russell**
Editor: **Ken Russell**
Costumes: Shirley Russell
Choreography: Helen May
Cast: Mercedes Quadros, Mika van Bloemen (Mike Sniver), Helen Ulman (the artist's model), E. Collins (the stallholder), Elisha Manasseh (the artist), Helen May (the dancing teacher), Nicholas O'Brien (the brother), Elizabeth Collings, Evangeline Averre
Black & white, 26 minutes

MAKING AN ACTION PAINTING (1957)
Director: **Ken Russell**
Cinematography: **Ken Russell**
Cast: William Green
Black & white

LOURDES (1958)
Director: **Ken Russell**

Cinematography: **Ken Russell**
Black & white, 40 minutes

POET'S LONDON (JOHN BETJEMAN, A POET IN LONDON) (1959)
Monitor, BBC-TV (first telecast March 1)
Producer: Peter Newington
Director: **Ken Russell**
Writer: John Betjeman
Editing: Allan Tyrer, Huw Wheldon
Cast: John Betjeman
Black & white, 12 minutes

GORDON JACOB (1959)
Monitor, BBC-TV (first telecast March 29)
Producer: Peter Newington
Director: **Ken Russell**
Cinematography: John McGlashan
Editing: Huw Wheldon
Cast: Humphrey Burton, Gordon Jacob, Huw Wheldon
Black & white, 17 minutes

GUITAR CRAZE (1959)
Monitor, BBC-TV (first telecast June 7)
Producer: Peter Newington
Director: **Ken Russell**
Cast: Davy Graham, Fritz Kortner, Robert Robinson
Black & white, 17 minutes

VARIATIONS ON A MECHANICAL THEME (1959)
Monitor, BBC-TV (first telecast September 27)
Producer: Peter Newington
Director: **Ken Russell**
Writer: Alex Atkinson
Cast: Frank Duncan, Jerome Robbins
Black & white, 13 minutes

SCOTTISH PAINTERS/TWO SCOTTISH PAINTERS: COLQUHOUN AND
MACBRYDE) (1959)
Monitor, BBC-TV (first telecast October 25)
Producer: Peter Newington

Director: **Ken Russell**
Editing: Allan Tyrer
Cast: Robert Colquhoun, Robert MacBryde
Black & white, 12 minutes

PORTRAIT OF A GOON (1959)
Monitor, BBC-TV (first telecast December 16)
Director: **Ken Russell**
Cast: Spike Milligan
Black & white, 14 minutes

MARIE RAMBERT REMEMBERS (1960)
Monitor, BBC-TV (first telecast January 17)
Producer: Peter Newington
Director: **Ken Russell**
Cinematography: John McGlashan
Cast: Marie Rambert
Black & white, 22 minutes

JOURNEY INTO A LOST WORLD (ARCHITECTURE OF ENTERTAIN-
MENT) (1960)
Monitor, BBC-TV (first telecast March 28)
Producer: Peter Newington
Director: **Ken Russell**
Writer: John Betjeman
Editing: Huw Wheldon, Allan Tyrer
Cast: John Betjeman, Mary McCarthy
Black & white, 22 minutes

CRANKO AT WORK (1960)
Monitor, BBC-TV (first telecast April 24)
Director: **Ken Russell**
Cinematography: John McGlashan
Editing: Huw Wheldon
Cast: John Cranko, Bernard Cribbins, David Lee, Gillian Lynne, Carole Shelley,
Johnnie Wade, Huw Wheldon
Black & white

THE MINERS' PICNIC (1960)
Monitor, BBC-TV (first telecast July 3)

Producer: Peter Newington
Director: **Ken Russell**
Cinematography: John McGlashan, Alex Pearce
Editing: Huw Wheldon
Cast: Huw Wheldon, Douglas Cooper, John Berger, Pablo Picasso
Black & white

A HOUSE IN BAYSWATER (1960)
BBC Film Department (first telecast August 26)
Producer: **Ken Russell**
Director: **Ken Russell**
Writer: **Ken Russell**
Cinematography: John Ray
Music: John Hotchkis
Editing: Allan Tyrer
Cast: James Burr, Elizabeth Collins, Margaret Ann Croft, David Hurn, Louisa
May Laden, Thomas Raymond Laden, Helen May
Black & white, 28 minutes

SHELAGH DELANEY'S SALFORD (1960)
Monitor, BBC-TV (first telecast September 25)
Producer: Humphrey Burton, Nancy Thomas
Director: **Ken Russell**
Cinematography: Tony Leggo
Editing: Allan Tyrer, Huw Wheldon
Cast: Shelagh Delaney, Joe Delaney
Black & white, 15 minutes

THE LIGHT FANTASTIC (1960)
Monitor, BBC-TV (first telecast December 18)
Director: **Ken Russell**
Writer: Ron Hitchens
Cinematography: Tony Leggo
Editing: Allan Tyrer
Cast: Ron Hitchens (presenter), Jim Fowell (horn dancer)
Black & white, 24 minutes

LOTTE LENYA SINGS KURT WEILL (1961)
Monitor, BBC-TV (first telecast March 26)
Producer: Huw Wheldon

Director: **Ken Russell**, Humphrey Burton
Cinematography: Michael Bond
Music: Kurt Weill
Editing: Huw Wheldon
Cast: Lotte Lenya
Black & white, 45 minutes

OLD BATTERSEA HOUSE (PRE-RAPHAELITE MUSEUM) (1961)
Monitor, BBC-TV (first telecast June 4)
Director: **Ken Russell**
Black & white, 17 minutes

PROKOFIEV: PORTRAIT OF A SOVIET COMPOSER (1961)
Monitor, BBC-TV (first telecast June 18)
Producer: Huw Wheldon
Director: **Ken Russell**
Editing: Allan Tyrer
Cast: V. P. Gregory (Zhdanov), Boris Ranevsky (Rimsky-Korsakov/Prokofiev),
Joyce Rathbone (music teacher)
Black & white, 28 minutes

LONDON MOODS (1961)
Monitor, BBC-TV (first telecast November 5)
Director: **Ken Russell**
Black & white, 10 minutes

ANTONIO GAUDI (1961)
Monitor, BBC-TV (first telecast December 3)
Producer: Humphrey Burton, Nancy Thomas
Director: **Ken Russell**
Black & white, 15 minutes

LONELY SHORE (1962)
Monitor, BBC-TV (first telecast January 14)
Producer: Nancy Thomas, Humphrey Burton
Director: **Ken Russell**
Writer: Jacquetta Hawkes
Editing: Allan Tyrer
Black & white, 16 minutes

POP GOES THE EASEL (1962)
Monitor, BBC-TV (first telecast March 25)
Producer: Huw Wheldon
Director: **Ken Russell**
Cinematography: Ken Higgins
Editing: Allan Tyrer
Cast: Peter Blake, Derek Boshier, Pauline Boty, Peter Phillips
Black & white, 44 minutes

PRESERVATION MAN (1962)
Monitor, BBC-TV (first telecast May 20)
Producer: Humphrey Burton, Nancy Thomas
Director: **Ken Russell**
Cast: Bruce Lacey, Barbelle Martin
Black & white, 16 minutes

MR. CHESHER'S TRACTION ENGINES (1962)
Monitor, BBC-TV (first telecast July 1)
Director: **Ken Russell**
Black & white, 15 minutes

ELGAR (1962)
Monitor, BBC-TV (first telecast November 11)
Producer: Humphrey Burton
Director: **Ken Russell**
Writer: **Ken Russell**
Cinematography: Ken Higgins
Editing: Allan Tyrer
Cast: Peter Brett (Mr. Elgar), Rowena Gregory (Mrs. Elgar), George McGrath
(Sir Edward Elgar)
Black & white, 55 minutes

WATCH THE BIRDIE (1963)
Monitor, BBC-TV (first telecast June 9)
Director: **Ken Russell**
Cast: David Hurn, Alita Naughton
Black & white, 28 minutes

FRENCH DRESSING (1964)
Associated British Picture Corporation

Producer: Kenneth Harper
Director: **Ken Russell**
Screenplay: Peter Brett
Cinematography: Kenneth Higgins
Art Direction: Jack Stephens
Costumes: Shirley Russell
Music: Georges Delerue
Editing: Jack Slade
Cast: James Booth (Jim Stephens), Roy Kinnear (Henry Liggott), Marisa Mell (François Fayol), Alita Naughton (Judy), Bryan Pringle (The Mayor), Robert Robinson, Germain Delbat (French Woman), Norman Pitt (Westbourne Mayor), Henry McCarty (Bridgemouth Mayor), Sandor Elès (Vladek)
Black & white, 86 minutes (cut to 65 minutes for North American release)

BARTOK (1964)
Monitor, BBC-TV (first telecast May 24)
Producer: David Jones
Director: **Ken Russell**
Writer: **Ken Russell**
Cinematography: Charles Parnall
Editing: Allan Tyrer
Cast: Boris Ranevsky (Béla Bartók), Pauline Boty (Prostitute), Sandor Elès (Client), Peter Brett (Bluebeard), Rosalind Watkins (Judith), Huw Wheldon (narrator)
Black & white, 50 minutes

THE DOTTY WORLD OF JAMES LLOYD (1964)
Monitor, BBC-TV (first telecast July 5)
Producer: David E. James
Director: **Ken Russell**
Cast: James Lloyd
Black & white

DIARY OF A NOBODY (1964)
Six, BBC-2 (first telecast December 12)
Producer: John McGrath
Director: **Ken Russell**
Writer: John McGrath, **Ken Russell**
Cinematography: Ken Westbury
Production Design: Stewart Marshall
Costumes: Shirley Russell

Music: Ivor Cutler
Editing: Michael Bradsell, Michael Johns
Cast: Murray Melvin (Lupin Pooter), Brian Murphy (Mr. Gowing), Vivian Pickles (Mrs. James), Bryan Pringle (Charles Pooter), Avril Elgar (Mrs. Caroline Pooter), Jonathan Cecil (Mr. Cummings), Anne Jameson (Sarah), Anne Strunk (Daisy Mutlar), Bartlett Mullins (Farmerson), John H. Moore (Mr. Finsworth), Violet Dix (Mrs. Finsworth), Norman Dewhurst (curate), John Langley (greengrocer's boy), Junia (Bibbs)
Black & white, 38 minutes

(MONITOR SPECIAL PRESENTING) THE DEBUSSY FILM (1965)
Monitor, BBC-TV (first telecast May 18)
Producer: **Ken Russell**
Director: **Ken Russell**
Writer: **Ken Russell**, Melvyn Bragg
Cinematography: Ken Westbury, John McGlashan
Costumes: Velma Buckle
Editing: Allan Tyrer
Cast: Oliver Reed (Claude Debussy), Vladek Sheybal (Pierre Louÿs/Director), Annette Robertson (Gaby), Iza Teller (Madame Bardac), Penny Service (Lily), Vernon Dobtcheff (The Actor), Jane Lumb (Saint Sebastian), Yvonne Antrobus (stage Lily), Verity Edmett (Zohra, the slave girl), Stephanie Randall (secretary), Janet Fairhead (Chouchou at thirteen), Alison Fisk (Maeterlinck's girlfriend), Ian Flintoff (stage Debussy), Elna Pearl (Vasmer daughter), Yvette Rees (stage Mme. Bardac), Victoria Russell (Chouchou)
Black & white, 82 minutes

ALWAYS ON SUNDAY (1965)
Monitor, BBC-TV (first telecast June 29)
Producer: **Ken Russell**
Director: **Ken Russell**
Writer: **Ken Russell**, Melvyn Bragg
Cinematography: John McGlashan
Production Design: Luciana Arrighi
Costumes: Joyce Hammond
Editing: Larry Toft
Cast: James Lloyd (Henri Rousseau), Annette Robertson (Alfred Jarry), Bryan Pringle (Pere Ubu), Jacqueline Cook (Mere Ubu), Roland MacLeod (Apollinaire), Iza Teller (Josephine), Dorothy-Rose Gribble (Eugénie), Sheila Van Bloemen (first

neighbor), Ann Mitchell (second neighbor), Joanna Rigby (daughter), Mihael Van Bloeman (picture dealer), Oliver Reed (narrator)
Black & white, 45 minutes

DON'T SHOOT THE COMPOSER (1966)
Sunday Night, BBC-TV (first telecast January 9)
Producer: **Ken Russell**
Director: **Ken Russell**
Cinematography: Ken Westbury
Music: Georges Delerue
Cast: Georges Delereu, **Ken Russell**
Black & white

ISADORA DUNCAN, THE BIGGEST DANCER IN THE WORLD (1966)
Omnibus, BBC-TV (first telecast September 22)
Producer: **Ken Russell**
Director: **Ken Russell**
Teleplay: **Ken Russell**, Sewell Stokes
Cinematography: Dick Bush, Brian Tufano
Production Design: Luciana Arrighi
Costumes: Joyce Hammond, Shirley Russell
Choreography: Bice Bellairs
Editing: Michael Bradsell, Roger Crittenden
Cast: Vivian Pickles (Isadora Duncan), Peter Bowles (Paris Singer), Alex Jawkokimov (Sergei Yessenin), Murray Melvin (photographer), Jeanne Le Bars (Wilma), Alita Naughton (journalist), Sandor Elés (Bugatti)
Black & white, 65 minutes

BILLION DOLLAR BRAIN (1967)
United Artists
Producer: Harry Saltzman
Director: **Ken Russell**
Screenplay: John McGrath, based on the novel by Len Deighton
Cinematography: Billy Williams
Production Designer: Syd Cain
Costumes: Shirley Russell (as Shirley Kingdon)
Music: Richard Rodney Bennett
Editing: Alan Osbiston

Cast: Michael Caine (Harry Palmer), Karl Malden (Leo Newbigen), Ed Begley (General Midwinter), Oskar Homolka (Colonel Stok), Françoise Dorléac (Anya), Guy Doleman (Colonel Ross), Vladek Sheybal (Dr. Eiwort), Milo Sperber (Basil), Janos Kurutz (gangster), Paul Tamarin (gangster), Iza Teller (gangster)
Color, 111 minutes

DANTE'S INFERNO: THE PRIVATE LIFE OF DANTE GABRIEL ROSSETTI (1967)
Omnibus, BBC-TV (first telecast December 22)
Producer: **Ken Russell**
Director: **Ken Russell**
Writer: **Ken Russell**, Austin Frazer
Cinematography: Nat Crosby
Production Design: Luciana Arrighi
Costumes: Shirley Russell
Editing: Michael Bradsell, Roger Crittenden
Cast: Oliver Reed (Dante Gabriel Rossetti), Judith Paris (Elizabeth Siddal), Andrew Faulds (William Morris), Iza Teller (Christina Rossetti), Christopher Logue (Algernon Charles Swinburne), Gala Mitchell (Jane Morris), Pat Ashton (Fanny Cornforth), Clive Goodwin (John Ruskin), David Jones (Charles Augustus Howell), Norman Dewhurst (Edward Burne-Jones), Tony Gray (W. M. Rossetti), Douglas Gray (Holman Hunt), Derek Boshier (John Everett Millais), Caroline Coon (Annie Miller), Janet Deuters (Emma Brown)
Black & white, 90 minutes

SONG OF SUMMER (1968)
Omnibus, BBC-TV (first telecast September 15)
Producer: **Ken Russell**
Director: **Ken Russell**
Writer: **Ken Russell**, Eric Fenby, based on Fenby's memoir *Delius as I Knew Him*
Cinematography: Dick Bush
Production Design: Judy Steel
Costumes: Shirley Russell
Music: Frederick Delius
Editing: Roger Crittenden
Cast: Max Adrian (Delius), Christopher Gable (Eric Fenby), Maureen Pryor (Jelka Delius), David Collings (Percy Grainger), Geraldine Sherman (girl next door), Elizabeth Ercy (maid), Roger Worrod (Bruder), Norman Jones (doctor)
Black & white, 74 minutes

WOMEN IN LOVE (1969)
United Artists
Producer: Larry Kramer, Martin Rosen
Director: **Ken Russell**
Screenplay: Larry Kramer, based on the novel by D. H. Lawrence
Cinematography: Billy Williams
Art Direction: Ken Jones
Costumes: Shirley Russell
Music: Georges Delerue
Editing: Michael Bradsell
Cast: Oliver Reed (Gerald Crich), Alan Bates (Rupert Birkin), Glenda Jackson (Gudrun Brangwen), Jennie Linden (Ursula Brangwen), Eleanor Bron (Hermione Roddice), Alan Webb (Thomas Crich), Catherine Willmer (Mrs. Crich), Vladek Sheybal (Loerke), Phoebe Nicholls (Winnifred Crich), Christopher Gable (Tibby Lupton), Michael Gough (Mr. Brangwen), Norma Shebbeare (Mrs. Brangwen), Nike Arrighi (Contessa), James Laurenson (minister), Richard Heffer (Loerke's boyfriend)
Color, 131 minutes

DANCE OF THE SEVEN VEILS (A COMIC STRIP IN SEVEN EPISODES ON THE LIFE OF RICHARD STRAUSS) (1970)
Omnibus, BBC-TV (first telecast February 15)
Producer: **Ken Russell**
Director: **Ken Russell**
Writer: **Ken Russell**, Henry Reed, Richard Strauss
Cinematography: Peter Hall
Costumes: Shirley Russell
Music: Richard Strauss
Editing: Dave King
Cast: Christopher Gable (Richard Strauss), Judith Paris (Pauline Strauss), Kenneth Colley (Adolf Hitler), Vladek Sheybal (Joseph Goebbels), James Mellor (Herman Goering), Sally Bryant (Life), Gala Mitchell (fallen woman), Rita Webb (Salome), Imogen Claire (Salome—dancer), Maggie Maxwell (Potiphar's wife), Otto Diamant (Jewish man), Dorothy Grumbar (Jewish woman), Martin Fenwick (Baron Ochs), Anna Sharkey (Octavian)
Black & white, 59 minutes

THE MUSIC LOVERS (1971)
United Artists
Producer: **Ken Russell**
Director: **Ken Russell**

Screenplay: Melvyn Bragg, based on the book *Beloved Friend: The Story of Tchaikovsky and Nadejda von Meck* by Catherine Drinker Bowen and Barbara von Meck
Cinematography: Douglas Slocombe
Production Designer: Natasha Kroll
Costumes: Shirley Russell
Music: Peter Tchaikovsky
Editing: Michael Bradsell
Cast: Richard Chamberlain (Peter Tchaikovsky), Glenda Jackson (Nina Milyukova), Christopher Gable (Count Anton Chiluvsky), Kenneth Colley (Modest Tchaikovsky), Max Adrian (Nicholas Rubenstein), Sabine Maydelle (Sasha Tchaikovsky), Maureen Pryor (Nina's mother), Iza Teller (Mme. Nadedja von Meck), Andrew Faulds (Davidov), Bruce Robinson (Alexei Sofranov), Ben Aris (young lieutenant), Xavier Russell (Koyola), Dennis Meyers (von Meck twin), John Myers (von Meck twin), Joanne Brown (Olga Bredska)
Color, 123 minutes

THE DEVILS (1971)
Warner Bros.
Producer: **Ken Russell**, Robert H. Solo
Director: **Ken Russell**
Screenplay: **Ken Russell**, based on the play *The Devils* by John Whiting and the book *The Devils of Loudun* by Aldous Huxley
Cinematography: David Watkin
Production Designer: Derek Jarman
Costumes: Shirley Russell
Music: Peter Maxwell Davis
Editing: Michael Bradsell
Cast: Oliver Reed (Urbain Grandier), Vanessa Redgrave (Sister Jeanne), Christopher Logue (Cardinal Richelieu), Graham Armitage (King Louis XIII), Dudley Sutton (Baron de Laubardemont), Max Adrian (Ibert), Brian Murphy (Adam), Gemma Jones (Madeleine du Brou), Murray Melvin (Father Mignon), Michael Gothard (Father Barré), Georgina Hale (Philippe), John Woodvine (Trincant), Andrew Faulds (Rangier), Kenneth Colley (Legrand), Judith Paris (Sister Judith), Catherine Willmer (Sister Catherine), Iza Teller (Sister Iza)
Color, 111 minutes

THE BOY FRIEND (1971)
MGM-EMI
Producer: **Ken Russell**

Director: **Ken Russell**
Screenplay: **Ken Russell**, based on the play by Sandy Wilson
Cinematography: David Watkin
Production Designer: Tony Walton
Costumes: Shirley Russell
Music: Peter Maxwell Davies, Sandy Wilson, Nacio Herb Brown and Arthur Freed
Choreography: Christopher Gable
Editing: Michael Bradsell
Cast: Twiggy (Polly Brown), Christopher Gable (Tony Brockhurst), Max Adrian (Max), Bryan Pringle (Percy), Murray Melvin (Alphonse), Moyra Fraser (Moyra Parkhill), Georgina Hale (Fay), Antonia Ellis (Maisie), Sally Bryant (Nancy), Vladek Sheybal (De Thrill), Tommy Tune (Tommy), Brian Murphy (Peter), Graham Armitage (Michael), Cary Little (Dulcie), Ann Jameson (Mrs. Peters), Glenda Jackson (Rita)
Color, 137 minutes

SAVAGE MESSIAH (1972)
MGM-EMI
Producer: **Ken Russell**
Director: **Ken Russell**
Screenplay: Christopher Logue, based on *Savage Messiah* by H. S. Ede
Cinematography: Dick Bush
Production Design: Derek Jarman
Costumes: Shirley Russell
Music: Michael Garrett
Editing: Michael Bradsell
Cast: Scott Antony (Henri Gaudier), Dorothy Tutin (Sophie Brzeska), Lindsay Kemp (Angus Corky), Helen Mirren (Gosh Boyle), Michael Gough (M. Gaudier), John Justin (Lionel Shaw), Audrey Richards (mayor), Peter Vaughan (museum attendant), Ben Aris (Thomas Buff), Eleanor Fazan (Mme. Gaudier), Otto Diamant (Mr. Saltzman), Imogen Claire (Mavis Coldstream), Maggy Maxwell (tart), Susanna East (Pippa), Judith Paris (Kate)
Color, 97 minutes

MAHLER (1974)
Goodtimes Enterprises
Producer: Roy Baird
Director: **Ken Russell**
Screenplay: **Ken Russell**
Cinematography: Dick Bush

Production Designer: John Comfort
Costumes: Shirley Russell
Music: Gustav Mahler, Richard Wagner
Editing: Michael Bradsell
Cast: Robert Powell (Gustav Mahler), Georgina Hale (Alma Mahler), Lee Montague (Bernard Mahler), Miriam Karlin (Aunt Rosa), Rosalie Crutchley (Marie Mahler), Gary Rich (young Mahler), Richard Morant (Max), Angela Down (Justine Mahler), Antonia Ellis (Cosima Wagner), Ronald Pickup (Nick), Peter Eyre (Otto Mahler), Dana Gillespie (Anna von Mildenburg), George Coulouris (Dr. Roth), David Collings (Hugo Wolfe), Arnold Yarrow (grandfather)
Color, 115 minutes

TOMMY (1975)
Columbia Pictures
Producer: **Ken Russell**, Robert Stigwood
Director: **Ken Russell**
Screenplay: **Ken Russell**, based on the rock opera by the Who
Cinematography: Dick Bush, Ronnie Taylor, Robin Lehman
Art Direction: John Clark
Costumes: Shirley Russell
Music: Peter Townshend, John Entwistle, Keith Moon
Choreography: Gillian Gregory
Editing: Stuart Baird
Cast: Roger Daltry (Tommy Walker), Oliver Reed (Frank Hobbs), Ann-Margret (Nora Walker Hobbs), Elton John (Pinball Wizard), Eric Clapton (the preacher), John Entwistle (himself), Keith Moon (Uncle Ernie), Paul Nicholas (Cousin Kevin), Jack Nicholson (the specialist), Robert Powell (Captain Walker), Pete Townshend (himself), Tina Turner (the Acid Queen), Arthur Brown (the priest), Victoria Russell (Sally Simpson), Ben Aris (Rev. Simpson)
Color, 111 minutes

LISZTOMANIA (1975)
Goodtimes Enterprises
Producer: Roy Baird, David Puttnam
Director: **Ken Russell**
Screenplay: **Ken Russell**
Cinematography: Peter Suschitzky
Production Design: Philip Harrison
Costumes: Shirley Russell
Music: Franz Liszt, Richard Wagner, Rick Wakeman

Choreography: Imogen Claire
Editing: Stuart Baird
Cast: Roger Daltry (Franz Liszt), Sara Kestelman (Princess Carolyn), Paul Nicholas (Richard Wagner), Ringo Starr (the Pope), Rick Wakeman (Thor), John Justin (Count d'Agoult), Fiona Lewis (Marie d'Agoult), Veronica Quilligan (Cosima Liszt Wagner), Imogen Claire (George Sand), Nell Campbell (Olga Janina), Andrew Reilly (Hans Von Buelow), David English (Captain), Rikki Howard (Countess), David Corti (Daniel), Anulka Dzuibinska (Lola Montez), Murray Melvin (Hector Berlioz), Andrew Faulds (Richard Strauss), Ken Parry (Gioachino Rossini), Kenneth Colley (Frederic Chopin), Otto Diamant (Felix Mendelsohn)
Color, 103 minutes

VALENTINO (1977)
United Artists
Producer: Irwin Winkler
Director: **Ken Russell**
Screenplay: **Ken Russell**, Mardik Martin, based on the book *Valentino: An Intimate Exposé of the Sheik* by Brad Steiger and Chaw Mank
Cinematography: Peter Suschitzky
Production Design: Philip Harrison
Costumes: Shirley Russell
Music: Stanley Black, Ferde Grofé
Choreography: Gillian Gregory
Editing: Stuart Baird
Cast: Rudolf Nureyev (Rudolph Valentino), Michelle Phillips (Natacha Rambova), Leslie Caron (Alla Nazimova), Felicity Kendal (June Mathis), Huntz Hall (Jesse Lasky), David de Keyser (Joseph Schenck), Alfred Marks (Richard Rowland), William Hootkins (Mr. Fatty), Carol Kane (Fatty's girlfriend), Seymour Cassel (George Ullman), Peter Vaughan (Rory O'Neil), Anton Diffring (Baron Long), Jennie Linden (Agnes Ayres), Bill McKinney (cop), Don Fellows (George Melford), **Ken Russell** (Rex Ingram, uncredited)
Color, 128 minutes

CLOUDS OF GLORY: WILLIAM AND DOROTHY (1978)
Granada Television (first telecast July 9)
Producer: Norman Swallow
Director: **Ken Russell**
Teleplay: **Ken Russell**, Melvyn Bragg
Cinematography: Dick Bush
Production Design: Margaret Coombes, Michael Grimes, Alan Rutter

Costumes: Shirley Russell
Music: Benjamin Britten
Editing: Anthony Ham
Cast: David Warner (William Wordsworth), Felicity Kendal (Dorothy Words-
worth), William Hootkins (Reverend Dewey), Bridget Ashburn (Joanna
Hutchinson), Freddie Fletcher (Tom Hutchinson), Thomas Henty (Jack Hutchin-
son), Robin Bevan (young William), Susan Withers (young Dorothy), Anthony
Carrick (Uncle), Preston Lockwood (Dr. Carr), Trevor Wilson (John Words-
worth), Amanda Murray (Mary Wordsworth), Patricia Quinn (Annette Vallo),
Sally Sheridan (Mrs. Hutchinson)
Color, 52 minutes

THE RIME OF THE ANCIENT MARINER (1978)
Granada Television (first telecast July 16)
Producer: Norman Swallow
Director: **Ken Russell**
Writer: **Ken Russell**, Melvyn Bragg
Cinematography: Dick Bush
Production Design: Margaret Coombes, Michael Grimes, Alan Rutter
Costumes: Shirley Russell
Music: Arnold Bax
Editing: Anthony Ham
Cast: David Hemmings (Samuel Taylor Coleridge), Kika Markham (Sara
Coleridge), David Warner (William Wordsworth), Felicity Kendal (Dorothy
Wordsworth), Ronald Letham (Thomas de Quincey), Murray Melvin (Robert
Lovell), Ben Aris (Robert Southey), Imogen Claire (specter), Peter Dodd (Hartley
Coleridge), Barbara Ewing (Asra), Patricia Garwood (Edith Southey), Henry
Moxon (Dr. Gillman), Iza Teller (Mrs. Gillman), Diana Mather (Mary Fricker),
Annette Robertson (servant)
Color, 52 minutes

ALTERED STATES (1980)
Warner Bros.
Producer: Howard Gottfried
Director: **Ken Russell**
Screenplay: "Sidney Aaron" (Paddy Chayefsky), based on the novel by Chayefsky
Cinematography: Jordan Cronenweth
Production Design: Richard MacDonald
Costumes: Ruth Meyers
Music: John Corigliano

Editing: Eric Jenkins
Cast: William Hurt (Prof. Eddie Jessup), Blair Brown (Emily Jessup), Bob Bala-ban (Arthur Rosenberg), Charles Haid (Mason Parrish), Thaao Penghlis (Prof. Eduardo), Miguel Godreau (primal man), Dori Brenner (Sylvia Rosenberg), Peter Brandon (Hobart), Charles White-Eagle (The Brujo), Drew Barrymore (Margaret Jessup), Megan Jeffers (Grace Jessup), Jack Murdock (Hector Orteco), Frank Mc-Carthy (Obispo), Deborah Baltzell (patient), Evan Richard (young Rosenberg
Color, 102 minutes

THE PLANETS (1983)
The South Bank Show, London Weekend Television, ITV (first telecast June 12)
Director: **Ken Russell**
Music: Gustav Holst, performed by Philadelphia Symphony Orchestra, Eugene Ormandy conducting
Color, 50 minutes

VAUGHAN WILLIAMS: A SYMPHONIC PORTRAIT (1984)
The South Bank Show, London Weekend Television, ITV (first telecast April 8)
Producer: **Ken Russell**
Director: **Ken Russell**
Teleplay: **Ken Russell**, Ursula Vaughan Williams
Cinematography: Mike Humphreys
Music: London Philharmonic Orchestra
Editing: Xavier Russell
Cast: **Ken Russell**, Ursula Vaughan Williams, Iona Brown (violin soloist), Peter Savidge (vocal soloist), John Sanders (Gloucester Cathedral organist), Molly Russell
Black & white/color, 60 minutes

CRIMES OF PASSION (1984)
New World Pictures
Producer: Barry Sandler
Director: **Ken Russell**
Screenplay: Barry Sandler
Cinematography: Dick Bush
Art Direction: Stephen Marsh
Costumes: Ruth Meyers
Music: Antonín Dvořák, Rick Wakeman
Editing: Brian Tagg
Cast: Kathleen Turner (China Blue/Joanna Crane), Anthony Perkins (Rev. Peter Shayne), John Laughlin (Bobby Grady), Annie Potts (Amy Grady), Bruce Davison

(Donny Hopper), Gordon Hunt (group leader), Dan Gerrity (group member), Terri Hoyos (group member), Vince McKewin (group member), Deanna Oliver (group member), Patricia Stevens (group member), John C. Scanlon (Carl), Janice Renney (stripper), Stephen Lee (Jerry), Pat McNamara (Frank), Annie Potts (Amy Grady)
Color, 107 minutes

ELTON JOHN: NIKITA (video short) (1985)
Color, 5 minutes

CLIFF RICHARD: SHE'S SO BEAUTIFUL (video short) (1985)
(part of *Now That's What I Call Music 6*)
Color, 3 minutes

FAUST (1985)
Österreichischer Rundfunk (ORF)
Producer: Franz Kabelka
Director: **Ken Russell**
Screenplay: Jules Barbier, Michel Carré (libretto), based on the novel by Johann Wolfgang Goethe
Production Design: Carl Toms
Costumes: Carl Toms
Music: Charles Gounod
Choreography: Alphonse Poulin
Editing: Kurt Zöhrer
Cast: Ruggero Raimondi (Mefistofele), Walton Grönroos (Valentin), Alfred Sramek (Wagner), Gabriela Benacková (Marguerite), Gabriele Sima (Siébel), Gertrude Jahn (Marthe), Ursula Hambsch-Pfitzner and Christian Herden (Valentin's children)
Color, 176 minutes

GOTHIC (1986)
Virgin Vision
Producer: Penny Corke
Director: **Ken Russell**
Screenplay: Stephen Volk
Cinematography: Mike Southon
Production Design: Christopher Hobbs
Costumes: Kay Gallway, Victoria Russell
Music: Thomas Dolby
Editing: Michael Bradsell

Cast: Gabriel Byrne (Lord Byron), Julian Sands (Percy Shelley), Natasha Richardson (Mary Shelley), Myriam Cyr (Claire Clairmont), Timothy Spall (Dr. John Polidori), Alec Mango (Murray), Andreas Wisniewski (Fletcher), Dexter Fletcher (Rushton), Pascal King (Justine), Tom Hickey (tour guide), Linda Coggin (Turkish mechanical woman), Kristine Landon-Smith (mechanical woman), Chris Chappell (man in armor), Mary Pickard (young William), Kiran Shah (Fuseli monster)
Color, 87 minutes

ELTON JOHN: CRY TO HEAVEN (video short) (1986)
Color, 3 minutes

CLIFF RICHARD & SARAH BRIGHTMAN: ALL I ASK OF YOU (video short) (1986)
Color, 4 minutes

SARAH BRIGHTMAN AND STEVE HARLEY: THE PHANTOM OF THE OPERA (video short) (1986)
Color, 4 minutes

ARIA (1987)
Virgin Vision
Segment, Puccini's "Nessun Dorma" ("None Shall Sleep") from *Turandot*
Producer: Don Boyd
Director: **Ken Russell**
Writer: **Ken Russell**
Cinematography: Gabriel Beristain
Art Direction: Paul Dufficey
Costumes: Victoria Russell
Editing: Michael Bradsell
Cast: Linzi Drew, Andreas Wisniewski, Bella Enahoro, Bunty Mathias, Angela Walker
Color, 6 minutes

RICHARD GOLUB: TRIAL OF THE CENTURY (DANCING FOR JUSTICE) (video short) (1987)
Color, 4 minutes

KEN RUSSELL'S ABC OF BRITISH MUSIC (1988)
The South Bank Show, London Weekend Television, ITV (first telecast February 4)
Producer: **Ken Russell**

Director: **Ken Russell**
Writer: **Ken Russell**
Editing: Melvyn Bragg, Dave Simpson
Cast: **Ken Russell**, Thomas Dolby, Rita Cullis, Evelyn Glennie, Nigel Kennedy, John Lill, Julian Lloyd Webber, Eric Parkin, The Fairer Sax
Color, 75 minutes

SALOME'S LAST DANCE (1988)
Vestron Pictures
Producer: Penny Corke
Director: **Ken Russell**
Screenplay: **Ken Russell**, based on the play by Oscar Wilde
Cinematography: Harvey Harrison
Production Design: Michael Buchanan
Costumes: Michael Arrals
Choreography: Arlene Phillips
Editing: Timothy Gee
Cast: Glenda Jackson (Herodias/Lady Alice), Stratford Johns (Herod/Alfred Taylor), Nickolas Grace (Oscar Wilde), Douglas Hodge (John the Baptist/ Lord Alfred "Bosie" Douglas), Imogen Millais-Scott (Salome/Rose), Denis Lill (Tigellenus/Chilvers), Russell Lee Nash (pageboy), **Ken Russell** (Cappadocian/Kenneth), David Doyle (A. Nuban), Warren Saire (young Syrian), Kenny Ireland (first soldier), Michael Van Wijk (second soldier), Paul Clayton (first Nazarean), Imogen Claire (second Nazarean), Tim Potter (Pharisee)
Color, 89 minutes

THE LAIR OF THE WHITE WORM (1988)
Vestron Pictures
Producer: **Ken Russell**
Director: **Ken Russell**
Screenplay: **Ken Russell**, based on the novel by Bram Stoker
Cinematography: Dick Bush
Production Design: Anne Tilby
Costumes: Michael Jeffery
Music: Stanislas Syrewicz
Choreography: Imogen Claire
Editing: Peter Davies
Cast: Amanda Donohoe (Lady Sylvia Marsh), Hugh Grant (Lord James D'Ampton), Peter Capaldi (Angus Flint), Sammi Davis (Mary Trent), Catherine

Oxenberg (Eve Trent), Stratford Johns (Peters), Paul Brooke (P. C. Erny), Imogen Claire (Dorothy Trent), Christopher Gable (Joseph Trent), Chris Pitt (Kevin), Gina McKee (Nurse Gladwell), Lloyd Peters (Jesus Christ), Miranda Coe (maid/nun), Linzi Drew (maid/nun), Carol Anne Kelly (maid/nun)
Color, 93 minutes

THE RAINBOW (1989)
Vestron Pictures
Producer: **Ken Russell**, Neville Cawas Bardoliwalla
Director: **Ken Russell**
Screenplay: **Ken Russell**, Vivian Russell, based on the novel by D. H. Lawrence
Cinematography: Billy Williams
Production Design: Luciana Arrighi
Costumes: Jane Law
Music: Carl Davis
Choreography: Imogen Claire
Editing: Peter Davis
Cast: Sammi Davis (Ursula Brangwen), Amanda Donohoe (Winifred Inger), Christopher Gable (Will Brangwen), Glenda Jackson (Anna Brangwen), David Hemmings (Uncle Henry), Paul McGann (Anton Skrebensky), Dudley Sutton (McAllister), Jim Carter (Mr. Harby), Judith Paris (Miss Harby), Kenneth Colley (Mr. Brunt), Glenda McKay (Gudrun Brangwen), Mark Owen (Jim Richards), Ralph Nossek (vicar), Nicole Stephenson (Ethel), Molly Russell (Molly Brangwen)
Color, 113 minutes

IL MEFISTOFELE (TV movie) (1989)
Valiant SRL
Director: **Ken Russell**
Writer: Arrigo Boito (libretto)
Cinematography: Paolo Bellani, Sergio Cavandoli, Rocco Laparelli, Enzo Tosi, Luca Vasco
Production Design: Paul Dufficey
Costumes: Paul Dufficey
Music: Arrigo Boito
Choreography: Richard Caceres
Cast: Paata Burchuladze (Mefistofele), Ottavio Garaventa (Faust), Adriana Morelli (Margherita), Silvana Mazzieri (Marta), Fabio Armiliato (Wagner), Josella Ligi (Elena), Laura Bocca (Pabtalis), Saverio Bambi (Nereo)
Color, 137 minutes

A BRITISH PICTURE, PORTRAIT OF AN ENFANT TERRIBLE (1989)
The South Bank Show, London Weekend Television, ITV (first telecast October 15)
Producer: Ronaldo Vasconcellos
Director: **Ken Russell**
Writer: **Ken Russell**
Cinematography: Dick Bush
Art Direction: Michael Buchanan
Costumes: Victoria Russell
Editing: Xavier Russell
Cast: Melvyn Bragg, **Ken Russell**, Molly Russell, Rupert Russell, Victoria Russell, Vivian Russell
Color, 50 minutes

PANDORA'S BOX: IT'S ALL COMING BACK TO ME NOW (video short) (1989)
Color, 7:48 minutes

WOMEN AND MEN: STORIES OF SEDUCTION (1990)
"Dusk before Fireworks" segment (first telecast August 19)
HBO
Producer: William S. Gilmore
Director: **Ken Russell**
Teleplay: based on the story by Dorothy Parker
Cinematography: Billy Williams
Costumes: Jane Robinson
Music: Marvin Hamlisch
Editing: John Jympson, Robert K. Lambert
Cast: Molly Ringwald (Kit), Peter Weller (Hobie)
Color, 25 minutes

THE STRANGE AFFLICTION OF ANTON BRUCKNER (1990)
The South Bank Show, London Weekend Television, ITV (first telecast October 14)
Producer: Ronaldo Vasconcellos
Director: **Ken Russell**
Writer: **Ken Russell**
Cinematography: Robin Vidgeon
Costumes: Victoria Russell
Music: Anton Bruckner
Editing: Brian Tagg

Cast: Peter Mackriel (Anton Bruckner), Catherine Neilson (Gretel), Carsten Norgaard (Hans)
Color, 50 minutes

ROAD TO MANDALAY (TV movie) (1991)
Home Sweet Home, TVS
Producer: Maureen Murray
Director: **Ken Russell**
Writer: **Ken Russell**
Editing: Xavier Russell
Cast: Muriel Codd or "Aunt Moo," June Codd, **Ken Russell**, Rupert Russell
Color, 35 minutes

WHORE (1991)
Trimark Pictures
Producer: Dan Ireland, Ronaldo Vasconcellos
Director: **Ken Russell**
Screenplay: **Ken Russell**, Deborah Dalton, based on the play by David Hines
Cinematography: Amir M. Mokri
Production Design: Richard B. Lewis
Costumes: Leonard Pollack
Music: Michael Gibbs
Editing: Brian Tagg
Cast: Theresa Russell (Liz), Benjamin Mouton (Blake), Antonio Fargas (Rasta), Elizabeth Morehead (Katie), John Diehl (derelict), Daniel Quinn (brutal man), Sanjay Chandani (Indian), Jason Saucier (Bill), Michael Crabtree (man in car), Jered Barclay (dead trick in car), Doug MacHugh (man in diner), Amanda Goodwin (Martha), Frank Smith (Charlie), Jason Kristofer (shy kid in van), Robert O'Reilly (younger man in car), Ginger Lynn (wounded girl)
Color, 95 minutes

PRISONER OF HONOR (1991)
Dreyfuss/James Productions and HBO Films (first telecast November 2)
Producer: Richard Dreyfuss, Judith Rutherford James
Director: **Ken Russell**
Writer: Ron Hutchinson
Cinematography: Mike Southon
Costumes: Michael Jeffrey
Music: Barry Kirsch
Editing: Mia Goldman, Margaret Goodspeed, Brian Tagg

Cast: Richard Dreyfuss (Colonel Picquart), Oliver Reed (General de Boisdeffre), Peter Firth (Major Henry), Shauna Baird (Henry's wife), Jeremy Kemp (General de Pellieux), Brian Blessed (General Gonse), Peter Vaughan (General Mercier), Kenneth Colley (Captain Dreyfus), Judith Paris (Mme. Dreyfus), Catherine Neilson (Eloise), Lindsay Anderson (war minister), Murray Melvin (Bertillon), Martin Friend (Emile Zola), Christopher Ashley (orator #1), David Bamford (boy prostitute), Duncan Bell (army doctor), John Bennett (magistrate), John Carter (new war minister), Imogen Claire (cabaret singer), Paul Dufficey (sketch artist), Nick Musker (vampire Dreyfus)
Color, 98 minutes

ANDREW LLOYD WEBBER: THE PREMIERE COLLECTION ENCORE (video) (1992)
Phantom of the Opera, All I Ask of You, Wishing You Were Here Again, The Music of the Night segments
Cast: Michael Ball, Sarah Brightman, José Carreras, David Essex, Cliff Richard
Color, 58 minutes

THE SECRET LIFE OF ARNOLD BAX (1992)
The South Bank Show, London Weekend Television, ITV (first telecast November 22)
Producer: Maureen Murray
Director: **Ken Russell**
Writer: **Ken Russell**
Cinematography: Robin Vidgeon
Costumes: Victoria Russell
Music: Arnold Bax
Choreography: Hetty Baynes
Editing: Xavier Russell
Cast: **Ken Russell** (Sir Arnold Bax), Glenda Jackson (Harriet Cohen), Hetty Baynes (Annie), Kenneth Colley (John Ireland), Melissa Docker (Sybil Chadwick), Maureen Murray (the Manageress), Alan Arthur (waiter), Maurice Bush (doorman)
Color, 60 minutes

THE MYSTERY OF DR. MARTINU (1992)
RM Associates (first telecast May 16)
Producer: Maureen Murray
Director: **Ken Russell**
Costumes: Victoria Russell

Music: Bohuslav Martinu
Editing: Xavier Russell
Cast: Patrick Ryecart (Bohuslav Martinu), Shauna Baird (Charlotte Martinu), Hannah King (Slava), Martin Friend (Prof. Mirisch), Mac MacDonald (the official), Dylan Brown (Jason), Nick Boothby (Martin), Mark Adell (the alien), Robert Northwood (G.I.), Tamzin Outhwaite (girlfriend)
Color, 61 minutes

LADY CHATTERLEY (1993)
London Film Productions and BBC (4 episodes, first telecast June 6–27)
Producer: Michael Haggiag
Director: **Ken Russell**
Teleplay: **Ken Russell**, Michael Haggiag
Cinematography: Robin Vidgeon
Production Design: James Merifield
Costumes: Evangeline Harrison
Music: Jean-Claude Petit
Editing: Mick Audsley, Peter Davies, Alan Mackay, Xavier Russell
Cast: Joely Richardson (Lady Connie Chatterley), Sean Bean (Mellors), James Wilby (Sir Clifford Chatterley), Shirley Anne Field (Mrs. Bolton), Hetty Baynes (Hilda), **Ken Russell** (Sir Michael Reid), Brian Blessed (petty officer), Breffni McKenna (Donald Forbes), Pat Keen (Mrs. Mellors), Amanda Murray (Mrs. Draycott), Molly Russell (Molly), Rupert Russell (Rupert)
Color, 205 minutes

BRYAN ADAMS: DIANA (video short) (1993)
Color, 4 minutes

CLASSIC WIDOWS (1995)
The South Bank Show, London Weekend Television, ITV (first telecast February 5)
Producer: Maureen Murray
Director: **Ken Russell**
Teleplay: Melvyn Bragg
Cinematography: Hong Manley
Music: Benjamin Frankel, Humphrey Searle, Bernard Stevens, William Walton
Choreography: Amir Housseinpour
Editing: Xavier Russell
Cast: **Ken Russell**, Xenia Frankel, Fiona Searle, Bertha Stevens, Susana Walton, Hetty Baynes (performer), Fiona Cross (performer)
Color, 53 minutes

THE INSATIABLE MRS. KIRSCH (1995)
Regina Ziegler Filmproduktion
Producer: Ronaldo Vasconcellos
Director: **Ken Russell**
Writer: **Ken Russell**, Hetty Baynes
Cinematography: Hong Manley
Editing: Xavier Russell
Cast: **Ken Russell** (Mr. Kirsch), Hetty Baynes (Mrs. Kirsch), Simon Shepherd (narrator)
Color, 29 minutes

MOMENTOUS EVENTS—RUSSIA IN THE 1990s: ALICE IN RUSSIALAND (1995)
Channel 4 Films
Producer: Ronaldo Vasconcellos
Director: **Ken Russell**
Writer: **Ken Russell**
Music: Richard Niles
Editing: Xavier Russell
Cast: Hetty Baynes (Alice), Peter Majer (various), Amanda Ray-King (Alice's sister)
Color, 60 minutes

TREASURE ISLAND (1995)
Channel 4 Films (first telecast December 24)
Producer: Maureen Murray
Director: **Ken Russell**
Writer: **Ken Russell**, based on the novel by Robert Louis Stevenson
Cinematography: Hong Manley
Music: Adrian Sutton
Editing: Xavier Russell
Cast: Hetty Baynes (Long Jane Silver), Michael Elphick (Billy Bones), Gregory Hall (Jim Hawkins), Georgina Hale (Mum)
Color, 63 minutes

MINDBENDER (1996)
Major Motion Pictures (TV Movie) (first telecast October 2)
Producer: Doran Eran
Director: **Ken Russell**
Screenplay: **Ken Russell**, Yael Stern
Cinematography: Hong Manley

Production Design: Jacob Turgeman
Music: Bob Christianson
Editing: John Orland, Xavier Russell
Cast: Ishai Golan (Uri Geller), Terence Stamp (Joe Hartman), Hetty Baynes (Kitti Hartman), Idan Alterman (Shipi), Delphine Forest (Sharon), Rachel Elner (Hanna), Rafi Tabor (Uri's father), Aviva Yoel (Uri's mother)
Color, 93 minutes

TALES OF EROTICA (1996)
"The Insatiable Mrs. Kirsch" segment
Producer: Ronaldo Vasconcellos
Director: **Ken Russell**
Screenplay: **Ken Russell**, Hetty Baynes
Cinematography: Hong Manley
Costumes: Rosie Russon
Music: Wendy Blackstone
Editing: Xavier Russell
Cast: **Ken Russell** (Mr. Kirsch), Hetty Baynes (Mrs. Kirsch), Simon Shepherd (narrator)
Color, 29 minutes

DOGBOYS (1998)
Showtime Networks, Inc. (first telecast April 4)
Producer: **Ken Russell**
Director: **Ken Russell**
Writer: **Ken Russell**, David Taylor
Cinematography: Jamie Thompson
Production Design: Ed Hanna
Costumes: Csilla Márki
Music: John Altman, Spencer Proffer
Editing: Xavier Russell
Cast: Bryan Brown (Captain Robert Brown), Dean Cain (Julian Taylor), Tia Carrere (D. A. Jennifer Dern), Ken James (Warden Adam Wakefield), Sean McCann (Pappy), Richard Chevolleau (Willy B.), Hardee T. Lineham (Watkins), Von Flores (Miguel), Robbie Rox (Bull), Jody Racicot (Rego), Matthew Bennett (Carl Ewing), James Bearden (J. B. Diggs), Robert Collins (Cates), Bruce Tubbe (bus guard), Scott Wickware (prison guard #1), Billy Otis (Smitty), Rick Demas (monster), Bernard Browne (tower guard), Wayne Best (prison guard #2), Roger McKeen (guard #1), Raymond Hunt (guard #2), Joe Matheson (newscaster)
Color, 92 minutes

IN SEARCH OF THE ENGLISH FOLK SONG (1998)
Channel 4 Films (first telecast August 31)
Producer: Maureen Murray
Director: **Ken Russell**
Writer: **Ken Russell**
Editing: Sean Mackenzie
Cast: **Ken Russell** (presenter), So What ("Kick It"), Garry Fenna ("Going to Put a Bar in My Car and Drive Myself to Drink"), Bob Appleyard ("The Fawley Flame"), Lynne Fortt ("Down at Greenham Common on a Spree"), June Tabor ("The King of Rome"), Fairport Convention ("Seventeen Come Sunday"), Osibisa ("Sunshine Day"), Eliza Carthy ("Good Morning, Mr. Walker"), Chris While and the Albion Band ("Young Man Cut Down in His Prime"), Waterson Carthy ("Stars in My Crown"), Donovan ("Nirvana"), Edward II ("Shepherd's Hey"), Percy Grainger Chamber Orchestra ("Country Gardens"), Sian Elizabeth Rees ("Brigg Fair")
Color, 50 minutes

LION'S MOUTH (2000)
Gorsewood Productions
Director: **Ken Russell**
Writer: **Ken Russell**
Art Direction: Alex Russell
Editing: Tim Arrowsmith, **Ken Russell**
Cast: Diana Laurie (Josephine Heatherington), **Ken Russell** (Ken the Clown), Tulip Junkie (Nipply/Lion), Emma Millions (tart/Androcles)
Color, 27 minutes

THE FALL OF THE LOUSE OF USHER: A GOTHIC TALE FOR THE 21ST CENTURY (2001)
Gorsewood Productions
Producer: **Ken Russell**
Director: **Ken Russell**
Screenplay: **Ken Russell**, based on several short stories of Edgar Allan Poe
Cinematography: **Ken Russell**
Costumes: Victoria Russell
Music: James Johnston
Editing: **Ken Russell**
Cast: James Johnston (Roderick Usher), Elize Tribble (Madeline Usher, Masked Mary, Mummy, Dr. Wells), Marie Findley (Nurse AB Smith), **Ken Russell** (Dr. Calahari), Lesley Nunnerly (Berenice), Emma Millions (Annabelle Lee), Peter Mastin (Ernest Valdemar), Sandra Scott (Beulah Von Birmingham), Barry

Lowe (Dr. Glynn/Gory the Gorilla), Alex Russell (Igor/Gory the Gorilla), Roger Wilkes (Gory the Gorilla), Claire Cannaway (young Leonore Usher), Sam Kitcher (young Allan Usher), Suki Uruma (screw)
Color, 83 minutes

ELGAR: FANTASY OF A COMPOSER ON A BICYCLE (2002)
The South Bank Show, London Weekend Television, ITV (first telecast September 22)
Producer: **Ken Russell**
Director: **Ken Russell**
Teleplay: **Ken Russell**
Costumes: Victoria Russell
Cast: James Johnston (Edward Elgar), Elize Tribble (Lady Elgar)
Color, 50 minutes

REVENGE OF THE ELEPHANT MAN (2004)
Producer: **Ken Russell**
Director: **Ken Russell**
Screenplay: **Ken Russell**
Cinematography: **Ken Russell**
Cast: **Ken Russell** (Dr. Henry Horenstein), Lisi Tribble (Nurse Randy Ravensworth), Barry Lowe (Ella, the Elephant Man)
Color, 27 minutes

HOT PANTS: 3 SEXY SHORTS (2006)
Gorsewood Productions
   1. "The Revenge of the Elephant Man"
Producer: **Ken Russell**
Director: **Ken Russell**
Screenplay: **Ken Russell**
Cinematography: **Ken Russell**
Production Design: H. K. A. Russell
Costumes: Lisi Tribble
Music: Merv Greenslade, Carl Chamberlain, Mike Bradsell
Choreography: Lisi Tribble
Editing: Michael Bradsell
Cast: **Ken Russell** (Dr. Henry Horenstein), Lisi Tribble (Nurse Randy Ravensworth), Barry Lowe (Ella, the Elephant Man)

   2. "The Mystery of Mata Hari"
Producer: **Ken Russell**

Director: **Ken Russell**
Screenplay: **Ken Russell**
Cinematography: **Ken Russell**
Production Design: H. K. A. Russell
Costumes: Elize Tribble
Music: Hugo Wasserman
Choreography: Alf and Elf Russell
Editing: Michael Bradsell
Cast: Elize Tribble (Mata Hari/Sister Claire), **Ken Russell** (Henri Rousseau),
Barry Lowe (O. C. Firing Squad)

3. "The Good Ship Venus"
Producer: **Ken Russell**
Director: **Ken Russell**
Screenplay: **Ken Russell**
Cinematography: **Ken Russell**
Production Design: H. K. A. Russell
Costumes: Elize Tribble
Music: Hugo Wasserman
Choreography: Elize Tribble
Editing: Michael Bradsell
Cast: The Vulgar Boatmen: **Ken Russell**, Elize Tribble, Barry Lowe, Mike Bradsell

TRAPPED ASHES (2006)
segment "The Girl with the Golden Breasts"
Producer: Dennis Bartok, Yoshifumi Hosoya, Yuko Yoshikawa
Director: **Ken Russell**
Screenplay: Dennis Bartok
Cinematography: Zoran Popovic
Production Design: Robb Wilson King
Costumes: Toni Rutter
Music: Kenji Kawai
Editing: Marcus Manton
Cast: Rachel Veltri (Phoebe), Richard Ian Cox (Doug), Scott Heindl (Zack), Glynis
Davies (nurse), Rob deLeeuw (Ben), Mina E. Mina (Dr. Judith), Winston Rekert
(Dr. Larry), **Ken Russell** (Dr. Lucy), John R. Taylor (Dr. Charlotte)
Color

EIN KITTEN FÜR HITLER/A KITTEN FOR HITLER (2007)
Producer: Emma Millions
Director: **Ken Russell**
Screenplay: **Ken Russell**
Cinematography: **Ken Russell**
Production Design: James Merifield
Costumes: Victoria Russell
Music: Hugo Wassermann
Editing: Michael Bradsell
Cast: Rusty Goffe (Lenny), Lisi Tribble (Rachel), Phil Pritchard (Adolf Hitler), Rosie Thewlis (Eva Braun), Rufus Graham (Pres. Truman), Steve Mullins (storm trooper 1), Paul O'Shea (storm trooper 2), **Ken Russell** (Santa)
Color, 8 minutes

BOUDICA BITES BACK (2009)
Producer: Steve Sullivan
Director: **Ken Russell**
Screenplay: **Ken Russell**
Cinematography: Mark Veysey
Costumes: Kimberly Hazell, Angharad Spencer
Music: David Massengill, Lisi Tribble, Hugo Wassermann
Editing: Michael Bradsell
Cast: Lisi Tribble (Boudica), **Ken Russell** (Roman Senator)
Color, 16 minutes

Ken Russell: Interviews

Shock Treatment

Gordon Gow / 1970

From *Films and Filming* 16, no. 10 (July 1970): 8–12. Reprinted with permission.

In view of the commercial success of *Women in Love*, Ken Russell is in a strong position to direct films exactly as he chooses. His film about Tchaikovsky is to be followed by a study of the seventeenth-century French priest Urbain Grandier, whose sexual libertarianism provoked scandal and hysteria, and in both cases the opportunities to startle an audience are part of Russell's interest in the subjects: "There are certain points in every film I do, where I deliberately want to shock people into awareness. If you treat a situation in unexpected terms, by suddenly doing something in an extraordinary way, or even a very funny way, I think it makes them doubly aware.

"People can grow jaded and bored—virtually blind—by looking at things which are done in the expected way time and again. But to turn everything upside down will make everyone, including myself, look at a situation from a different point of view and gain a fresh perspective. So I often do that. I'm doing it more and more."

For the Tchaikovsky film he has extended the controversial and technically zestful approach that earned him widespread attention throughout the 1960s, when he made a number of antidocumentary films about the arts for BBC television. He recalls that in 1959, for a TV-film with John Betjeman called *Poet's London*, there was official resistance to his idea of bringing in a child actor to represent the poet when young, and likewise it was considered unseemly to engage any actor to personify a dead artist within a documentary format. This opposition evaporated in time. The Russell films grew increasingly provocative, reaching a peak with his Isadora Duncan essay in 1966. The artists whose careers and private lives he examined were frequently composers: Prokofiev, Elgar, Bartók, Debussy, Delius, and most recently a "comic strip" impression of Richard Strauss which many regarded as outrageous.

Perhaps the cinema-film on Tchaikovsky will prove equally contentious. When the work of an artist is interwoven with impressions of his personal life, especially when that life was riddled with psychological troubles, the result can seem to denigrate the work itself. This is far from being Russell's intention. He has a deep admiration for Tchaikovsky's music: "The television films, as well, have all been about composers whose music I love. And my tastes in music cover a very wide range, from thirteenth-century polyphony to Stockhausen. In my films there has been, basically, a great love for the music of these men. Then I have also been attracted by the fantastic lives they have led. Each film is about a certain aspect of life, perhaps love or patriotism."

At the time when he talked to me, Russell was eager to change the title of his Tchaikovsky film from "The Lonely Heart" (adopted from one of the composer's many songs, "None but a Lonely Heart," which has a corny ring to it now) to "Opus 74" (the Symphony No. 6 in B minor—*The Pathétique*—given its first performance in 1893, just before Tchaikovsky's death). "Near the end of the film, we have him saying that all his life is in this symphony, and it does contain all his torments and joys and triumphs and despairs, so this seems a fair reason for using 'Opus 74' as our title. Of course, it would be lovely just to call it 'Tchaikovsky,' but I'm told nobody would go to the cinema if it were called that."

Presumably Dimitri Tiomkin has no such reservation, because his film about the same composer is still being advertised as *Tchaikovsky* pure and simple. One might hazard a guess that it will be decidedly "pure" as a whole by comparison with Russell's, as well as concentrating more upon performances of the music. Russell believes in merging the psychology of the individual with the presenta-tion of his creative work: "I don't think you can tear one from the other. I won't just stop the film and play a bit of music. What interests me is the position of the artist in society—his responsibility towards it—his neglect of it. If you use his music to tell things about his life, you're doing two things at the same time. You're letting his own art have its say, and you're recognizing that the music is an integral part of some psychological aspect of his life.

"Quite early in the film, we have the First Piano Concerto—not all of it, but quite a lot of it—and the slow movement is entirely devoted to an exploration of his relationship with his sister; I think this slow movement is probably one of his happiest compositions, and it's different from the first hackneyed movement that we usually hear—all crashing out. The slow movement is very poetic and while it's being played we show a summer he spent at Kamenka with his sister. This suggests the ideal life he was always trying to achieve and never could. I doubt if there was any sexual activity between them, but I think his sister prob-ably loved him more than she loved her husband, and he loved her more than any other woman he ever met, except perhaps his mother.

"The sister was the ideal woman he could worship and wouldn't have to have sexual relations with. He couldn't, because it was outside the bounds of society. He liked her husband very much, anyway, and maybe in his own mind he felt that here was a safe solution to his problem. At the same time, we bring in a sort of symbolic dream sequence, which doesn't look like a dream because the whole thing has a slightly heightened feeling to it, and here he is confronted with a choice he has to make between two people in his life, the idealized sister and Count Anton Chiluvsky, the homosexual friend he was always trying to get rid of and at the same time not wanting to do so.

"Tchaikovsky's homosexuality worried his sister. His father knew nothing about it, but there was gossip at the Moscow Conservatoire, and it looked as though he might be thrown out and his name disgraced. So he was always on the lookout for some ideal woman to marry, and he happened to be working on the opera *Eugene Onegin*—he'd just got to the 'Letter Song,' where Tatiana writes to Onegin declaring her love, after which he turns her down flat and consequently ruins both their lives—and while he was composing this, Tchaikovsky had a letter from a woman who declared herself in almost the same terms as Tatiana, saying that she wanted to marry him. All his friends thought it was ridiculous, but he was a great believer in fate, and he felt it was too much of a coincidence. So he did agree to see the girl, and he married her. And I think this sequence is the most complete thing I've done in a film, by carrying the story through in terms of the music. One hears the 'Letter Song' being sung, and it's all intercut."

Russell's account differs slightly from the commonly held opinion that the "Letter Song" was composed in advance of the opera, although it became eventually a dominant theme of *Eugene Onegin*. As dramatic license, this minor alteration of fact would seem reasonable. In other areas, however thorough the research, Russell has indulged in conjecture. For example, Tchaikovsky's wealthy patroness Mme. Von Meck is shown as withdrawing her support when she discovers that Tchaikovsky is a homosexual: "You won't find in any book the reason why she did finish with him, but I think this is the only possible solution. These personal matters weren't documented, but one reads between the lines.

"If you try to reconstruct something and use as much of the truth as you can, in an odd sort of way—and I've done enough of these films to be sure I'm not just dreaming it—something begins to happen. You feel instinctively that this is the way it really was, and the actors feel it too. It's almost a psychic thing. You reconstruct, as best you can, a room, the clothes, the situations; and the characters begin to take on the personalities of those real people. From there you can fill in gaps. It's like a detective story.

"You can also reject things that you feel to be false. And one thing that I feel to be utterly false, as far as the biographies are concerned, is the tendency to put the blame for Tchaikovsky's breakdown and near-suicide upon his wife. She had nobody to stand up for her. She was just an ordinary girl, lower middle class. And she's been very hard done by in the biographies. They say she was a nymphomaniac, but there are no grounds to prove this. They say she drove him to attempt suicide, but the girl just married him expecting a normal sex life, and he kept trying to get her drunk all the time so that she wouldn't know where she was. This is never mentioned. She, poor dear, was abandoned by him. I suppose the marriage lasted about a year, all in all. He left her and came back to her, and she ran away and came back. I suppose they actually lived together for two or three months at the most. He did give her money, it's true, but money without love is nothing. Her mother took most of that anyway. And she ended up in a lunatic asylum.

"The thing is that the private lives of artists up until the present time were very carefully shielded. Tchaikovsky is a pertinent case in point. His brother Modeste wrote the official biography and burnt all the letters from Nina, the wife, and destroyed the diary of Tchaikovsky in which he had written about his homosexual liaisons with various people. So, as I say, it has become detective work. One may be totally wrong, but I always find in most of the films I do that the facts are more extraordinary than anything I can make up. Why I think the Hollywood biographies are all boring is because they all follow the same path. They're totally interchangeable. The Liszt and Chopin films were almost identical.

"I'm not saying that every word in the Tchaikovsky film is true, but many of the words have been taken out of the context of letters he wrote, and we've used them in conversations. The pity is that truthful biographies aren't written about these people at the time. Maybe they should be put away, locked up in vaults—not to be opened for fifty years. But these people I've made films about have all been big enough, I think, to be able to withstand any accusation or any sort of skeletons that might be in their closets.

"I always try to take a dispassionate view. In the film, Tchaikovsky's homosexuality is just stated—there it is. He's always trying to fight against it. The attitude towards it is sympathetic, I suppose, because we treat it as I think he must have felt it himself. There's no moral. We don't disapprove.

"We use the Sixth Symphony, the most tortured music he wrote, in this nightmare honeymoon experience he has. And we base it on a letter of his—there is no dialogue in the sequence. He said in the letter he felt he was going mad at the realization of what he had let himself in for, when he found himself locked in a sleeping compartment with Nina on a train, hurtling through the snow at sixty miles an hour, rocking violently. It's like hell. Almost like *Huis clos*. It's a little box six feet square. And he gets her drunk in it—as he did; he said himself he got her drunk. We show her taking off her things, and suddenly he's with a piece of meat."

Wondering if he meant literally, and envisaging a shock cut to some item from the abattoir, I interrupted him to make sure. But no: "I was speaking metaphorically. She's a naked drunk. She passes out cold. And she just rocks about on the floor, and he is trapped with this . . . piece of meat."

These combinations of the music with portions of biography have been selective. As a consequence, many of Tchaikovsky's most familiar works are not represented. There is nothing of *The Queen of Spades*, for example, and from the ballets there is only a portion of the Black Swan (*Swan Lake*: ballroom scene). Russell filmed the initial pas de deux and the coda, but not the variations, on a stage built outdoors beside a real lake in the grounds of a stately home at West Wycombe. The dancers are Georgina Parkinson, of the Royal Ballet, and Alain Dubreuil, of the London Festival Ballet. It rained steadily for three days, making the going pretty slippery. Evidently Russell was of the opinion that the rain would be no disadvantage to the effect he needed: "Again, this section has a point. I'm telling a story, not giving a canned performance of the composer's works. *Swan Lake* is very relevant to Tchaikovsky's own particular dilemma, because it's about a prince who falls in love with a vision and is deceived into thinking that the evil woman who takes on the form of the vision is the actual person he loves. So we point the parallel. Nina is watching the ballet with him, and he has begun to think that she isn't the pure dreamlike creature he had in his mind when he proposed to her. To him she isn't the white swan but the black swan. And this is put into his mind by the evil genius who is his boyfriend Chiluvsky, who turns up and sits with them. So you get the evil magician on the stage, and Chiluvsky there in the audience with Tchaikovsky and Nina. And you get the pure white swan appearing for a moment or so during the pas de deux, and through Tchaikovsky's eyes she is juxtaposed with an image of his sister."

Russell was a dancer himself at one time: "Terry Gilbert, the choreographer I used on the Tchaikovsky film, and myself were the entire male corps de ballet in *Swan Lake* on the pier at Eastbourne, one summer many years ago. I was twenty-six then, and now I'm forty-two. I'd trained in classical dance at the International Ballet School, and I toured Scandinavia with the Norwegian Ballet and Sheffield and Leeds and Nottingham in the third touring company of *Annie Get Your Gun*. All great experience. I've used a lot of what I learned from ballet in my film work. What one does with the camera, and the way actors are moved about, is really choreography, even when there are just two people in a room."

His initial excursions into filmmaking for the cinema were *French Dressing* (1963) and *Billion Dollar Brain* (1967). The first was a comedy about efforts to convert a British seaside town into as glamorous a resort as St. Tropez, by promoting a film festival and luring a seductive French actress to the place; the second continued the adventures of Harry Palmer, the reluctant spy played by Michael

Caine, who had already established the character, based on the anonymous figure in Len Deighton's novels, in Sidney J. Furie's film of *The Ipcress File* (1965) and Guy Hamilton's *Funeral in Berlin* (1966). In neither case was Russell entirely content with the material: "In their own way, I'm not ashamed of them. *Billion Dollar Brain* was a complicated and difficult novel, though, and when one came to analyze it and try to make a film script, it just didn't add up. Probably one should have abandoned it then and there, but I was promised I could do other films, the sort I'm doing now, if I made *Billion Dollar Brain*. That was the reason I did it. I don't think it's any worse than many films of that kind. It had some pretty things in it. Maybe it wasn't very exciting. I saw *French Dressing* again a couple of months ago, for the first time in about six years, and although there's some absolutely awful stuff in it, I still think it has a weird, strange atmosphere. If it had come out a little later than it did, it might have stood a better chance. In fact, I think if it were reissued now and given the treatment it should have had at the time, it might go. It's no masterpiece, it's not even very good, but it's weird and odd.

"I learned a lot of things on both those films that I couldn't learn on the TV films I did for the BBC. There's no comparison, really. The television sort of thing is like a group of friends who get together and just rush out in a car and start filming. It's not very easy to plan properly, for all sorts of reasons, mostly lack of numbers. The relationships are entirely different." Between the two features for cinema he returned to television filming, but his breakthrough as a cinema director was achieved in 1969 with *Women in Love*. Finding a visual equivalent for the psychological and erotic themes of the Lawrence novel, he worked in the more expansive medium with considerable assurance.

Glenda Jackson, who plays the dominant Gudrun in *Women in Love*, is cast as Nina in the Tchaikovsky film. Christopher Gable, the ill-fated bridegroom Tibby Lupton in the Lawrence film, progresses to the more demanding character of Chiluvsky: since his departure from a flourishing career with the Royal Ballet, Gable's determination to become a straight actor has already been aided considerably by Russell, who gave him the difficult task of impersonating Eric Fenby in a TV film about Delius, *Song of Summer*; the result was subtle and perceptive, and it will be interesting to see what has emerged from the Chiluvsky assignment. The most surprising casting, however, is that of Richard Chamberlain for the role of Tchaikovsky, although one gathers that his Hamlet in the theater has been creditable and, like Robert Vaughn and Warren Mitchell and many another, he must have felt a strong compulsion to overcome the image established in a long-running television series. As Russell puts it: "One always associates Chamberlain with the person he hates most in the world, Doctor Kildare. One had nothing else to go on. It would never have occurred to me to consider him until I saw him in a television serial of a Henry James story, *The Portrait of a Lady*, and in that he gave a wonderful performance, very sensitive. We wanted a romantic sort of hero, and he's certainly that. And I investigated and discovered that he could play the piano well enough to give a convincing semblance. I didn't want just to have long shots of him playing and then cut in somebody else's hands on the keyboard. It's essential for the audience to see him actually playing if they're to believe in him as a composer."

The pianist who will actually be heard is Rafael Orozco, but Chamberlain's preparation for giving the "semblance" was arduous: "We recorded Orozco playing it and gave Chamberlain the tape and tutor. And after six months of practice—working on it every day for six months—he could do it."

Areas of Russia in the last century were simulated in sundry parts of the UK. The interior of the stately home at West Wycombe served for the house of Mme. Von Meck, Hampstead Lock provided the setting for the composer's suicide attempt, and the Pump Room at Bath represented the Moscow Conservatoire, while other locations ranged through Southampton, Salisbury, and Milford-on-Sea, in addition to studio work at Bray and an outdoor set on the back lot to represent a fairground.

Such details, along with the meticulous business of showing Tchaikovsky at the keyboard (reputedly he did play the piano quite well at the age of six), might have the customary ring of the filmed biographies that Russell dislikes. One gathers, however, that the pursuit of authenticity is an adjunct to the director's own flights of imagination. If this is not sufficiently implicit in his accounts of the equations of concerto and idealism, symphony and nightmare-honeymoon, and evocative swans, he really lets himself go when he describes the way he has treated the *1812 Overture*—fair game, of course.

"I used it to show Tchaikovsky's dilemma in doing something he absolutely hated, which was conducting in public and becoming a public figure. He's egged on in this by his brother Modeste, after he's been rejected by Mme. Von Meck. Modeste tells him that if it's love he wants, an audience will give him that. Tchaikovsky hated the *1812 Overture* anyway. He thought it was a vulgar piece, and he only did it for a commission. We show him being totally caught up in it and turned into stone by it.

"The sequence shows all those who have been in his life, his sister and Mme. Von Meck, and Nina, with cannons—because we've done it with the cannons and the bells. And in his mind they're shooting at him with the cannons, and they're chasing him. And there's a huge wind which they're battling against. The crowd get hold of him and carry him away and put him right up on top of the cathedral, and he's conducting there. And there's this whirlwind again, and his brother is chasing banknotes and stuffing them into a black bag and becoming a financier.

And then Tchaikovsky's conducting the can-can, doing a commercial thing—and finally Modeste, his brother, gets on a cannon and blows off the heads of all the family and friends, and Tchaikovsky's carried out to a great pealing of bells, and Modeste is on one of the bells, swinging it. And Tchaikovsky's put up on a great plinth and he turns to stone—becomes a statue—and snow falls."

Russell's belief in the value of shock to promote awareness should be amply expressed as well in his next film, *The Devils*. This is the account of Urbain Grandier's life and of the events that led to his trial for diabolism, taken from the play of the same name by John Whiting, which was performed at the Aldwych in London by the Royal Shakespeare Company in 1961. In the same year a Polish film on much the same subject, but set in Poland rather than France, took an award at the Cannes Festival: this was *Mother Joan of the Angels*, also known as *The Devil and the Nun*, directed by Jerzy Kawalerowicz. Whiting's play was based on Aldous Huxley's book *The Devils of Loudun*, an examination of seventeenth-century hang-ups, and of the particular circumstances in which the prioress of St. Ursula's Convent in Loudun was believed to be possessed by an evil spirit, an infection which spread through the entire nunnery, and for which Grandier was blamed.

Huxley's book records that Grandier held a view not uncommon at the time, namely that a priest's vow of celibacy was not binding, since "for the young male, continence is impossible." In respect of young females who take religious vows, sexual problems are also considered in some detail by both Huxley and Whiting. And now by Russell, too.

An Interview with Ken Russell

Gene D. Phillips / 1970

This interview first appeared in the Fall 1970 issue of *Film Comment* and is reprinted with the permission of *Film Comment* and Film at Lincoln Center.

With *Women in Love*, forty-two-year-old British director Ken Russell suddenly burst upon the film scene as a director of international importance, and American filmgoers wondered where this considerable talent had been keeping itself all this time. British viewers, however, were not in the least surprised by the craftsmanship that Russell displayed in *Women*, since for a decade they had been treated to a series of excellent documentaries which Russell had made for BBC-TV. Recently Russell invited me to his favorite London pub, near the place where he was supervising the final editing of his latest film, *The Music Lovers*, to discuss his career past, present, and future.

Gene D. Phillips: Like John Schlesinger, you broke into films by way of TV. How did you get into TV in the first place?

Ken Russell: In 1959 I got the chance to do some ten-minute segments for a TV series called *Monitor*. Huw Weldon, who is now managing director of BBC-TV, worked on the series too. After awhile I was allowed to make some longer documentary shorts for use on the program. I did one on the dance craze, the guitar craze, and one on pop artists called *Pop Goes the Easel*. My segment on photographers probably influenced *Blow-Up*.

Finally, I was asked to do some full-length biographies on the lives of great artists of the past: composers like Elgar, Debussy, Bartók, Prokofiev, and Delius; the poet Rossetti; and dancer Isadora Duncan. I did a film in 1964 called *French Dressing*, a kind of seaside comedy, but it was an ill-conceived project from the start: the chemistry of the characters was wrong and the story never quite gelled. It was a flop, so I continued on in television.

GDP: Among all of the TV biographies which you have done, which ones are among your favorites?

KR: Three of the ones I most enjoyed doing are *Isadora, the Biggest Dancer in the World* [1966], *Song of Summer* [1968], about the composer Delius, and *Dance of the Seven Veils* [1970], which was suggested by the life and music of Richard Strauss.

GDP: I have seen all of the ones you have named; I admired Karel Reisz's subsequent film on Isadora Duncan very much, but I must say that I enjoyed your TV version much more than Reisz's film.

KR: Reisz's film version used most of the incidents in Isadora's life that I used, but I managed to tell her story with a little more economy in about half the time that his film runs.

GDP: This is partially due to the fact that you ran through the whole of Isadora's life in a kind of kaleidoscope-newsreel fashion at the beginning of your TV film (à la *Citizen Kane*) which gave the viewer a capsule view of her life that you could then easily expand as you went through the rest of the story.

KR: And Vivian Pickles, an excellent actress, who had not done many important roles, was perfect as Isadora. Since Isadora's life was so pathetic and tragic, I tried to lighten the material at times. For example, I used the old Betty Hutton recording of "The Sewing Machine" from the 1947 Hollywood film *The Perils of Pauline* on the soundtrack when Isadora was falling in love with Paris Singer, the sewing machine manufacturer.

GDP: Nevertheless, your *Isadora* has some darker tones at certain points than Reisz's film. For example, you showed that Isadora's Russian husband was an epileptic and a kleptomaniac and how this complicated their relationship, while the movie *Isadora* ignored these facts. With your interest in biographies of this kind, how did you wind up doing the film of *Billion Dollar Brain* [1967]?

KR: I had a contract with Harry Saltzman to film the life of the Russian dancer Vaslav Nijinsky with Rudolph Nureyev in the lead. Then Nureyev decided that he could not play the role of a dancer who was inferior to himself, and the project was off. So I directed the spy film *Billion Dollar Brain* for Saltzman instead, since at that time he was doing a series of these films hoping to make the Harry Palmer character played by Michael Caine as popular as the James Bond character.

GDP: I understand that Nureyev has at last decided to do the role of Nijinsky and that Tony Richardson is now going to make the film. At any rate, *Brain* flopped like your first film had done, and so it was back to television.

KR: One of the biographies that I did at this time was that of the composer Delius, who spent the last years of his life blind and crippled by syphilis while living in an English country cottage with his faithful wife and his amanuensis. It was a difficult TV film to make, since I felt that I didn't know enough about Delius and his milieu, so I couldn't formulate just how I wanted to approach the material. I did not feel that way about D. H. Lawrence at all, incidentally. But I went ahead with the Delius biography anyhow, since making films is a voyage of discovery. I used a lot of location shots in the country, since Delius's music deals so often with nature and because he died there. While working in TV I always shot out of doors as much as possible, since the indoor sets always seemed to me to look like sets: four blinking flats with pictures hung on them. I have shot almost all of my TV films outside of a TV studio on location. In general, I always disregarded the fact that I was doing them for television, although working in TV has made me partial to big close-ups, and I still use them often in motion pictures.

GDP: You said that you felt at home working on material from D. H. Lawrence when you filmed *Women in Love* [1969].

KR: I had immersed myself in the book and worked on the script, so that by the time I went on the floor to shoot the film, I knew what I wanted. Nevertheless, I am a great believer in inventing things on the set. Working in TV you learn how to cut costs and prune down the project to essentials. When you work fast you get a certain spontaneity from your cast and crew, and they make suggestions about how to improve a scene during shooting.

GDP: I understand that Glenda Jackson, who worked for you both in *Women* and in *The Music Lovers*, is particularly good at suggesting things that you can use in a scene.

KR: Glenda Jackson is my kind of actress. Some actresses talk about the character they are playing incessantly—not Glenda; you have a preliminary discussion of the character with her, and then she sticks to that throughout the filming. She makes a great many suggestions, and I usually accept about half of them. I only work with people who understand what I am trying to do, because of the short time we have to work. In order to make a period picture on the same budget as a film in a contemporary setting, you have to sacrifice something, and I sacrifice time. I assemble around me a cast and crew that can intuit what I want and to whom, therefore, I have to say very little. Glenda is the prime example of the kind of person with whom I like to work.

GDP: Most of your work for TV and motion pictures has had a period setting. Why are you drawn to the past for subject matter?

KR: I love period films: the possibility of opening a book into the past fascinates me. You don't have to worry that every last detail is historically accurate; a lack of total authenticity doesn't matter; in the end a little roughness is not a bad thing. I generally select period material because all of the stories I do are about the relationships of people to their environment and to each other, and other eternal questions that we are just as concerned about today as people were in the past. Topics of the moment pass and change; besides, one's feelings toward contemporary topics tends to distort one's presentation of them. We can be much more dispassionate and objective, and therefore more truthful, in dealing with the past. To see things of the past from the vantage point of the present is to be able to judge what effect they have had on the present.

GDP: You said that you worked on the script of *Women in Love*. Since so many critics commented on how faithful the film is to Lawrence's novel, could you tell me how much of this fidelity to Lawrence was due to yourself?

KR: The first script was done by an excellent screenwriter, but it had nothing to do with Lawrence. He had the old idea that unless you change something beyond recognition, you are not being creative. This attitude is a terrible affront to the original author of the novel, especially if the author in question happens to be a writer like D. H. Lawrence. A second version of the script was done by another screenwriter and it was appalling: at the final fadeout Alan Bates and Jennie Linden were to gallop off into the sunset. At this point I took a hand in writing the script. I used as much of Lawrence's dialogue as I possibly could. Nearly all of the conversation is verbatim from the novel. For the storyline, I pulled out of the novel's action bits that would hang together as a narrative. So I suppose that I am as responsible as anyone for the film's fidelity to Lawrence.

GDP: Was the nude wrestling match between Alan Bates and Oliver Reed your idea, then?

KR: The wrestling match was in the novel and I wanted to use it in the same symbolic fashion that Lawrence had used it. At its conclusion Birkin [Bates] says to Gerald [Reed], "We are mentally and spiritually close. Therefore, we should be physically close too." This is not a plea for a homosexual relationship between them. Birkin believes that two men can each get married and yet maintain an intimate relationship with each other that is different from, but which neverthe-less complements the heterosexual relationship that each has in marriage. Gerald could not commit himself to Birkin on this level not only because he thought such a relationship unconventional but because he really could not reveal himself or commit himself to anyone. I originally thought of a swimming context for the scene, since how else could you explain the two men stripping off for the match? But Oliver Reed said that that setting would be too poetic. He suggested that it should be more of a real physical confrontation between the two men locked in a room sweating and straining, and that is how we did it.

GDP: Since *Women in Love*, as frank as if is, was so well received, were you surprised at the dismay in England caused by your TV film on the life of Richard Strauss, *Dance of the Seven Veils*?

KR: I saw that television biographies were becoming filled with terrible clichés that had grown out of imitation of my TV films—deification of the artist is wrong; he should be presented as a human being who, despite his faults, managed to create lasting works of art. The telecast began with an announcement that what was to be presented was a harsh and violent personal interpretation of Strauss's life and work, but one which was nevertheless based on real events. This should have been a sufficient warning to those who might be offended by watching it.

Those who were offended by it took the film much too literally. It was meant to work on a deep symbolic level. For example, in order to get across the fact that Richard Strauss was uninterested in the Second World War because it didn't touch him personally, I presented a dream sequence in which Strauss is forced to watch his wife raped and his child murdered by the Nazis. Just as a Nazi holds a gun to Strauss's head, the image dissolves into that of his son with a toy gun, and then the camera pulls back to show the Strauss family in a kind of *Sound of Music* Tyrolean setting completely removed from the realities of the war. This is the insulated atmosphere in which Strauss wrote his *Alpine Symphony*, as if the war didn't exist.

GDP: What about your treatment of Strauss's capitulation to the Nazi regime? That offended a lot of admirers of his work.

KR: Strauss was one of the most famous people in Germany at that time, and if he had taken a stand against the Nazis, this would have had a tremendous effect. I was trying to shock people into a realization of their responsibilities. Strauss thought of himself as an ageless superman. He based his *Zarathustra*—which has since become identified with Kubrick's use of it in *2001*—on Nietzsche's conception of the superman. Then in later years when he was out of favor with Hitler, he wrote an obsequious letter to Hitler. At this point I have his wife put on him the mask of an old man, for Strauss has finally admitted his weakness and dependence on Hitler's favor. Later, after the war, when he is conducting the *Zarathustra* in London after he has been completely exonerated by the Allies of having endorsed the Nazi regime, the music swells to a crescendo, and I have Strauss rip off the mask of the old man; he is still the crypto Nazi with the superman fantasy underneath the facade of the distinguished elderly composer.

GDP: The day after the program was screened on BBC-TV, a motion was introduced in Parliament condemning your version of Strauss's life and music as vicious, savage, and brutal. Some TV critics suggested that you were trying to increase the limits of what is permissible on television.

KR: The BBC got an enormous number of phone calls after the film was televised, as many for as against. The television audience are all asleep in their armchairs. It's a good thing to shake them up; even if it's only as far as the phone. Huw Weldon defended *Dance of the Seven Veils* when it was shown for fifty members of Parliament, and John Trevelyan, the British film censor, supported the film as well.

GDP: To me your *Dance of the Seven Veils* is the most visually brilliant piece of work you have done so far, especially in the fantasy scenes.

KR: In every film I have made, the style has been dictated by the subject. *Delius* was an austere, restrained film, mainly about three people in a bare, white room. That was the way to do that particular story. Strauss, on the other hand, was a self-advertising, vulgar, commercial man. I took the keynote of the film from the music, a lot of which is bombastic. I also built up the portrait from the man himself; and 95 percent of what Strauss said in the film he actually said.

GDP: You even gave him a screen credit for contributing to the dialogue. You are undoubtedly in for more criticism from music lovers for presenting Tchaikovsky as a homosexual in *The Music Lovers*.

KR: There is a Russian version of Tchaikovsky's life coming out as well. When I went to United Artists with the idea of doing his life, they pointed this out to me, and I replied that my approach to the composer's life was sure to be different from the Russian version. For one thing, the Russians have never admitted that Tchaikovsky was homosexual. I have been quoted as saying that my film is about a homosexual who marries a nymphomaniac. This is a flip way of putting it, but basically it boils down to this, and this is what the film explores. It takes only two years in Tchaikovsky's life, the period when he was married. This was the turning point in his life. Tchaikovsky himself said that his inner conflicts are there in his music and they are. His Sixth Symphony is tortured and terrible. In one scene in my film, Tchaikovsky [Richard Chamberlain] is shown in bed with the rich Vladimir Shilovsky [Editor's note: named Anton Chiluvsky in the film and played by Christopher Gable], whose possessiveness helped push Tchaikovsky into thoughts of marriage. Besides, he had always longed to have a family. In addition, he believed that man was governed by fate. He had written an opera, *Eugene Onegin*, in which a girl writes love letters to a man who turns her down and thereby ruins his own life and that of the girl. Tchaikovsky started getting letters from a girl, Antonina Milyukova [Glenda Jackson]; he decided the situation was too much of a coincidence with the story of his opera to be ignored, and so he met and married her. The marriage, of course, was a disaster. As in my television lives of composers, I make a definite connection between the man's life and his music. The composer-conductor of the film's music, André Previn, has drawn on Tchaikovsky's music throughout the film, and there is not one piece of music that is there for its own sake. It's all there to reflect some aspect of Tchaikovsky's life and personality.

GDP: What future projects do you have in mind?

KR: I would like to do *The Devils* and have done a script based on both Aldous Huxley's book and John Whiting's play. I also used the available documentation, but I had to thin it out since it is so vast. It is based on the same historical incident which served as the basis of Kawalerowicz's 1961 Polish film *Mother Joan of the Angels*, which I saw about five years ago. A frustrated mother superior in a convent, whom 1 hope will be played by Glenda Jackson, gets dreamy about a priest. Cardinal Richelieu does not like the priest and has evidence planted on him to discredit him. My version of the story will bring in more of the political background of the period than did the Polish film.

GDP: In defending you against the negative criticism of your TV film about Strauss, Huw Weldon said that you happen to be a Roman Catholic and would not set out to offend any religious group in your work. Do you feel that your background as a convert to Catholicism will be a help to you in making *The Devils*?

KR: Possibly. My Catholic background helps me to distinguish between normal religious practices and the bizarre things attributed to the nuns in *The Devils*. Since Kawalerowicz is not a Christian, the whole idea of convent life would seem bizarre to him. At any rate, I don't mind now if I am not able to make the film, since I have worked it out shot by shot in my imagination; 1 can run it in my head any time I want to. Although I must admit a finished film is often very different from the way one has initially pictured it in one's mind.

GDP: Do you intend to adapt any more novels for the screen?

KR: I am interested in Evelyn Waugh's 1934 novel *A Handful of Dust*, but I will not attempt to update it to the present as did the recent film of his 1928 novel *Decline and Fall*. Waugh's novels are relevant to the present, and they do not have to have the setting updated to prove it. I would also like to do Graham Greene's *A Burnt-Out Case*, which is one of the few novels that Greene has written that has yet to be filmed.

GDP: Greene, who has done some of the scripts himself, once told me that the initial script that he does from one of his novels usually has a great deal of the original dialogue from the novel in it; but he deletes most of this as he revises the script, and in the end most of the original dialogue is gone. Yet you told me that most of the dialogue in *Women in Love* is directly from the book. Do you then disagree with Greene's approach to adapting a novel to the screen?

KR: Not really. If a man adapts his own novel to another medium, he feels that he's done it this way once; in the interim it has grown in his mind, since one's ideas about any subject change and grow over a period of time. But if I adapt something written by someone else to the screen, I am approaching it fresh and want to leave the thing the way it is as much as possible.

GDP: I understand that Lesley Hornby—alias Twiggy—has said that she will take out time from her modeling career to do a film with you if the right part turns up.

KR: Yes, and I hope the right part does turn up. If so, she will be the greatest thing to hit the screen since Marilyn Monroe.

GDP: I gather that you have achieved total artistic control over your films.

KR: While I was at the BBC, I was my own boss, and after *Women in Love* I was ready to go back to television for good, since I was allowed to act as my own producer on any of my previous films. I found that when someone else is producing, I have a battle royal with him most of the time. After one has poured his lifeblood into a project, it is difficult to accept the fact that someone else is really controlling the project. Now that I do have the same artistic freedom in making films that I had in television, I think I will stick with films.

An Interview with Ken Russell

Max Tessier / 1971

From *Cinéma* 71 (December 1971): 119–22. Translated by Claudia Gorbman. Reprinted with permission. From a conversation in Paris on October 22, 1971, translated from English by Max Tessier.

Facing the prospect of interviewing the director of *Women in Love* and *The Devils*, you might worry what kind of blasphemous monster will appear before you, and whether he might seize you in his powerful claws and drag you into a crypt full of maniacs, tormentors, and sexual obsessives. Instead, we found ourselves in the company of an affable fellow, alert and solid, his ruddy British complexion brimming with health, who has braved sea tempests as well as cinematic ones. He was an inexhaustible source of details about his motley and eventful adolescence that might have been that of a character in one of his films. He was quite chatty in recounting these stories as he sat on a couch, I before him, feeling bizarrely like an amateur psychoanalyst . . .

Ken Russell: My father, who had a shop in Southampton, had never really made the grade in his career as a seaman. Accordingly, he sent me to naval school, which I perfectly detested. At the school I eventually staged a musical show, dressed up as Carmen Miranda and the other guys played South American girls. That is when I realized I wanted to perform, not be a sailor. But I did sail to Australia at age seventeen. When I returned, my mother issued an ultimatum: go back to my father or make the break and change careers. So I started to study music. I was playing Tchaikovsky on the piano, and I felt that something extraordinary was happening to me. It so transported me that I started to dance Stravinsky's *Rite of Spring* naked in the living room, breaking half the furniture! Since I couldn't in any case continue to break more furniture, I joined the Royal Air Force.

There I met a sailor who loved music and had organized a kind of music club where people listened to records and watched films. The sailor danced *Swan Lake* during the concerts at the club. I asked him, "What are you doing?" "I'm doing a dance." "A dance? What do you mean?" "Try it yourself." So I started dancing with him, and found it quite amusing. He suggested I go to London to properly learn choreographic technique, which I eventually did. But also during my time in the RAF, I often went to the cinema with my mother. She was quite a movie buff, seeing at least one film per day.

When I left the air force, I tried to get hired as an actor in film studios, but it didn't happen. So I tried my hand at working as a dancer; I performed in a lot of musicals such as *Annie Get Your Gun*. But I also made attempts at stage acting in a traveling company, the Garrick Players—which disbanded after a particularly rainy summer.

Then I became a photographer. I took my wife and children to Scotland and photographed them dressed up as Charlotte Brontë characters. I purchased a movie camera and made three amateur films. The most original of them was *Amelia and the Angels*; it's the story of a little girl who has lost her angel wings for the school play and who goes off to find some other wings. At that time, over ten years ago, the English film industry was in a bad slump, and all the studios were occupied by television production. TV people were looking for young directors, and after seeing *Amelia*, they hired me at the BBC, and I worked there for several years. I made very direct and personal documentaries, very symbolic, about various poets, artists, and musicians such as Debussy, Bartók, Elgar, Prokofiev, and so forth. The connection between those films and the ones I make now is logical enough.

Max Tessier: Do you think there is an autobiographical component to films like *The Music Lovers*?

KR: Yes, in the sense that the artist is fighting against the society around him and feels misunderstood. Since I made many biographical films for TV for several years, I always thought it was an excellent way to express what I myself was thinking and feeling. The difference between television and film is that the budget is considerably smaller in television; this is a good thing in a way, since one must use imagination to find other less obvious means to achieve what the film is trying to express.

MT: Apparently for *The Music Lovers* and your other films you needed substantial financial means; could you have made it without a big budget?

KR: In fact, my films have not been as expensive as they might appear. I think my last film (*The Boy Friend*) also breaks a record in this respect—I did it for much less money than someone else could. This comes from my television training, where you use small budgets and a small crew, but often a crew who are really committed, passionate, and capable. The next film I will be making, which is the story of the French sculptor Henri Gaudier-Brzeska, who was killed in the

First World War, will be financed by me, no American companies involved. The reality is that American companies collect 25 percent of the budget for "general expenses," which means their girlfriends and their trips on jumbo jets from Paris to San Francisco. Twenty-five percent of the budget, meaning tens of thousands of dollars that go over the film. So the solution is to produce films by yourself, to make sure this money is on the screen, not in the pockets of some guys traveling with their "companions." When there have been problems with my budgets, it's that I have exceeded them because of these bogus "general expenses."

MT: All your recent films are set in the past, either recent or far removed. Does this have a particular significance, or does the particular era have no importance?

KR: I think I'm more concerned with the past—that the present is on television every day, in the news. If I made films about the events in Ireland or other current political issues, I think in a year's time they would ring false and feel outdated. I prefer to situate these problems in the past, fifty or a hundred or four hundred years back, in order to consider them in a new way.

MT: Would you say that, in this sense, *The Devils* is a kind of parable about Ireland?

KR: Yes, but not only about Ireland—it's about fanaticism in general. The trial you see at the end is reproduced every day in our world, and more now than ever.

MT: But don't you think the spectacular side of the film lessens its significance and masks its deeper intentions?

KR: No, not really. This could be a danger, but I don't think it's the case here. Given the current situation of cinema in England, audiences prefer watching TV to going to the movies. For *The Devils*, the critics said it was a horrible, dreadful film, to be avoided at all costs, etc. And because of *that*, people have been running to see it—the very opposite of what they expected. And the critics have been utterly silent regarding the political aspect of the film. As long as people go see the film, the game is on: once the audience can see it, they can make up their own minds about it and "get the message." Now, if I had made a much subtler film, requiring reading between the lines like so many others do these days, critics would surely not talk it up and the audience wouldn't have gone to see it. I see no harm whatsoever in getting the audience's attention: to get your film seen, you have to be able to hook them in the first twenty-five seconds!

MT: We have the impression that in *The Devils* you devoted less attention to historical credibility than in your previous films. None of the characters resemble the image history has given us of them.

KR: You are entirely right, but I think that the time has come when treating historical subjects involves focusing more on the spirit than on the details of the reenactment. What is really important is seeing the relationship between past events and the present. This is why I maximally stylized the sets and the acting, to avoid the usual clichés. I also see my film as a modern equivalent of a medieval mystery play, in which religious devotion, farce, comedy, and melodrama are all mixed together to give an idea of what could (and still can) happen in a place such as Loudun.

MT: What do you say to those who accuse you of sadism, voyeurism, and piling on lurid details?

KR: I think that in cinema it is very boring to be sadistic, unless one is a complete sadist, which I am not. Putting sadistic details on screen demands the clinical stance of a surgical operation: you have to calculate the amount of hemoglobin, see what color will be obtained, and all this is devoid of any passion whatsoever. What truly thrills me is the idea one has of the film *before* shooting; that's where I really feel emotion. In any case, if I were a true sadist, I would torture my children at home instead of making movies.

MT: Did you immediately see the symbolic ramifications of *The Devils*?

KR: To a point. When I saw the play in England around 1960, it really struck me, but it didn't show much of the horrible side of the story; it muted it to remain in the bounds of "good taste," which does not interest me by any means. If there is bad taste in the world, why not show it as well as good taste? Why not show it all? What was important to me was the way we would show how Grandier had been used and destroyed by a political faction. As for Huxley's book, I think it is one of the greatest works of English literature; when I began the film, it couldn't be found in any bookstore.

MT: Would a science fiction film from a work of Huxley's interest you, such as *Brave New World*?

KR: I would perhaps like to make a film from a book by Huxley that is a novel written in 1948 about the possible effects of an atom bomb, *Ape and Essence*. But I wonder if I could do it, because even if people can tolerate reading the most horrific things, they lose their defense mechanisms when they are *shown* them. They would be terribly shocked, because it moves too fast.

MT: Your preoccupations do not seem to appear in your musical *The Boy Friend*. What is this movie for you?

KR: This film has nothing to do with the others. I think it will be quite popular and people will enjoy it, but it's very different from the "intense" films I have made so far. It's an homage to Busby Berkeley—I grew up on his great musicals of the thirties. I think each subject demands its own style, and that I couldn't treat *The Boy Friend* like my previous films.

MT: You also plan to make a biographical film about Sarah Bernhardt? Are you eager about the idea of working with Barbra Streisand?

KR: I think it's a good subject, she is a good actress, and that it's worth the risk. Barbra herself will produce the film, and I think she's excited about the subject, since she has spent several months studying it. Sarah Bernhardt was a woman who acted out her own life onstage. She had a repertoire of about twenty plays made for her, half of which she used to interpret aspects of her private life, from the intoxication of drugs to her lesbianism, her nymphomania, and so forth. She could not face all that in her life, so she projected her obsessions onstage. I find this quite interesting.

Conversation with Ken Russell

Terry Curtis Fox / 1973

From *Oui* (June 1973): 63–64, 102–8. Reprinted with permission.

An American walking into a movie theater in 1967 expecting to see the newest Len Deighton-Harry Palmer thriller received quite a shock when *Billion Dollar Brain* came on the screen. There was Michael Caine, alright, being his usual reluctant secret-agent self, but this time he was the butt of some strange cosmic joke about how much snow there is in Finland. Halfway through the movie, Ed Begley suddenly prepared to invade Russia by dancing around a Texas bonfire, and the climax of the thriller turned out to be nothing more than a musical and cinematic joke.

Although few took notice at the time, *Billion Dollar Brain* was America's introduction to Ken Russell, a self-educated former British sailor out to set the film world on end. For years the enfant terrible of the BBC, Russell had been busily puncturing national sensitivities and enraging conservative artistic sensibilities with his irreverent biographies of famous artists. Isadora Duncan was shown ascending to heaven accompanied by Beethoven's Ninth Symphony and a horde of prancing children, her death-dealing scarf floating jauntily in the ephemeral wind. Richard Strauss was portrayed as a comic-strip Nazi. While the stodgy screamed, the public remained glued to its tellies.

Russell gained international recognition with his film of D. H. Lawrence's *Women in Love*. Though some Lawrentians complained that it was not the movie they would have made, none could accuse Russell of avoiding the sensual issues of the book. Puritans were enraged that Russell dared to show two nude men wrestling erotically in a fire's orange glow, especially since the public and the press appeared enraptured.

Never one to rest on his laurels, Russell immediately offended a host of film and music critics with *The Music Lovers*. A biography of Tchaikovsky, the film played heavily upon the composer's homosexuality and included a sequence to the *1812 Overture*. There were more accusations of self-indulgence when Russell

presented *The Devils*, a story of religious persecution and witch hunting in medieval France, adapted from a book by Aldous Huxley and a play by John Whiting.
Always disrespectful, Russell plunged into the decadence and death pervading
society and the church. Strange coming from a Catholic convert.

Next came *The Boy Friend*, once a happy spoof of twenties musicals. Russell
cast Twiggy in the film's lead and turned the project into a cynical look at sex and
the theater. MGM took one look at what he had done and emasculated the film for
American release. Russell sputtered but went back to MGM with *Savage Messiah*,
a study of the early twentieth-century sculptor Henri Gaudier-Brzeska. Evoking
Russell's favorite theme of a self-centered artist in conflict with society, *Savage
Messiah* was played at a single near-hysterical level. While some critics saw it as
his most controlled work, audiences were generally confused. Russell remained
unperturbed. This was his art, and the public would damn well get used to it.

Oui: You've said you came from a working-class family that never read books.

Ken Russell: That's right.

Oui: Where did you grow up?

Russell: I grew up in a port, Southampton, which was a very colorful place.
It's a rather strange mix-up, really. The road I lived on was a side street, and traffic never came down it. I never saw another child until I went to school. But as
soon as I could walk, my mother would take me down to the center of town,
which was a teeming, marvelous, fantastic place. I always imagined it rather like
Marseilles once was. It was a great mixture of sailors and rather shady-looking
individuals, prostitutes, and God knows what. In the middle of this was a place
called the High Street, which had a couple of variety theaters and was full of
picture palaces. Every afternoon we'd plunge into this seething mass and go to
the pictures. The next morning, I'd just sit in my quiet road by myself, thinking
about what I'd seen and probably acting out various scenes.

Oui: And your interest in art and artists developed out of your immersion
in all of this?

Russell: I went through the process of going to naval college and went to
sea a bit, but I didn't like that. I used to put on shows at college. We used to get
the cadets up in drag. Carmen Miranda and things like that, which was very
different from the usual concerts they had there, where they'd stand in gray
flannels, white sweaters, and naval caps, singing "The Fisherman of England."
I did the shows by breaking bounds and getting caned and beaten for it, but it
was well worth it. I realized I preferred show business to being a sailor. I made a
very, very short film there which I never saw. It was a mad Chaplinesque farce,
again using all the college students dressed up as men and women. I still had no
interest in art at all. I didn't know about painting or music until I came out of

the merchant navy and went into the air force. I got interested in music when I was recovering from a breakdown I had after coming back from sea. We had a very mad disciplinarian of a captain who made life hell on the ship. If you were ever beaten, which I was fortunate enough not to be, you were practically cut in two with a rope. Where were we?

Oui: The music.

Russell: Well, when I had this sort of breakdown, I just happened to be listening to the radio, and I heard some music I couldn't believe. The man announced that it was Tchaikovsky's First Piano Concerto. I rushed out and bought the records. From then on, I couldn't have enough music. I would buy every record I could afford. And then I went to the air force and ran this music circle with another sailor, named Bert Woodfield. We put on the records in the projection theater, and the audience would sit in the auditorium and listen. One day, Bert suddenly got up, and this very fat sailor with his figure-hugging bell bottoms did a fantastic dance. He did the male *Bluebird* variation from Tchaikovsky's *Sleeping Beauty*, which is very difficult. To see this fifteen-stone gentleman suddenly flying through the air was rather an extraordinary sight, which has never left me. I said, "What's that?" and he said, "It's ballet." He told me what ballet was—I'd never heard of it. Then he said, "When we're demobbed, why don't you come to London? Anyone can dance." I thought it was rather fantastic, but he said, "You can come to the Hamester Ballet Club," which I did. I got a job working in an art gallery during the day. That's where my interest in art started. To get that, I wrote to every gallery in London. They used to have a great list of art galleries in the Underground, the London subway. I just wrote the whole list down and wrote to them all. I ended up getting one call to a gallery named Le Favre. I went there the day before I was supposed to and saw that the paintings on the wall were by someone called Sickert, whom I'd never heard of—didn't like him much, actually. I read up on Sickert, and when I went back the next day, I said, "Ah, your Sickerts are marvelous. That was his blue period in Camden Town." I was very knowledgeable about the whole thing, which I'd just read overnight. They were greatly impressed, and I got the job. In the evenings, I did the ballet business, but I was twenty-one when I started, and you've really got to be five, or twelve at the latest.

Oui: Did you get into films through dance?

Russell: I'd tried to get into films as soon as I came out of the air force. But to get into the British film industry in those days—that was about 1948—was impossible. It was a dying industry. It was dying because they really wouldn't take anyone fresh. They would just use old school friends and old directors and so forth. So then I took an audition with the International Ballet School. I couldn't dance much, but I could jump very high. They said that was good enough. For three years, I was a student, but my limbs were too stiff. I was always straining ankles and kneecaps. So I thought, I've got to get some job dancing—if not in *Sleeping Beauty* or *Swan Lake*, it'll have to be—and it was—*Annie Get Your Gun*. I was in the chorus of *Annie Get Your Gun* for some time.

Oui: Between the ballet and your joining the BBC, you were a still photographer.

Russell: Yes, well, let me go on about ballet. I did one or two things. I went to the Norwegian ballet. There was a group called London Theatre Ballet. They were small companies with two pianos, and they played one tattered seaside resort, off season. Places like the Flora Hall Eastbourne. I was given a chance to do *Dr. Coppelius* there, which was quite good because I did it like *Dr. Caligari*, which I'd just seen. It was very unusual to see this fair-type ballet done with an expressionist mad doctor, but I was no good at ballet, really. So I gave it up for acting. I was hopeless as an actor. I lasted three weeks, precisely. A placed called the Garrick Players, Newton Poppleford, South Devon. We acted in the pouring rain to three people in deck chairs. I gave that up and thought, "I really want to go into films, and it's still impossible. The nearest thing is photography." Dancers and actors always wanted portraits. So I thought, well, I can make a living that way. I started at a technical college to learn photography, which I did very quickly. I also met my wife there. She was a fashion designer, and I used her as a model. I thought I'd become a fashion photographer.

Oui: Did you make a living?

Russell: I made a living not as a fashion photographer but as a features photographer with magazines called *Illustrated* and *Picture Post*. They're not around anymore. Television killed them. I did feature work for them, but the things I liked doing best were things like we did on our honeymoon. We had our honeymoon at Howard, where the Brontë sisters lived. I dressed Shirley up in Victorian gear, and we tramped all over the moors, evoking the spirit of the Brontës, against the backlit grass and mud. I photographed the churchyard, the couch where Charlotte died, and so forth. They were evocative, moody, atmospheric things, but there wasn't much call for them. I sold one or two. We always liked dressing up and doing things like that. As the years went on, I managed to save enough to make three amateur films—two fantasies and a documentary.

Oui: One of those films, *Peepshow*, is something of a metaphorical statement about the relationship between art and magic.

Russell: I suppose it is. It also has elements of *Dr. Coppelius*, which has the same thing. It was about somebody who brings something to life and about people trying to destroy that. I suppose that's often the theme of my films. I hadn't thought of it before, but they are about creation and destruction. So I suppose that was an early start.

Oui: How did you get to the BBC?

Russell: There was this one arts program, and there were about four produc-ers on it. John Schlesinger was there before I was. I really took over his place. He got a chance to do a feature film and they needed another director. To get into the program, I showed them the amateur films I'd made myself, and I was taken on a freelance basis.

Oui: Who chose the subjects for your BBC films?

Russell: I did. I gave the editor of the program, Huw Wheldon, who is now managing director of the BBC, a list of six subjects. He picked one, and I made it. Afterwards, he said, "I'll give you another chance. I liked that. What do you want to do?" I said, "Well, I'll do a New Forest composer I know," and he said, "OK." It went on from there. The first two films were about living people. Then we started doing documentaries about dead people. We weren't allowed to show them. We had to show just photographs. It was a very purist documentary. One had all the boredom of two decades of English documentary behind one to shake off.

Oui: *Listen to Britain* and that sort of thing?

Russell: Yes, that's right. They were very good in their way, but nothing had progressed. Over the years, we were given the freedom to experiment. Gradu-ally, we were allowed to show the hands of the composer playing, then the com-poser in long shot, still never speaking, intercut with newsreel material. Then we showed them in close-up, and *then* we actually were allowed to show them speaking. They turned from little documentaries into quite long feature films. The programs were generally forty-five minutes, and there were usually four items to them. So you can see, the films were very short to start with. As our films got longer, we got more ambitious. They'd take up the whole program. Sometimes the program would be longer than forty-five minutes; some were an hour and a half. It was the only film school England's ever had. They didn't think a program on the arts would last more than a month. Actually, it ran for about ten years, and it developed into about twenty other arts programs. It was all due to this fantastic man who ran it, Huw Wheldon, who has the most analytical mind I've ever encountered. He is terribly articulate and intellectual. I could always think in pictures, but I couldn't really express in words what I wanted to do. He made me sit down and write the commentary. He'd say, "Come on, say what you feel there." And I'd *try* and say it, and he'd say, "No, say it more succinctly than that, get it more crisp." Then I'd try again, and eventually, after about five years, I could do my own writing. He would analyze the films and say, "That's self-indulgent; take that out." I did a film on dancing. It was about twenty minutes, and I said, "Oh, it's twenty minutes long, it's great." He said, "We don't want *length*, we want *brilliance*—cut it." That's been my credo ever since. I cut them down—all my ideas—to the bare minimum before anyone gets a chance to be bored. At least I hope I do. Of course, when you're making films for television, you've really got to grab the audience. Our program came on every other Sunday, after the feature film, and people who would watch a feature film wouldn't necessarily watch an arts program. So before they could get up and turn us off, we had to grab them. A lot of my early films had terrific impact starts. I don't think you've seen *The Debussy Film* in America.

Oui: No.

Russell: The start of that was a girl in a modern T-shirt being shot full of arrows by teenagers on a beach. You hesitate before you turn *that* off.

Oui: Is it common in Britain for a television director to be well known? American TV directors are really unknown quantities.

Russell: I should think it's the same in Britain. There are many good TV directors who occasionally get a chance to make a film. Things being what they are, their first film is often their last. *My* first film was nearly my last. The thing is that you don't have any choice. If someone comes up to you and says, "Would you like to make a feature film?" you think, "My God, yes, that's a wonderful opportunity." But in my own first two cases, the subjects were ones I'd never have chosen in a million light-years. Things I don't know much about and which I shouldn't have done. I made one feature film very early on in my TV career, called *French Dressing*, which I don't think was ever shown in America. I think it has some fun things in it. It's rather heavily based on French films, sort of a poor man's Jacques Tati. It's got a bit of Truffaut tucked away. It's quite a lyrical film, but it's not very funny. Rather unfortunate, since it was supposed to be a comedy. It's about a terrible English seaside resort which is dying on its feet. The owners think they'll have a film festival to attract people. They go over to France and get a girl to come over. The whole thing ends in disaster. It's quite a bizarre film. I think it might go down now.

Oui: The humor in your second film, *Billion Dollar Brain*, is also a bit bizarre. For example, the idea of choreographing an invasion of Russia to the Shostakovich *Leningrad Symphony*.

Russell: That came from John McGrath and myself. He's an excellent playwright who won't have his stuff done in London's West End. In a sense, he's a bit like me.

Oui: What sort of relationship do you have with your screenwriters?

Russell: It's a very intimate one. I've worked with three, Christopher Logue, Melvyn Bragg, and John McGrath. They are friends, and it's a very close thing. I usually tell them how I would like the story. We discuss it: they will say why they don't like something or how they think something can be improved or come up with their own idea. They read it to me, and we revise as we go along. Usually, when I'm shooting, I revise yet again according to the necessities of the day. I believe in using what is available, and when I've changed my mind, I rewrite the whole thing. They know how I feel, and they know my work. They've seen all the films. It's a very good relationship.

Oui: Throughout *Billion Dollar Brain*, Michael Caine plays Harry Palmer as if he's always at a loss. The final shot of Caine deserted on the ice is almost a savage joke. Did you have any trouble getting him to play the role that way?

Russell: Not at all. I suppose he might have thought it was quite a bit different. I'd seen the other Palmer films, but they hadn't made much of an impression on me. It just seemed right, because that's how he was in the book, somewhat a victim, unwitting. It's so long ago, I can hardly remember, actually. I haven't seen that since we made it. You were talking about the battle on the ice. Well, John and I loved *Alexander Nevsky* and thought it would be quite hilarious to do a modern *Nevsky*. I can't quite remember what happens in the book. I know they do invade, but we deliberately built it up. A tribute to Eisenstein, as it were.

Oui: Was *Billion Dollar Brain* a project that was more or less just something to get you into features?

Russell: It was a bit of a hoax, in a way. Harry Saltzman saw my Debussy film. At the time Saltzman was setting up, in his mind only, a consortium of six up-and-coming directors to do films of their choice on low budget. Two of my ideas were Tchaikovsky and Nijinsky. He said, "Before we get you going, you can get your hand in by doing this feature film with Mike Caine. He'd like you to do it, and I'd like you to do it. You'll get a feel of what it's like." I thought, "Well, I think I do know what working a feature film is about," but I did it against my better judgment. I found what I'd found on *French Dressing*, that the film industry was still pretty alienated from television directors. They never liked one changing one's mind, and I change my mind quite a lot. Everybody who works in my films knows that one thing is certain, and that is that nothing is certain. They never know whether we're going to be in or out. If the schedule says "studio tomorrow," they know they're going to turn up, and I'll come out and say, "I saw a hill there yesterday and I'd like to do a shot up there instead." Everyone's ready to jump immediately in the cars, go off, and do it in a couple of minutes. We are terribly fast and mobile. I can ask for any props. I've got a band of thieves, almost, who go out and steal, if necessary. That's how we used to work in the BBC with these small units. Now I can get the same mobility with a big unit. It's taken quite a few years to organize it.

Oui: So you don't plan your shots?

Russell: Well, it depends, you see. I know where we're going to do it and what I want out of the scene. Usually, I try and do it in one shot, which we work out on the day. I'm a great believer in sudden inspiration. Everyone chips in ideas, from the actors to the carpenters. When I've got a party scene—my bête noire—

I simply know I'm lumbered. I've got to place the camera and just shoot static setups, which I don't like. They are absolutely horrible.

Oui: In both *Billion Dollar Brain* and *Women in Love*, you set many scenes in the snow.

Russell: I have used snow a bit. I always use all the elements. I use fire a lot. Rain, too. In *Debussy*, there was an awful lot of water. You know, we're all from the womb; we're all from the sea. The elements of nature are irresistible. They give the film another dimension. They usually crop up in my films at certain moments, except for *Billion Dollar Brain*, which was virtually all snow anyway. I mean, it was shot in Finland. Actually, it wasn't that easy. The Finns have got the snow problem so well organized that a flake of snow never touches the ground. They've got the shovels out catching it before it does. It was a strange sight to see lorries bringing the snow into Helsinki instead of carrying it out. The citizens couldn't believe what they were seeing.

Oui: How did you decide on the period for *Women in Love*?

Russell: It was either 1920 or 1921. I can't honestly remember now. We never said what date it was, because Lawrence was writing it for some time. I can't remember when he finished it. I think it was after the war. He wanted a timeless time. We chose 1920 because dresses weren't getting short, but they weren't Edwardian. The hit song of the year was "I'm Forever Blowing Bubbles," so we had that as our theme. I was criticized for that, as though those girls of Lawrence had never heard of pop songs, which is quite ridiculous. Lawrence never mentions popular songs, but the characters were schoolteachers who probably had a gramophone and played records.

Oui: There is a perpetual controversy over adaptations. How do you approach a novel?

Russell: I am faithful to what I consider the central idea of every character and situation I tackle. Now, there are as many different interpretations of any particular idea or character of any stature as there are interpretations of Beethoven's *Pastoral Symphony*. What I think most critics should do—but don't—is take an artist's view as one particular view and just absorb *that*. In films, mostly, people don't make the same story twice. We did in *Isadora*, and that's quite an interesting case. There are two versions of that, mine and the one by Karel Reisz. There may well be two versions of quite a few other films. You've got to say, well, that's his point of view, I disagree or I agree. There's nothing else to be said about it. What's important is the director's point of view.

Oui: Otherwise you get that awful Russian *War and Peace*, which is just like a picture book.

Russell: Right. You've got to grab hold of what you think is the central theme. All my films have one central theme, except the musicals. *The Music Lovers* wasn't just about Tchaikovsky, which a lot of people make the mistake of thinking. It was about the effect of dreams on reality.

Oui: Did you really describe *The Music Lovers* as the story of a homosexual who married a nymphomaniac?

Russell: I said that to get the money.

Oui: And it was only to get the money?

Russell: Well, it's a film that can be taken on many levels. It can be taken on that level. There are unsophisticated audiences who would just get that out of it. Fine. But it's also about Tchaikovsky and the exploitation of dreams on constitutions and minds that can't handle them. Dreams are right for some people who can handle them. Most people can't. Today we're inundated with dreams, and the film is about the danger of the dream mentality. Nina represents the public, in a way. Tchaikovsky represented the sort of ad man who was concocting fantasies. People wallow in dreams, daydreams. I think it's dangerous, and the film is about the danger of decadent art coming in touch with reality.

Oui: You consider Tchaikovsky's art decadent?

Russell: Yes, really. That sort of romantic music had gone to the extremes. It was over-defined. That sort of expression was at its top, and it just had to crash. It's dangerous to put your own uncontrolled emotions into a work of art. I think there are some sublime moments in his Sixth Symphony, but, generally, there is a little too much hysteria. It only shows that he was in a very bad state of mind.

Oui: I get the impression you still hold a fondness for his First Piano Concerto.

Russell: Yes, I do, but it depends on how it's taken. He himself said that it reminded him of the summer at Braillov with his sister. He would have loved nothing more than to wallow in the very cozy ambience of a relationship with his sister that was almost incestuous. He could put all his adoration onto her and feel secure in the knowledge that nothing could ever come of it physically. He was at his happiest, and in his most self-fooling state, when he was with the family at Braillov and imagined he was a family man himself. It was his ideal, but it was a dream like anything else. And doomed to disaster. He ruined his sister, as he ruined everyone he came in contact with through his music. He *allowed* his music to ruin other people's lives. That's another theme that keeps cropping up in my work. It was in the Richard Strauss film, and it's in my next film. What value do you actually get out of art? What sacrifice is made because of it? What use is it put to—a good use, a bad use, or a self-indulgent use? Whether it's just a means of escape? If so, an escape to what? The questions it raises are endless. Music can be a prop to keep one in a dreamworld. I think music nowadays has reached the other extreme. It shatters one out of the dreamworld but also puts one in yet another world of unreality—the unreality of strange sonic sounds that are only motorcar horns and New York traffic disguised very thinly as something else. That's not art, it's an evasion.

Oui: Are you talking about concert music?

Russell: That's the only music that lasts. I think pop music is all very well and fun. I buy quite a few pop records, but when I play them twice, I never want to hear them again. I think the greatest modern popular music, although I don't think it ever became really popular, was by Charles Mingus. He, for me, is one of the great serious concert composers in this century because his is an indigenous music coming out of the people. He's a great musician, but it's also a matter of roots, the roots of suffering transmuted into art. I think if there is a music in this century of that kind that will last, it's certainly his.

Oui: Are the fantasy sequences in *The Music Lovers* intended as program music?

Russell: Well, nothing in this film is meant as pure description. There's a meaning behind all the music, apart from the face value. All composers have to live. That's another theme in my films. Unfortunately, composers are often remembered for their worst music. I mean, there are more recordings of the *1812 Overture* than there are, let us say, of the *Hamlet Overture*, which is unquestionably a far greater piece of music. Tchaikovsky really hated the *1812 Overture*. It was giving in to commercialism, writing potboilers, and being untrue to his own ideals. I also think that in films, people get used to a certain way of doing things, and you need a certain change in gear to make them sit up. That was what I tried to do with the Richard Strauss film.

Oui: And you were embroiled in controversy, as usual.

Russell: Yes. But I think if all people can say is, "It's a stupid film," they're making a stupid criticism. Critics seem to be rooted in what they expect to see, rather than what is. They're so used to seeing a film on a romantic composer which is just a "from birth to the grave" thing. There's very little drama in it, usually, although those composers had much more dramatic lives than one is ever led to believe. The critics were prepared for *The Music Lovers*.

Oui: In *The Devils*, how much did you take from John Whiting's play and from Aldous Huxley's book, and how much was original?

Russell: It's very difficult to say offhand. I'd say there's about a third from the play, but some of that is superimposed over Huxley, anyway. I suppose mainly Huxley for the atmosphere. I thought the play was rather sentimental. When I first saw it in 1961, I was knocked out by it. Dorothy Tutin played Sister Jeanne, and she was wonderful. Then I read it again just before I started the screenplay. It was very good dialogue, but I thought it evaded the central issue. I thought it soft-centered: it wasn't hard enough. I sent my wife's brother, who teaches medieval French, to London. He dug up a lot that Huxley had missed, presumably because he couldn't translate the stuff. About the plague, for instance. I don't think Huxley mentions the plague. I thought that was a very fine background for what was going on. Death was common, a quarter of the population died. Death was being laughed at, avoided, just jeered at. It was this marvelous dance-of-death period.

Oui: The subject of decadence invariably comes up in discussions of both *The Devils* and *The Music Lovers*.

Russell: I don't know much about it, actually.

Oui: It's just that you show so much of it. Particularly in those two films.

Russell: Well, we *are* living in the most decadent period of all. I like to keep reminding people that we are. My films, although they're set in the past, are not just about the past. They're all about today. If people would only look at them in that way. I mean, just look at them freely and try and think, is there anything to do? That's why I say *The Music Lovers* is really about the ad man and the exploitation of people who sit in front of their television night after night. *The Devils*, in terms of today, is about religious exploitation and about the state destroying the individual who stands in its way. I like to keep reminding people that there's no happy ending. That's the trouble. Everyone wants a happy ending to life. People are used to watching television and the Korean War or the Vietnam War or Ireland. I think even that, in the end, becomes associated with fantasy. It becomes a fantasy of reality, of handheld cameras running down the street. That's why I would never do a modern film like that. People have come to expect that sort of violence. They don't stop eating while it's going on. I do want to shock people into a sense of awareness.

Oui: Couldn't the heavy emphasis you place on this sort of awareness be described as insane?

Russell: It *could* be described as insane, but my feeling is that it is sane and everyone else is insane. The artists in my films have a heightened sense of awareness that's totally impossible for the ordinary person to grasp. If everyone could grasp it, everyone would be writing symphonies and would live in this heightened state of nerves. Van Gogh was put in a madhouse, so obviously people branded him insane. I mean, he wasn't insane. You look at his paintings. They're not disordered paintings. They have a fantastic order about them. They've also got the feel of a god looking into reality, looking into the reality of a sunflower and seeing all the possibilities. Seeing life glowing in that sunflower. Seeing life in other plants glowing there. Seeing madness and angels in the sky. That isn't madness. That's being a visionary. That's almost being a god. But anyone who watches commercials on television and doesn't get up and destroy the set is insane.

Oui: Let's go back to *The Music Lovers*. Can't the same genius/awareness lead an artist to believe he has a godlike right to exploit?

Russell: That often happens, in which case the human being begins to take over, or the human feelings take over. I think they usually do, and that's when the character disintegrates. The artist has the pressure of producing extraordinary works, the likes of which have never been heard or seen, plus the pressures of his private life. I mean, there's going to be a clash somewhere. There have been very few great men—Beethoven or anyone else—who have managed to survive these two clashes of personality, the artist and the man.

Oui: Do you see the sexual difficulties of many of your film characters as part of that?

Russell: I think everything in one's psyche is, every thought in one's mind. That's just one part of it. It might be a strong part of it, but it is only a part of the problem. For some people, it's more profound. Tchaikovsky, for instance. It had no effect on Brahms at all—he led a celibate life, didn't seem to have any particular sexual problems, and his music was pretty good. You know, every man has his own demon within him. It can destroy him or make him. It can be a sexual demon. In Tchaikovsky's case, it was; in Richard Strauss's case, it certainly wasn't. It was an egocentric demon that made Strauss feel he was a superman, which fitted in very well with Hitler's scheme.

Oui: You are a convert to Catholicism.

Russell: Yes.

Oui: What prompted your conversion?

Russell: When I was a photographer, I was at a rooming house in Bayswater. There was an intellectual Catholic convert there. He talked to me night after night for two years, and I found that the things he said seemed to make sense. I didn't have any philosophy at the time. I was converted, and I suddenly found a direction. I've known exactly what I've been trying to do ever since.

Oui: Do you feel the influence of Catholicism on your films?

Russell: All my films are religious films. They're about Catholic subjects. They're about redemption and things like that.

Oui: Do you have any desire to do the story of a sacred artist?

Russell: You see, I don't differentiate. Take Bach and Vivaldi. They were contemporaries. Bach was a layman, Vivaldi was a priest. Bach's music is full of religious fervor, while Vivaldi's is very superficial and for the courts of Italy. I feel the same thing about life. Just because you happen to wear a dog collar doesn't mean you're a religious person.

Oui: Have you ever found yourself in conflict with the church over the presentation of sex in your films?

Russell: I suppose. I know there was a great outcry over *The Devils*. Especially in Italy. It's only an outcry of fear. But, you know, if they can't take it, that's too bad. That's what I see to be the truth, and it's no use hiding out. Urbain Grandier, in my view, should have been a saint, should have been a martyr. Instead of that, they got Sister Jeanne, toured her around France, and made her a saint. They did phony marks on her hands and pretended she had the stigmata to further denigrate Grandier. Well, I'm not going to forgive them for that. Or allow them to forget it. You see, they'd like to forget, that's the point.

Oui: Given all that, why did you choose to do *The Boy Friend* when your heavier films were making such an impact?

Russell: It was a reaction against *The Devils*. Also, it was a show that my wife and I saw when we'd just met, when I was about twenty-six or so. There was a sort of phase we went through twenty years ago, being mad about the twenties. Then we forgot it. We'd met Twiggy just before we did *The Devils* and liked her very much, and I thought I should do a film with her. Anyway, all my films are reactions, one subject to another. It seemed a wonderful change, a bit of a holiday, a chance to get away from drama, horror, and so forth. It was quite a horrendous experience making *The Devils*. I've been criticized for self-indulgence, but believe me, *The Devils* was very hard work, anything but self-indulgent. It's very hard to keep up that sort of intensity and hysteria and not be affected by it. Some of the things in the film I couldn't quite believe in script. For instance, when Sister Jeanne was exorcized—I think that might have been cut a bit in America—she was put up on the altar of her own chapel and given an injection of holy water. When I was working it out, I thought, "How am I going to get the nuns to react? How are we going to get them into a state of hysteria? Just by watching?" I needn't have worried. When we actually did it, we grabbed Sister Jeanne and put her up on this altar, knocked all the candles down. Her legs were spread apart, and we got this huge syringe. They got into a state of hysteria, all right. I remember Justin de Villeneuve came on the set and he had to go off, he couldn't take it. *The Boy Friend*, by the way, turned out to be the hardest film I'd ever done. It was far harder than *The Devils*. It wasn't a very happy atmosphere, but it should have been. There were lots of petty jealousies and fights and rather violent incidents. It was nearly canceled.

Oui: During shooting?

Russell: No, well, yes. We were a bit doubtful about it ever going on, and during the shooting, one person said he was going to walk off. Or his manager said, "This person will walk off if I don't get my way by noon." So I had to devise an ending that would miss out about twenty minutes of the story but still make sense. So I shot the end before the deadline at noon. I'm sorry we didn't distribute the complete version.

Oui: Can you say what's cut out?

Russell: There's a point that everyone mentions—a screen drops down, and you don't see what's projected on it. Suddenly there's a cut and the screen just goes up. Well, there was a sort of Busby Berkeley number, done with old men in wheelchairs and nurses, all shot from the top. It was very charming. I won't go see the film now. I'd do something violent.

Oui: The first half hour seemed very carefully set up, but then the film got quite diffuse.

Russell: You see, reel ten wasn't shown. A lot of points of view were developed further in it. MGM said, "We've simply got to have it two hours. That's all there is to it." So I said, "Well, you could take out reel ten," thinking that would be bad, but it was better than nothing. But despite the fact that they took out reel ten, they kept chipping away at everything else.

Oui: Was it shown complete anywhere?

Russell: I'll get around to that. They did a ridiculous thing. Instead of taking out that Greek ballet, because it lasts about six minutes, they cut four minutes and left two minutes of meaningless stuff. Well, they'd have done better to cut it out totally. I did. I cut the entire six minutes out because nobody liked it, and the film *was* a bit long and slow. In England, the only thing I removed was the entire Greek ballet and a reprise of "I Could Be Happy with You," which is probably in this one. The European version, as I call it, is a great deal better. People who have seen both can't believe the difference. It was the same with *The Devils*. I mean, there's a European version and an American version for that.

Oui: Is there a great difference?

Russell: I haven't seen the American version. Ted Ashley had this ridiculous notion that he wanted an "R" for it. When he saw it, he said, "Your script isn't the same as the film." Then some of his lackeys started saying, "I've had every girl from San Francisco to Seattle. I've done the filthiest things you could imagine, but I'm appalled by this film. This is disgusting." Then they said, "You've got to cut out all the pubic hairs, to make it an 'R.'" We had a one-hundred-foot-high pile of pubic hairs in the cutting room. Then they showed it to the censor, and he still gave it an "X." All right, they're Philistines, not artists, but you'd think they should be good businessmen. A good businessman thinks, "I'm stuck with an 'X.' Let's grab all the pubic hairs we can and stuff them all over the place." But they were such frightened, scared little men. They thought it best to leave them out. So there's quite a big difference there. I also had a big chunk cut out in England by the censor. So it wasn't the film it might have been.

Oui: Why did you make another film for MGM after what happened to *The Boy Friend*?

Russell: Because I had their assurance in writing. I wouldn't take their word that *Savage Messiah* would be shown to the critics in the state that I made it and that it would be shown for three weeks in New York in my version. If they had to cut it then, well, I would come over and cut it. It's only one hundred minutes long. I honestly can't see what can be gained by cutting it. The only thing that might result is an "X" for the nude girl walking down the staircase.

Oui: I never thought that it might—

Russell: Neither did I, but if the pubic-hair law is still around, it might well operate. There might be a bit of a battle over that. But my next film, which they may be distributing, is financed privately. They will just have the right to distribute it. No cutting at all.

Oui: Where does the title *Savage Messiah* come from?

Russell: It's in the book. I don't think it's particularly appropriate as a title. It's a bit stronger than it should be. It's very hard to think of titles. I thought of dozens of different titles. I thought *Stoned* would be a good title, because it's about sculpture. But no one thought that would be very good. What was another one? Oh, there was an English joke—*Art and Soul*. It's really "Heart and Soul," but you drop the "H." That was a bit corny. We had twenty titles. On *Music Lovers* we had about fifty.

Oui: You tend to direct your actors toward large gestures.

Russell: I do it because in the ages in which my films are set, they used large gestures. They were very flamboyant. It was an age of rhetoric. Cinema didn't exist. There was only theater and rhetoric, and people did tend to use large gestures. They were far more flamboyant and red-blooded and outspoken. My people are usually physical people. Isadora Duncan was physical. Henri Gaudier-Brzeska was physical. I met only one man who knew Gaudier. He said Gaudier would do a leapfrog over people on the pavement and that he would jump on monuments and shout. They'd all been brought up on the French revolutionary posters and paintings. If you look at them, they're all full of huge gestures. It's just a question of period. *The Debussy Film* was set in today. It was about a film crew making a film on Debussy, and there were no gestures. Everyone is just terribly cool. They hardly move. They just look. It's a film of terrific understatement.

Oui: Both Dorothy Tutin and Glenda Jackson, who are very modern actresses, seem to have adapted extraordinarily well to your style.

Russell: That's the whole point of a good actress.

Oui: Do you like working with stage actors and actresses, or isn't that distinction made in Britain?

Russell: No, there's very little distinction between them, but I think I would rather work with people who've come from the stage. In a way, Oliver Reed and Michael Caine are harder to direct. They aren't used to physical movement, which you have to do on the stage, and they're not used to big projection. I think that Oliver and Caine would both be richer if they could do stage work. Oliver's afraid his voice would go. I have to do all the shouting things last with him, or know that we can do other things after we've done him, because his voice just cuts out.

Oui: In music, acting style, choice of subject, shooting style, there seems to be a general tendency toward extravagance in your work. You may be the most extravagant-looking director since Orson Welles. I was wondering if you felt this consciously and if you felt any affinity toward Welles.

Russell: Oh, yes. I mean, he is the director whose work inspired me more than anyone else. But only his first film, really. I haven't liked any of his other films. There were moments in *The Trial* that I thought were good. Some of the old Welles came through. I feel I've absorbed an enormous amount of *Citizen Kane*. I think it is just because I've done period films that you think I'm extravagant. I did a film on a photographer for the BBC called *Watch the Birdie*, which Antonioni saw before he made *Blow-Up*. Quite a few of my things are in that film. That's quite restrained. It's the subject. It just happens, I suppose, that the feature films I've done have all been period pieces. At least half of my new film is set today.

Oui: There's a very compressed tension in the shooting of your films. The result is that instead of entire sequences, what we remember are individual moments. For example, in *Savage Messiah*, there's a bit where Sophie says, "Look." The next shot is of Henri on the rocks. In effect, you cut out two shots—one of what Sophie sees and another of Henri walking to the rocks. But you manage to convey all the information.

Russell: I think when someone leaves, if you show him walking to the door, you tend to forget the individual moments. People are often saying to me, your films are too concentrated. Well, that's the way they are, and that's the way they're going to be. I think the one thing that Godard did that was any good was to scrap continuity in *Breathless*. That was a great leap forward. Hollywood films all seem so slow and tedious and boring to me because of these very points you're making. I think they are the death of film. Film wants to get more concentrated than ever. We're just on the borders of trying to get so concentrated that in the end you don't know what it's about. It's gone right within you, and you've got something out of it, but you're not quite sure what. That's what I'm interested in doing. So I'm just at the beginning of concentrating my films. I think if I can crack this Virginia Woolf film, *To the Lighthouse*, then I'm onto something.

Oui: In *Savage Messiah*, the war is seen passing in the background. I wonder what sort of link you find between historical events and personal artistic action.

Russell: That film is about the death of humanity. It's about the death of an artist. It's about the death of a way of life. Everyone knows about the Great War, that's why it wasn't necessary to show it.

Oui: At the end of *Savage Messiah*, Gaudier's artworks become enshrined; this is precisely what he'd lectured and harangued against. Is there any defense against that enshrinement?

Russell: I think it's bound to happen, and I don't think it matters much, as long as they don't enshrine the artist. Gaudier wouldn't have liked to have been enshrined, but I'm sure he would have loved to have his works in the Louvre.

It's all very well for him to say something, but I'm sure if he were alive now, he wouldn't be taking his works out of the Museum of Modern Art. They are there, and anyone can go and see them. It's sad when they become national institutions. I think people are really afraid of enjoying works of art. You see people going around in an art gallery. They're all whispering as if they were in church. There should be music playing loud. People should be shouting and dancing about. But that's not the fault of the artist. That's the fault of the people who think they have a million dollars hanging on that wall. People are in reverence of money.

Oui: I suppose it's nice working in film because it's not enshrined yet.

Russell: That's why I'm against film festivals. They tend to enshrine things. They tend to enshrine rubbish quite a lot. Or enshrine, as the New York Film Festival seems to do, things that are going to be shown next week anyway. Well, I don't see much point in festivals. I think festivals should be stopped, and the money that goes towards them go towards making the projection facilities better in cinemas. This is where the efforts of so-called film lovers should be directed. One cinema near me has had a bad lens on one projector for nearly two years, and they haven't bothered to change it. The picture is so out of focus you cannot look at it. The public is too apathetic. If only people got up and complained.

Oui: I hear you don't go to the cinema.

Russell: That comes from having to be sitting with my own films in projection booths for half my life. I don't want to go and do the same thing for the other half. That's one thing. The other thing is that I've seen enough films. I don't want to see any more. I get far less out of seeing films than I do out of reading books. So I've got about a billion books to get through before I see another film. That's how I look at it.

Ken Russell Faces the Music

Patrick McGilligan and Janet Maslin / 1975

From *Take One* 4, no. 12 (July–August 1974): 16–21. Reprinted with permission.

[Interview edited from conversations with Ken Russell and Janet Maslin (by telephone) and Ken Russell and Patrick McGilligan (in New York City) in January of 1975, before the release of *Tommy*.]

When these interviews were being conducted, Columbia was engaged in a marketing survey that would make it official: *Tommy* would not be the film to make Ken Russell's reputation with a wide audience after all. Columbia was discovering that the likeliest audience for the picture would be young Who fans, and that if advertising the presence of such Hollywood types as Ann-Margret and Jack Nicholson at the expense of various rock stars in the cast would be a mistake, even mentioning the director's name in the ads would spell disaster.

Russell was, at this stage, still hoping *Tommy* would attract a varied following, and he had no reason yet to suspect trouble—still, he seemed cheerfully resigned. The man whose *The Boy Friend* was recently cut from 140 minutes to 72 minutes for television is accustomed to unexpected disappointments.

Russell points out that, if *Tommy* was great fun to make, it is also one of his sloppier efforts, and deliberately so. The matching mistake that has a brown-eyed child growing up to be blue-eyed Roger Daltrey is especially striking, but throughout the film there are lesser examples of the same thing: curtains that aren't quite sewn together, props that keep changing, glimpses of the leading lady's underwear, even one fleeting shot of the director working a handheld camera while Elton John sings.

Incidentally, Russell does one other brief cameo in the picture, appearing as one of the cripples Tommy promises to (but ultimately cannot) heal. Just why he deemed this sort of role appropriate is anybody's guess.

Question: What do you like to do when you are not directing?

Ken Russell: Sit on a mountaintop and look at the sun. Yes, and go blind in the eyes. My favorite part of the world is the Lake District where I made *Mahler* and a dozen other films—or bits and pieces of films. It's this sort of great, rejuvenating place. It's a weird, mysterious place that I discovered about eight years ago quite by accident when I was doing some research on a film about Rossetti and the pre-Raphaelite poets. I happened to read, in my research, that one of the few places he had visited before he died was in the Lake District. I remember going up with my wife in a car in a very off season, March or something. One sort of went through this mountain pass and, suddenly, Shangri-La, the *Lost Horizon* bit. It did seem a very strange place, and I began to realize why so many Victorian poets—Wordsworth, Shelley, Keats, Southey, Coleridge, and De Quincey—gravitated towards it. It does have a very strange force behind it.

I intend, eventually, to go up there and stay up there and make my own films with a 16mm camera on, say, Wordsworth's *Preludes*—which is about his childhood up there and his mystical feelings about the place.

Q: And never come back?

KR: Well, rarely come back.

Q: What is your routine when in London? Do you see many films?

KR: I never see films if I can possibly help it. I see them for particular reasons—if I hear of an actor and people say, "Well, you're doing a film on so-and-so, so then you should certainly see so-and-so. He's a new actor." Or if I want to satirize something that I hear about—that I'm going to use in another film—like *The Exorcist*, for example, in the Liszt film. In the Liszt film, I have a scene where Liszt exorcizes Wagner, so I wanted to know what the latest popular conception of exorcism was. So I went to see *The Exorcist*. I saw the tricks and it was pretty obvious how they did them. Hilariously funny, I thought.

I go to films for that reason or when I'm a captive on a boat. After lunch, there isn't much to do—although I write scripts quite a bit on boats—but if I need a bit of relaxation, then I go and see the movies. When I'm actually working in London, one of the last things I want to do when I'm free is to go and sit in the black cinema when I've been in the black studio all day long. Also, I've seen so many films that I don't want to see any more. I've seen enough—whereas I haven't read enough books, and I haven't looked at enough sunsets or listened to enough music. I would prefer to do those things as a priority—insofar as they are refreshers and they also help me to make the films I make. Looking at other people's films wouldn't do that at all. I don't want to be influenced by films. I have assimilated all the influences I need to keep me going for the rest of my filmic life.

I've seen a couple of American films by accident. I occasionally go. Everyone kept saying, "*Blazing Saddles, Blazing Saddles*—you must see *Blazing Saddles*," so that was the last time I actually went into a cinema and paid money and sat down and saw. I was very glad I did. On the boat to New York, I saw *Mame*, which was better than I thought it was going to be from just hearing the record. Once, when Warner Brothers was in love with me, before they wanted to murder me, they wanted me to direct it. I heard the record and I hated it. It was like the antithesis of everything I like. It was despicable. So I was surprised by the film. It was nowhere near as bad as I thought it would be. Then I saw a film that I liked very much called *The Crazy World of Julius Vrooder*. It's about a mental casualty of the war, and it all takes place in a mental hospital overlooking the biggest war cemetery one's ever seen. It's a very light antiwar comedy with a very delicate touch. I gather it died the death here—no one seems to have heard of it. That was the best film I've seen in a long time. And I saw a terrible comedy with George C. Scott called *The Bank Shot*. Whew. It's the only film I've fallen off to sleep in in a long, long time. Oh, yes, and a quite hilarious film called *The Tamarind Seed*.

Q: Was it intended to be hilarious?

KR: I shouldn't have thought so—not with Omar Sharif and Julie Andrews.

Q: How would you describe your visual aesthetic—the flashy, showy Ken Russell style?

KR: The flashy, showy thing comes from Catholicism. I probably wasn't like that at all until I became a Catholic. Since Catholicism is a very flashy, showy religion, which isn't to say that it isn't devout or sincere or any of those things—but it just is flashy, showy, flamboyant, and God-knows-what—I certainly wasn't any of those things until I saw the . . . film. Film! Until I saw the film! Ha, ha, ha. I mean, until I saw the light. Well, everything's a film—*Jesus Christ Superstar*.

It's a very un-English characteristic, generally speaking, though, of course, there are exceptions. All the films that have impressed me were flamboyant. Eisenstein's films, Fritz Lang's early German expressionist films, early Griffith, *Citizen Kane*, my favorite American film. They were the ones that impressed me the most. It is as if out of kinship towards their way of looking at things. And, I suppose, being rather more inspired by music than literature, I can't hear a bit of music without seeing a picture or thinking about one. Since thoughts are pictures, it's inevitable.

Q: Where does your love of classical music—and classical composers—derive from?

KR: I suppose it's always there. It came when I was recovering from a slight nervous breakdown after a spell in the Merchant Navy at the end of the war. I just happened to be sitting like a vegetable in an armchair—the radio was on all the time—and, by accident, a piece of classical music came on. I sat up suddenly. I just couldn't quite believe what I was hearing. I had just never realized that such amazing sounds could be made. It was a simple, old B-flat minor Tchaikovsky piano concerto—the slow movement—which is very beautiful, absolutely sub-lime. From that moment, I simply rushed out and bought every classical record I could get my hands on. I have done that ever since.

Q: How do you research the lives of the composers you later portray in film, such as Mahler?

KR: Whenever you got a record, you just looked at the back and thought, "That's interesting." The old program note. I was always curious as to why they wrote that particular piece. From then on, the development is obvious.

By the time I came to do these musical biographies—for instance, with *Mahler*—I have read his biographies, his wife's letters, and everything I could lay my hands on years ago, before I ever thought of making the film. Because he interested me. I've been listening to his music for twenty years. So, when the opportunity came for me to make a film, when I felt I was ready—because there are a lot of films that I've put off because I don't feel that I'm ready to do them yet—when it actually came to doing the film, I had obviously been thinking about Mahler for twenty years. I just wrote it down, you know? It took a very short time, about three weeks. Given the facts of the man's life, given what he says about the symphonies, given the symphonies themselves, and given one's train of thought, that's all one needs. It's sort of like automatic writing. It has to be organized, of course, into a form. I always work with music playing. Or, no matter what I'm doing. I never write far away from the gramophone.

Q: What kind of attention do you give to historical fact?

KR: Well, there are about three or four books on him which more or less repeat the same sort of thing. I met his daughter, Anna, you see, as well—she's still alive. I talked with her a lot about him. And he did say these things were in his symphonies.

When one is doing a film that is a hundred minutes long, it is a question of condensation. The best example that I can give you is that there were about six men interested in his wife before Mahler died, which he knew about. I don't think she had any affairs with them, but they came pretty close. She nearly ran off with one of them. The film isn't about that, but that's an important part of it. He saw the threat to his marriage in terms of music—as a brutal, tough military march—so I condensed all the lovers, would-be lovers, and admirers into one figure, who was the soldier, who represents the military theme. There's a sequence in the film where the love theme comes up and it's disrupted suddenly when this man appears; I just let the music carry on, the military theme comes in, the threat diminishes, and the love theme comes back. So that's a good example. I get the facts, think how he handled it in his music, and that usually gives me a key as to how he condensed them in his music, and as to how I can condense them into the film.

There is a sequence on the mountaintop, where he converts from Judaism to Catholicism. I'm sure he took it with a bit of a pinch of salt, insofar as he thought it was a necessary step in his career as a conductor. He had to convince Cosima Wagner that he was an okay guy, and that's why he did it. It seemed a very cynical move. Since, even in a lot of his religious symphonies—his symphonies about death and so forth—he treats a lot of things as a joke (I mean, he has scherzos and things, a bit of light comic relief, and he put nature worship before everything else), I treated that conversion in the same sort of way, as almost a joke. I had him jumping through Christian hoops and hammering a Jewish star which he carries into a Wagnerian cross-cum-sword—things like that. It's a light-hearted, almost Charlie Chaplin sort of sequence. It seems to upset some people.

A lot of the film is about his relationship with his wife. I mean, she said, "Oh, I'm just your shadow," and there's a sequence where she *is* just his shadow, following behind him. I dressed her exactly the same as him and put a black stocking over her face; and she's just a vague shadow of herself, ignored by everyone, while the people are all crowding round him.

Mahler was preoccupied with death. She found he was writing some songs one day on the death of children. She was furious. She said, "Why do you tempt providence like that? Why don't you write songs about the life of children, the joy of children?" He says, "Oh, no, I've just got to do it." She then throws the music into the lake, and he says, "No, it's still in here," tapping his head. He went on writing, and his youngest child suddenly keeled over and died. These things seemed to happen throughout his life; he was compelled to do things which then happened.

He put a lot of his psychology, a lot of his personal life, into his music. When he became jealous of his wife and they were nearly breaking up, she said, "Oh, I'm nothing to you," and he said, "You remember the second subject of the first movement of the Sixth Symphony?" She said, "Yes, I copied it out for you, remember?" He said, "Well, that's you." And it is the most beautiful thing he ever wrote—but it's cut across by a brutal military march. He always associated the threat to love, or the death of love, with a military band. Because, when he was a kid, they lived next door to a barracks. His father was very brutal—beating up his mother and seducing the maidservant—and, always, a military band was playing whenever this was going on.

Q: How do you know that?

KR: Well, he said so.

Q: How much of the material is purely subjective—as with Tchaikovsky in *The Music Lovers*, things which you simply feel to be true?

KR: What I've done in *Mahler* is project things into the future a bit, because he was always going on about how no one ever really dies. In a way, that's the theme, also, of *Tommy*—a sort of continuing life cycle, spring-summer-autumn-winter, that eternal renewal thing. He was very taken up with Nietzsche's philosophy on that. The fact that he was terrified of death—he kept putting off his Ninth Symphony because he knew that Beethoven had died after his Ninth, and Bruckner died after his Ninth—he cheated, and called his Ninth Symphony "Song of the Earth." But eventually he wrote number nine, which is all about death, and then of course he never finished. So he was right; he did go.

He had a thing about changing his religion, and being afraid of being buried, and then being afraid of being cremated, and so forth. He changed his religion just because he had to in Germany at that point, just to get on; the Jews weren't popular even in those days, in 1900. I thought, what if he'd just been a few years later, and his music was banned by Hitler? I thought, I wonder what would have happened if he'd tried to change his religion then? It wouldn't have made any difference, he'd have gone to the ovens anyway. So I mixed all that, projected all those thoughts about his life, and what happened to musicians like him in the regime that followed—which Cosima Wagner was partly responsible for, because Hitler always said, to understand National Socialist Germany, you must read Wagner's philosophy and listen to his music. All those things subconsciously rose to the surface, and I put them in the film.

Q: Is it significant—to your choice of subjects—that the composers you have portrayed biographically, such as Mahler and Tchaikovsky, are beset by neuroses or some personal disorder?

KR: If they didn't have any neurosis, they wouldn't have written the music. You can't have one without the other. I think most artists have—I wouldn't go as far as to say a neurosis—but they have a different inner life or vision. I've got to like the music. The things that attracted me to Tchaikovsky were the agony of his life that he poured into the Ninth [*sic*] Symphony; I found that very moving, and very revealing. It seemed to tell me more about him, once you're given a clue, than all the biographies you can read put together. Obviously it should, because it's a distillation of his entire experience in forty-five minutes, the culmination of his life, a tortured life.

Symphonies, in particular, seem to be the greatest achievement that man's made in assimilating and putting forth remote human emotions and philosophies in an abstract way. They seem self-consciously, as far as I'm concerned anyway, to open up paths of perception that are denied one in literature. You can read very amazing philosophical books and so forth, but, to me, symphonies are almost like inner space science fiction music. It's a trip in the mind. I've never taken drugs, but I imagine it's the same sort of thing; you're in control in a sense, when you're listening to music, and, given a clue, you can go on this amazing journey, as it were.

Mahler was interested in things which interest me—like, the Third Symphony is an exploration of God through nature. Every moment is what the rocks tell me, what the flowers tell me, what the animals in the forest tell me, what loves me. He also said it could be what God tells me. I'm interested to know what those things did tell him, and so that is why I find his symphonies fascinating. I also find the Sixth Symphony fascinating—which he said was autobiographical. It has the most beautiful theme he ever wrote, but he didn't let on until quite late in life—in fact, he was estranged from his wife by then, and only mentioned it in desperation—that this theme represented her. If he had told her a few years before, it might have helped matters; but he didn't.

His music seems to throw a lot of psychological insight into his own personality, and what moved, affected, and shaped his life. I was very fortunate because, more so than any other composer, he said what his things hinted, what they were about. It's like this voyage of discovery combined with this sort of detective work to try and solve the mystery behind him. Which one can't do, but, at least by exploring, you can throw some light on him.

Q: What is the situation with distribution, in America, of *Mahler*?

KR: It's been finished over a year, and we did have an American distributor, but . . .

Q: Ely Landau of the American Film Institute?

KR: That's the chap, yes. Negotiations went on and eventually came to a close. He came to England and said, "Well, there are just one or two things we'd like to clip out." I said, "Tell me the first one." He said, "There's this conversion of Mahler on the mountain that's in rather bad taste; that would have to go." That's my favorite sequence, it lasts ten minutes, and it's the highlight of the movie. So I said, "Don't bother to tell me the rest," and showed him the door.

Q: How does it feel, then, to have the full backing and spiritual support of a major company like Columbia for *Tommy*?

KR: Somebody who shall be nameless—some high executive—saw the film and said, "Great, there's only two criticisms I have to make." I said, "Well, what are they?" He said, "There are two yawns in the picture. People in the film actually yawn, and nobody yawns in a Columbia picture."

He also said, "Oh, those black bits you've got on the screen with a few arrows, I appreciate the significance of it, but I just wonder about those." I said, "Oh, well, of course, that's just a storyboard for how we're going to shoot an optical sequence." I mean, all it was, was some black paper with white chalk marks with an arrow pointing to a pinball, to show the direction it was to go. A child would know it was just a guide for the people who were going to shoot the thing, to accompany the music. But they thought it was a part of the finished product. I don't think they know too much about movies.

Q: Why were you attracted to *Tommy*?

KR: Again, it's very religious. It's a pilgrim's progress, it's about somebody trying to find answers, it's about masses trying to find answers and the fact that answers are often not to be found in externals, but mostly in internals. It's all to do with "put on your eyeshades, put in your earplugs, put a cork in your mouth, turn inward and play pinball." I mean, that's a very good metaphor, it seems to me. Who wants to do that? Nobody. Very few people, anyway. It's about instant enlightenment, instant answers, an obvious solution, and it's about the exploitation of religion. One of the first straight documentaries I ever made—just cut to music, actually—was about Lourdes. It was the first time I learned to cut films to music, although I sure didn't cut it myself. It was about Lourdes—the pilgrims, the processions, the exploitation; and *Tommy* is about the exploitation of religious ideals, as much as anything else—the way, in this case, that people reject them. Chuck out the baby with the bathwater.

Q: Did you hear the Who album when it was originally released?

KR: Yes, it was played to me by some friends of mine who—they knew my interest in visuals with music—said, "You must do this." I played side one and I thought it was rubbish. I couldn't follow the story; I couldn't make head nor tail of it. I was unfamiliar with music of that kind, anyway. Then, a few years later, an album came out which was very badly orchestrated—it had nothing to do with the Who. I hated it, insofar as it was a big symphony orchestra, all bloated, and it sounded more like Leonard Bernstein—at least, though, the numbers were more dramatic. One could follow the story since there was a bit of a synopsis; it became much clearer.

About that time, I was approached by some people to see if I would be interested in doing a script; I met Townshend. Pete showed me all the scripts that had been submitted to him by various promoters over the years, and they were all, without exception, totally horrific. Mostly Julie Andrews–type scripts; some were amazingly awful, in that sense. One was set on a pinball table, for some extraordinary reason. They varied from that sort of pseudoscience-fiction thing to the Julie Andrews musicals. All the scripts were rubbish; they didn't seem to be what he seemed to be about.

I assimilated everything he'd written about the pieces. I wrote a little treatment in which I put forth the ideas I thought he was on about, and then we discussed that, made slight changes—very slight—and then I wrote the script, pointing out various gaps in the storyline which I thought needed opening out and amplifying and explaining, which he hadn't bothered about in the original.

Q: What changes did you make in Townshend's original score?

KR: We both said from the start we didn't want to use any dialogue. So that was that. I wrote the script with the songs where the dialogue would be, and the action written against the verse of the songs.

Q: How did you actually shoot the movie without dialogue?

KR: We wrote the script and, naturally, I knew the words for the songs. Occasionally, I said, "Could you alter one line here or so"—you know, to give a bit of emphasis to something—and he'd say, "Yeah." He'd written the new songs, given me the words for them, and so, basically, I had a whole lot. I told him where I thought there should be instrumental things to accompany visuals to link those sequences, and then we simply went into a recording studio for three months and recorded it, totally out of context. This person would be available, and then Ann-Margret would be flown over and she'd do all her songs. Because we had worked out exactly the way the story would go, I could say to Ann-Margret, "Sing this song yawning, because you are going to be bored with Tommy's problem by this time. Years have gone by or you've just had a breakdown; put this marshmallow in your mouth and sing with that. Or put a cigarette in your mouth and sing yawning because you're not interested." So it went on like that. Everyone we talked to, we filled in, and if they hadn't seen the script, at least they knew where they stood in context to that whole particular sequence.

So we had it dramatically sorted out before we actually got onto the floor; then it was just a question of doing it to playback, and knowing you had to get a certain sequence over by x number of lines. Which was a very good exercise, insofar as it made one very concise. You had to make sure the visuals didn't overrun the music and it stretched your imagination. The impact was greater because it was much more concise and stated in a much shorter time than one would naturally do.

Q: Did you have any trouble working with the musicians?

KR: Only insofar as I was naive enough at the very start, when we were doing the prerecording, to suggest to Pete Townshend, "When're we starting? Eight o'clock in the morning, nine?" He said, "I think we should start it a little later." I said, "Ten o'clock?" He said, "Just a wee bit later than that." I said, "Two o'clock in the afternoon, then." He said, "Well, if you think so, alright." Of course, I was in the studio at two o'clock, and he came in about five o'clock, knowing nobody would be there, and then we sat there until midnight. Then they started coming in. Well, that's when I got the message that they work a different time scale to filmmakers. Once I got over that hurdle, it was okay.

Q: The last I heard, you had no interest in rock music.

KR: I still haven't. What I've heard doesn't do anything for me. But the fact that *Tommy* is written in a rock idiom is, so far as I'm concerned, beside the point. It's a good piece of music and it's a very good opera. I don't care what style it's in. I mean, in the twenties, Kurt Weill could write symphonies that sounded like Richard Strauss, but when he came to do his operas they sounded like German jazz. He was just a good musician. Well, Townshend's been brought up with a rock background and has got a rock following. But *Tommy*, at least the film version, will reach those people, and I hope will reach millions more people, who've never dreamed of hearing rock.

Q: How did you cast the film if you are so unfamiliar with rock music?

KR: A lot of names were suggested, as I am not familiar with rock at all. A lot of the people I had never heard of at all. Somebody would be suggested, and one would hear their records and so forth.

I'd never heard of Eric Clapton or Elton John, for example, but I thought any performer who's any good at all could play the cameos if it's up their street, as it were.

I did know we needed good actors to play Tommy (Roger Daltry), his father (Robert Powell), his stepfather (Oliver Reed), and his mother (Ann-Margret). The mother had to do more singing than anyone else and most people in the film put together. Someone said, "Well, what about Ann-Margret?" I remembered her from the old days of *Bye Birdie* and the Elvis things, and I said, "Look, she can't act, can she?" They said, "Go and see *Carnal Knowledge*." So I saw it and thought, "Couldn't be better, really super." And she is, I think, very good in the film.

Q: What kind of an effect do you hope to have, with the kind of extravagant visuals you employ in *Tommy* and your other films?

KR: An effect that is going to illuminate music, if we are talking about music—or an effect that is going to illuminate the idea in the fastest possible way, in the most dramatic way, and in the most emotional way—with the most impact, because I like instant exposure to an idea. It doesn't give one time to put up the metal grille of censorship in the mind. The thing about reading—the thing about Aldous Huxley's *The Devils*—is that you can censor it as you go along. By the time you've translated the words into pictures—because one's brain obviously can't be open to horror all the time—there's this censorship thing that seems to operate, and it's transmitted into an acceptable picture. Whereas the thing I like about visual things is that before you get time for the defenses to go up, it's hit the brain; and you have to react simply as you would. There's no time for any sort of wall to go up, and I think that's what I like about it.

Q: I wanted to ask you about this week of interviews that you've given in New York City. The press has always been fairly hostile to you; what sorts of questions have you been asked, and what is your impression of their attitude?

KR: Well, they always start off with "Now, you're called a controversial director . . ." You can fill in the rest from there, I think.

A lot of people, when they met me, I was told they were going to be cowering in corners and absolutely terrified of facing up to the ogre who was going to come crashing in and probably pummel them to pulp. Most of them said, "Gosh, you look like Santa Claus." I've got this beard now, and a very benign expression, and I usually have a coat slung over my back, which they think is a sack full of presents. They see the dandruff on my shoulders, and they think it's snow. Santa Claus is the new image, but they'll probably still be saying, "I survived the ogre."

Q: I understand you had a bit of trouble on the *Tomorrow* show with host Tom Snyder.

KR: Oh, if I'd have known what he was up to, how boring and dead, what a piece of plastic surgery was sitting in the chair, well, I either wouldn't have done it or I would have approached it in a different way. That was the first thing he said: "Now, you're controversial . . ." He'd never seen any of my films—he had no intention of seeing them, didn't really want to. As far as he was concerned, I was just somebody sitting in a fur coat, talking. I think he was an idiot.

André Previn Meets Ken Russell

André Previn / 1974

From *The Listener* (September 19, 1974): 367. © 1974 British Broadcasting System. Reprinted with permission of Immediate Media Co.

André Previn: Did you always have this fascination, either aural or visual, with music? Were you a frustrated pianist when you were a child?

Ken Russell: No; nothing like that at all. I was just a very lonely child. I played in a large garden, made up stories, like all children do, imagined characters, and so on. It wasn't until I hit upon music that the imagination actually took over and became even more amazing. I found music just turned me on to fantastic ideas. It just overwhelmed me. The first time I really got an idea of how I could turn something into a film was when I heard *Romeo and Juliet*. I was in the air force then, away in the country, and I just heard this fantastic music and I felt— I can put pictures to that and I must put pictures to that.

Previn: And if you had been a musician?

Russell: I'd prefer to have been a musician. I'm only a film director because I can't compose music or conduct an orchestra or play anything. I'd far prefer to express myself that way because that, to me, is the ultimate form of expression. Filmmaking is way down the scale.

Previn: From your point of view as a director, or as a creator, of these imagined visions, if there is a piece of music that has within itself a programmatic story, and if you know that programmatic story, can you still clear your head of all those images and start from square one?

Russell: You can do, but it's not always necessary. In the Tchaikovsky film, which you were involved with yourself, it seems to me that all the programmatic stories in that were to do with him. *Swan Lake* was about frustrated love, a false love. *Romeo and Juliet* is about, well, we all know what that one is about. *Manfred* is about someone being in love with his own sister, which was Tchaikovsky's problem, I think. There are about a dozen stories which reflect aspects of Tchaikovsky's character to me in those symphonic poems and operas and ballets he wrote. And they showed me the pathway to follow when you're making the film.

Previn: But surely almost every great composer's compositions are about himself in one way or another?

Russell: Exactly. Therefore, you don't feel any compunction about adding another interpretation to it. Take Brigitte Bardot: there's a portrait Picasso did of her. It is his Brigitte Bardot, but it's also Brigitte Bardot; you could get any number of painters to paint her, and the fact is that there is more artistic license in art, high-art painting, than is allowed for in films. If you tend to interpret in films, you're going to be smashed down because, for years, in Hollywood in the thirties especially, they did biographies of composers that were all formula films. They were not interpretations of a director; they were *Woman's Own* stories, and it seems that we are stuck with that image today.

Previn: I must tell you something. The Disney studios were planning a rather serious, big film on Beethoven, and the script came back from whoever was the executive, and they said to the writer, "We'd prefer it if he were not deaf." The poor writer went up and argued, and he said: "Why should he not become deaf?" And Disney supposedly said, "In my pictures nobody gets sick."

Just one more thing about the interpretation—I remember I was conducting a symphony by an American composer called Walter Piston, a memorable old gentleman, and I had taken some rather radical liberties with it. I didn't know he was in the audience, and when he came round afterwards, I apologized to him, and he gave me an answer that I've really appreciated many times since. He said, "Look, there were two thousand people in the audience who didn't really know the piece, so while you were conducting, there must have been two thousand interpretations going on simultaneously; why not yours?"

Now, you always make films about composers you adore?

Russell: Not necessarily. I like Delius and Richard Strauss. They brought a lot of joy to people, and what makes them tick fascinates me.

Previn: Yes, because the obvious monsters, for instance, would be composers like Wagner.

Russell: I'm doing Franz Liszt meets Richard Wagner. It's going to be rather like Frankenstein meets Godzilla.

Previn: Do you read music?

Russell: I think I can vaguely follow it. Then I think I'm following it, and I find the music has come to the end and I have still got three pages on the score to go.

Previn: I know the feeling! Now, I have heard music in all your pictures that is relatively obscure and that you would not come across in casual encounters on records. How do you choose the music?

Russell: It is just by simply playing the music for hours on end. I mean that literally. There may be gems in Tchaikovsky and Strauss, or whoever, that I just simply don't know because they are not recorded. But, luckily, these days practically everything is recorded. I just play them over and over, and if I'm doing a film on Tchaikovsky, I play his music for six months solidly, and I just let it sink in. A piece of music can make you think of a scene, or if you know you have got to have a scene, a crucial scene in a man's life, then you just find a piece of music, like we did in *Manfred* in Tchaikovsky.

Previn: What is funny is that you put an image into a lot of people's heads, never to be erased, because I have, since then, done it, and every time we come to the end of the first movement, all I can see is poor Glenda Jackson in that railway carriage. I'm never quite sure whether I am doing a Tchaikovsky symphony or your film again. Now, you are going to make a whole further series of pictures about composers. Have you got them picked out?

Russell: Well, there is Liszt and Wagner and then Vaughan Williams, maybe George Gershwin, and Berlioz.

Previn: The fact that you are working in the cinema, which is a mass medium—does that influence your wish that the music should get across to a mass audience?

Russell: I have always wanted to transmit my enthusiasm for music. But working on *Tommy*, it seemed to me that one might be, in a way, preaching to the converted, because I don't think for a moment that a lot of the people I have met on *Tommy*, whom I found to be fantastic and the most exciting, imaginative people I've met for many years, have ever heard of Beethoven or Shostakovich or you or anyone else. It is all very well me making a film on Mahler and you touring the Soviet Union playing Vaughan Williams, but it might be more to the point if we began to think of a lot of the people who really have nothing whatsoever in the way of music, except rock music. It seems to me that *Tommy* is a very good opera on any level. If *Tommy*, instead of *The Knot Garden*, was put on at Covent Garden and toured around, it would do a lot to shake up the music world, because I think at this present moment too many composers are being supported by the Arts Council and producing work which is really of no interest except to a very, very small minority of people in this country and to themselves. I met some Hells Angels who said, "I'm glad you're making this rock film because at last we will have a film to go to that has got music in it that we like. We never hear music that we like." I said, "What do you do?" and one said, "Well, I've worked for seven years in a pottery. I work from seven in the morning to seven at night. I have half a day off a week, that's Saturday from one o'clock to six o'clock," and I said, "Where do you go to, then?" He said, "Nowhere," and it's for the nowhere people, maybe, that we should start thinking.

Fact, Fantasy, and the Films of Ken Russell

Gene D. Phillips / 1976

From *Journal of Popular Film* 5, no. 3 (1976): 200–210. ©1976 Heldref Publications. Reprinted with permission of Taylor & Francis, Ltd., http://www.tandfonline.com.

British director Ken Russell was forty-two when his film of D. H. Lawrence's *Women in Love* (1970) placed him in the ranks of movie directors of international stature. For more than a decade before *Women in Love*, however, British television viewers had been treated to a succession of his skilled TV biographies of great artists. The present interview consists of material garnered from three conversations with Russell in his London home, where he lives with his wife and costume designer, Shirley, and their five children. The third visit was before Russell went off to Spain to shoot his latest film, about the life of Rudolph Valentino starring Rudolph Nureyev, who a few years ago was slated to appear in the title role of Russell's film about Russian dancer Vaslav Nijinsky, a project which never materialized.

Russell has always gravitated toward the past in choosing subjects for filming because, as he says, "topics of the moment pass and change. Besides, we can be more dispassionate and therefore more truthful in dealing with the past. And to see the past from the vantage point of the present is to be able to judge the effect of the past on the present." His first TV documentaries corresponded to what he calls "the accepted textbook idea of what a documentary should be; you were supposed to extol the great artists and their work. Later I turned to showing how great artists transcended their personal problems and weaknesses in creating great art." But this more realistic approach upset some members of the audience of both his TV and theatrical films, as he advanced from the small screen to the large in continuing to turn out what have come to be called his "biopics."

Gene D. Phillips: Filmgoers not familiar with your highly imaginative television biographies were not prepared for your unconventional rendering of the life of Tchaikovsky in *The Music Lovers* (1971) or of the life of Father Grandier, the priest who led local opposition in the city of Loudun against Richelieu's attempts to centralize the French government, in *The Devils* (1971).

Ken Russell: What particularly drew me to the subject matter of *The Devils* was the fact that it reflected an instance of the collision of the individual with the state. We know from history that the state usually survives while the individual loses out in these cases; but I wanted to examine what lasting impact the individual still has, even when he loses.

Phillips: What upset many of the critics of the film was that you portrayed how Richelieu was able to discredit Grandier by first exposing his personal sexual indiscretions and then using them to suggest that he had corrupted a whole convent of hysterical nuns. They thought this antireligious.

Russell: I think *The Devils* is a Christian film about a sinner who becomes a saint. Grandier [Oliver Reed] is a mixture of good and bad qualities; he knows what he should do, but he often doesn't do it, as St. Paul once said. Then he gets the opportunity to stand up against Richelieu in order to preserve the rights of the city, and he does so. In this crisis his good qualities come to the surface, and he dies a Christian martyr for his people when Richelieu has him burned at the stake. The film has some things to say about the Church, but the Church will survive it. I happen to be a convert to Catholicism myself. When I was young, I really didn't know where I was going. But as soon as I came into the faith, my work, my philosophy, gained direction. With the possible exception of *The Boy Friend*, all of my films have been Catholic in outlook: films about love, faith, sin, guilt, forgiveness, redemption. Films that could only have been made by a Catholic.

Phillips: You were also excoriated for the vividness with which you portrayed the violent events in the film, such as Grandier's burning at the stake.

Russell: Once I had decided to do *The Devils*, I had to go along with the truth as it was reported. Historical films are often made as if the people living in the past thought of themselves as part of history already, living in museums. But people in the seventeenth century—or in any other century, for that matter—thought of themselves as contemporary, just as we think of ourselves as contemporary. I had to show the violent atmosphere that the plague had created at the time, for instance, in order to explain how ordinary people could stand by and allow a man they knew to be innocent to die a hideous death. They had become so calloused as a result of the plague; when there is death on every doorstep, the death of a man like Grandier becomes inconsequential, an everyday occurrence. That is why the crowd behaved at his burning as if they were attending a football match.

Furthermore, the film is a jolly sight less ugly than Aldous Huxley's book *The Devils of Loudun* (on which I based the script, along with John Whiting's play, *The Devils*). When one reads these events in Huxley's books, one can sift the words through one's imagination and filter out as much of the unpleasantness as one cares to. You cannot do this when you are looking at a film.

Phillips: Your next biopic was more subdued: *Savage Messiah* (1972).

Russell: The style of every film which I make is dictated by the subject matter. The story of the sculptor Henri Gaudier, who died in the First World War when he was twenty-three, and his love for Sophie Brzeska, a disillusioned Polish woman twenty years his senior, called for a quieter kind of treatment than did *The Devils*. It was the story of two people who were devoted to each other in a brother-sister relationship which they never consummated sexually, and how she sank into despair after his untimely death. I was attracted to this material because Gaudier was not what the general public considered to be an artist. He wasn't someone special tucked away at the top of an ivory tower making works which were totally obscure, to be admired by a few friends. He was somebody working for posterity and eternity, somebody who felt that there was something in him which he could transmit to his fellow human beings which might be of use to them.

I first read his biography when I was struggling to get started in my own career. I was impressed by the story of someone my own age at the time who was totally down-and-out, but who struggled onward nevertheless; and that gave me the courage to keep going. I was impressed by Gaudier's conviction that somehow or other there was a spark in the core of him that was personal to him, but which was worth turning into something that should be appreciated by others. I wanted to find that spark in myself and exploit it for the same reason. And my film of his life was my tribute to him for the inspiration which he gave me when I needed it.

Phillips: How did you manage to make such a personal film for a major studio like MGM without front office interference?

Russell: I invested in the production myself and set out to make the film as good as possible with as little financing as possible, because I have found that the smaller the budget a film has, the less likely the front office is to interfere with its production. I accordingly trimmed the budget and the schedule as much as possible, and even shot the picture in a small studio in London which is actually a derelict biscuit factory on the banks of a stagnant canal; but it served my purposes and kept the overhead down.

Phillips: I understand that you deleted a quarrel scene between Henri and Sophie from the film. Was that your idea or the studio's?

Russell: I took that scene out during the editing process. It may have happened in real life, but I found that it was too powerful for the film because the picture runs a hundred minutes and not several years, which is the time period covered by the story. I am not averse to making something better. Some of my colleagues found one of the production numbers in *The Boy Friend* overlong and rather out of tune with the rest of the film, and I also thought that the film played well without it. So I decided to cut it. I now have it stipulated in each of my contracts that any cuts that are made in a film of mine are made under my supervision.

Phillips: I gather that you never liked *The Boy Friend*, given the comments you have made about it.

Russell: After the strain of making a violent film like *The Devils*, I thought it would be a good change of pace to make a musical just for fun. But *The Boy Friend* turned out to be the most complicated project which I had attempted before *Tommy*. When I agreed to do the film for MGM, I got hold of a 16mm film of the original 1954 British production with Julie Andrews which had been made to assist the New York company during rehearsal. It was funny and touching at first, with everyone striking poses. But as the film went on, one got bored with the cardboard characters in a way that one didn't when watching them on the stage. That is when I realized that I would have to do the original musical as a show within-a-show if I was going to sustain the audience's interest throughout the film. I then decided to frame the original show within the context of a back-stage musical of the sort that Hollywood turned out in the 1930s. The opening credits set this tone for the movie by announcing "Ken Russell's Talking Picture of *The Boy Friend*."

I tried to get the extravagant, imaginative flair of the old Busby Berkeley musicals into the production numbers of the film, which in the story are projections of how a Hollywood producer in the audience at the show imagines that he would stage these songs in a lavish screen musical. But it was difficult to accomplish this in a British studio, where they had forgotten how to do an old-fashioned musical. Of course, they had done things like Carol Reed's *Oliver*, in which they just built naturalistic sets and then had the chorus dance around them. But I am referring to the kind of musical number which involves a lot of special effects and camera tricks. Take the song "There's Safety in Numbers" in *The Boy Friend*. By means of optical effects the chorines seem to spin into pinwheels and then turn into dancing dominoes. That took some doing because I was shooting with a British crew that had not done this sort of thing for a long time.

Phillips: But the experience which you gained in devising the musical numbers for *The Boy Friend* must have helped you create *Tommy*, which is really a succession of musical numbers with no spoken dialogue at all.

Russell: *Tommy*, as a film based on a rock opera, is of course highly imaginative throughout, until the ending when his fans rebel, and I employ a more realistic treatment as they destroy the national resort-shrine built in his honor once they discover that his mother and stepfather are using it for commercial exploitation of them. One is prone to fall back on clichés in scenes of straight reportage of this sort. The imaginative scenes which are meant to visualize the songs were more stimulating for me to do because in them I was exploring the interior world of the characters, particularly of Tommy. It was much harder to formulate images on the screen for the symphonic music in my biopics about composers, like *Mahler* and *The Music Lovers*, than it was to create visual metaphors for music that has lyrics as well, as in *Tommy*. Creating images to accompany symphonic music really stretches the imagination because one has to think of images that not only serve as counterparts to the music but which lead into other images as well. In working out the visuals for each successive musical number in *Tommy*, I was forced to imagine images that commented on the lyrics of the song in question but which also expanded its meaning. I didn't just want to illustrate the songs on the screen as if I were merely giving a slide lecture about the opera. The latter approach simply amounts to trading on the composer's hard work and contributing nothing of your own as a filmmaker. My task was to get the maximum amount of emotional feeling into a minimum number of images for each song.

The best sequences in *Tommy*, I think, are the ones in which reality and fantasy mingle. For example, when the Acid Queen injects Tommy with drugs, I tried to project onto the screen the experience which Tommy was having in such a way as to indicate that his acid trip triggered memories of his past life as well as caused him to hallucinate.

Phillips: Did you make any significant changes or additions in the story line of the opera in your screenplay?

Russell: I found that I had to fill in gaps in the story that went unnoticed when one listened to the recording of the show or saw *Tommy* done in a concert version on stage. The audience can only identify with people on the screen if they know something about them. So I added the prologue material which I felt was important to establish Tommy's background and the kind of people his parents and his stepfather were. Also, I felt that one shouldn't lose track of important characters as the story unfolded. While Tommy is busy becoming Pinball Wizard of the World, his mother drops out of sight in the original story. I told the composer, Peter Townshend, that we needed a number about how she is enjoying the luxuries which Tommy's success had brought her. He replied that he had toyed with the idea for a number called "Champagne," and I said that that would be fine.

Phillips: The scene in which Tommy's mother [Ann-Margret] takes him to a shrine to Marilyn Monroe to be cured of his traumatic deafness, dumbness, and blindness was criticized in some quarters as being antireligious, harkening back to similar accusations against *The Devils*.

Russell: The scene in which her faithful followers come to worship at the shrine of the dead superstar is not a criticism of religion but of the way that fans can deify superstars whom they idolize, whether they be movie idols or rock idols. The last shot in the scene, you recall, is of the statue of Monroe toppling over and crashing into rubble. My point was that no human being can live up to the idealized image of them which their fans build up for them, and the latter are therefore doomed to disillusionment. Through no fault of his, Tommy becomes such an idol and ultimately repudiates this kind of adulation, though his mother and stepfather exploit his fans for all they are worth. The Monroe scene foreshadows the disillusionment of Tommy's fans later in the film with the heroic image which they have created of him and which they demand that he live up to.

Phillips: In *Lisztomania*, your film about Franz Liszt, you present Liszt as the first superstar composer, thus combining the musical format of *Tommy* with the biography of a composer, which recalls your earlier biopics. The film, however, seemed to fail on both counts.

Russell: I got off on the wrong foot with *Lisztomania*, even though it starred Roger Daltrey, who played Tommy. It called for a bigger budget than we had, and so the film doesn't work as well as I wanted it to. The symbolism, moreover, is a bit too relentless and the fantasy sequences tend to submerge the reality of the characters. I think I had exhausted the vein of biographies of composers at the time I made *Lisztomania*, at least for a while.

Phillips: If you consider *Lisztomania* the weakest of your biopics, you have said that you think *Mahler* your best so far.

Russell: I think that *Mahler* has the best examples of the mingling of reality and fantasy of any film that I have made. Most of my films on composers evolve through a stream of consciousness in which the man and the myth, the music and its meaning, time, place, dream, and fact all blend into the mainstream of the film itself. As I mentioned earlier, the lifespan of a man is measured in years, but the screen time of a film on him is measured in minutes. Given this fact and the nature of the medium, so far as I am concerned the impressionistic techniques work best. When every second counts, it is often necessary to say two things at once, which is why I frequently introduce symbolism into scenes of reality. For example, during the last few years of his life Mahler was haunted by the fear that his wife would leave him. When he did die, Alma went through three husbands and God knows how many lovers before joining him. So time proved that Mahler's fears were justified. I therefore distilled all the men interested in Alma into one symbolic figure, a man named Max. In depicting the nightmare in which the dead Mahler sees his wife desecrating his memory with her lovers of the future, therefore, the most prominent is Max, who has already been established in the film as the symbolic threat to their love. This is just one example of my attempt to blend reality and fantasy in the film. There are many more for the audience to see and feel, at least subconsciously.

Phillips: And now you have turned to the life of an actor, Rudolph Valentino.

Russell: In my view, his story is about a man who wore a mask in public but was quite different in private. I have not seen the earlier film with Anthony Dexter as Valentino or the more recent TV movie starring Franco Nero. In choosing Nureyev to play the title role in my movie, I was not really worried about finding a Valentino lookalike. If you create the proper atmosphere around him, it will all be believable. In working out the script we have explored Valentino's sexual life and the rumors of his homosexuality more than any other screen treatment of his life has done. His sexuality is obviously something that must be dealt with. His first marriage lasted only one night. The big question is why, and the only person who can answer is eighty years old and will not see anyone. I am not really concerned about separating the man from the myth, because it's impossible to sort them out. And with my penchant for mixing reality and fantasy in my film biographies, I really am not inclined to do so anyway. I have devised one scene which looks like a Hollywood premiere and turns out to be his funeral. The film treats his second marriage, to Natacha Rambova, and then moves on to his final downhill plunge to death.

As I see it, Valentino killed himself to save his honor, not his pride; and since the idea of someone sacrificing himself to satisfy his honor seems right and inevitable to me, that is the way I am presenting it in the film.

We had originally planned to make the film in Hollywood, and I went out there to set things up. But the decision to shoot the movie at Pinewood Studios, near London instead, was made when we realized that 80 percent of the picture was to be done on interior sets. Production costs are almost double in the States what they are in England, and so there seemed to be little point in doing the film there after all.

Phillips: What do you have in mind to follow the Valentino film?

Russell: I am planning to do another film about a composer, this time Elgar. I made a TV film about Elgar when I was at the BBC, but I think that I have grown artistically since then. I showed Elgar in my TV film as having his ups and downs and not being recognized as a great composer until late in life. Basically, it was a sentimental, romantic film, showing Elgar galloping across the Malvern Hills on horseback in the early morning and so on. I was perhaps too much in love with the man's music to see what really produced it. The film was all too lovely, like a TV commercial for the Malvern Hills! In treating Elgar's life this time, I would be far truer to the man and his music than I was more than a decade ago. I would show the unfavorable parts of his life as well as all those lyrical things. I still love him, but I want to depict the complete man, "warts and all," as they say.

Phillips: Is Henri Gaudier still your guiding light as you pursue your career?

Russell: Yes, indeed. I am still firm in the conviction that I learned from his short life, and which I tried to get across in the film which I made about him. That everyone is a potential artist who has something in him which he can transmit to his fellows and which might well be of use to them. It is a pity when one, either through force of circumstance or because one is afraid of being ridiculed by others, won't produce and expose to everyone that little spark of something special which is unique to him alone. That is what I am still trying to do in my work. How well I have succeeded, of course, is not for me to judge.

The Gospel according to Russell

Marjorie Bilbow / 1976

From *Screen International* (November 20, 1976): 8. Copyright © 1976 by *Screen International*.
Reprinted with permission of Screen Daily.

A reincarnation of Attila the Hun is how many critics and purists see Ken Russell. He rides roughshod over the sensitivities, raping and pillaging their most cherished illusions.

This is not how I see him. Other directors of screen biographies may stick more precisely to the better-known facts; Ken Russell alone conveys the pain and effort that goes into creating a work of art.

His films never fail to speak to me loud and clear. Even at his most outrageous and infuriating, he stimulates me into reassessing attitudes that have become dangerously habit-forming.

When he adapts, he adapts as a creator, not as a copyist. He is faithful to what he is adapting within his own terms, as he sees the novel or the character whose life story he presents.

At EMI Elstree, where I watched him directing a scene for his eleventh feature film (*Valentino*), Ken agreed with my definition of his very personal approach.

"Yes, I think that is it in a nutshell. Practically all the feature films I've done have been adaptations of one sort or another. I've done a great number of biographies of composers among others.

"It's a question of putting a point of view onto the information one has about the man; otherwise one is doing a documentary with straightforward reportage—a pic of his house, say, photographs if there is no film available, and a voice-over—I did that for years at the BBC.

"If you haven't got a point of view about a man and you just want to show the facts of his life, that's okay. But facts aren't really what a person's about. A man isn't the sum of his diary—got up at 8 o'clock, got married on December 27, etc.—it's what he thought or what music he was writing or the emotion behind those actions that interest me.

"My films are about real people, most of them, and they are really investigations into the lives of those people and my theories on what they were about.

"They often come out of my subconscious. Out of, say, the music of the person. A lot of the Tchaikovsky film, for instance, came out of my having listened to Tchaikovsky for twenty years and absorbed what he said. In a very few words he said what his music was about: he said his Sixth Symphony was about 'my life,' and he went on to say it was about some of the worst aspects of his life.

"Well, knowing all that, you just have to absorb yourself totally in the music, be taken over by the composer—almost get back into a time machine and try and relive what you do know about him, what he said about himself, and what other people said about him, in terms of his music and the emotions expressed in it. Then, translate those into visual terms. For me, it's very exciting, like a detective story. You get all the fragments and you deduce the solution not to the crime but to the man's life through the study of his music."

"Critics Generally Get Things Mixed Up"

I reminded him that in *Lisztomania* Liszt says, "Time kills all critics."

Said Ken: "In the preface of the new book about me by Joseph Gomez,[1] to which I wrote the introduction, I start off by leading the reader up the garden path a bit by saying 'Here are extracts from my favorite reviews,' then follows a page of the most vitriolic, hateful, spiteful, vicious, nasty writing that can be concentrated onto a page. Then I ask if the reader remembers the names of the people who wrote those things, and there's a whole string of names which are totally forgotten. Those are the people who are responsible for the words. Then I say: 'Have you heard of . . . Bartók, Debussy, Prokofiev, Shostakovich, Delius?' because these are the people they were attacking.

"And I say the only connection I have with these people is that I love them very much, that I've made films about them.

"It's reassuring to know that they were viciously attacked, quite unjustifiably, by people who couldn't take the trouble to look into their motives and people who could just lash out and react without really giving it any thought.

"Critics generally get things mixed up. They say, 'Oh, Tchaikovsky's Second Piano Concerto was never played at Christmas Eve,' and I reply that we weren't actually playing Tchaikovsky's Second, it was his First. Then they'll say, 'Oh, all this tired old music in Tchaikovsky that we've all heard before.' Actually, there are about twenty-five pieces that have never been played in England for the last twenty years. . . .

"They just lash out, say anything that comes into their head, whereas the guy who wrote this book, for example, and people who make films seriously, as

I do, do an awful lot of research. I worked for a year and a quarter researching *Valentino*. I dare say, quite a few guys will come along at the end and demolish it in two minutes over a pink gin."

The Devils, I commented, was just the time when many critics turned against you—you could do no wrong before. It was said that this film was too violent, too horrific, but I remember Ollie Reed saying the scene where Grandier's legs are broken is only eight frames.

"It is. Oddly enough, just before that I'd seen another film—I was thinking of using a certain actress—a horror film, set in the same period, about an exorcist judge who went around maiming people, and there was a scene where someone attacked him with an axe, and they just showed as much blood and gore as they could, and the scene went on for about two and a half minutes. And I remember the censor saying when he saw my scene where Grandier was being tortured with the stake being driven between his legs so the legs are crushed between two boards, 'It's too long.'

"And I said to him that it couldn't be much shorter, 'It's twelve frames.' Now, twelve frames is exactly half a second. And he said that I had to shorten it. So I took four frames off, so I made it a third of a second. Now the rest is in people's imagination.

"The scene was about interrogation and how the State and the Church broke a man's will. So it was really all on their faces and the sound effects of the hammer hitting the wood.

"Now I suppose that created an image in everyone's head of his bones being crushed. In my films a lot of things are suggested, and all this violence that's supposed to be there . . .

"I mean, I go to films to see things I think are terribly violent. There was one I saw the other day which I thought was the most obscene film I'd ever seen. I think it should have been banned. I'm not for censorship in general, but I thought it degraded humanity.

"It was *To the Devil a Daughter*. And I think that this sort of stuff which is ground out just so the British film industry can be perpetuated, well, it would be better if the industry just died the death rather than have the abomination of a woman giving birth to a child with her legs tied together and blood spurting everywhere.

"It's not even horrible. It's depravity. It's the depths to which humanity can sink to think that it is entertainment, and to perpetuate it on a gullible public is grotesque.

"No one seemed to attack that film. They just said, 'Oh, a mild horror film,' and so on. But I've just got to show eight frames in a serious film about an individual being crushed by the State, which is a very serious theme, and I'm crucified. I suppose it's because my films are serious statements and people don't like the way I do them because life is mixed up like that.

"The carpet is usually pulled out from beneath people's feet. It just seems to be that there is a divine fate that stops us taking ourselves seriously even in tragic moments."

"I Identified Very Closely with It"

Was *Savage Messiah* to any extent a self-portrait, I asked him.

"It has a lot to do with the feeling I have about life and art mixed up and what one does with one's life and the struggles one has when younger. I identified very closely with it.

"I was in the struggling position of once trying to make a living and knowing that one had something within oneself to express, and there was that feeling of "How on earth do you do it, how do you get through to the public, how do you make something for people to see?" These are things probably everyone wants, to communicate at some point in their lives at whatever level it is. That's what the film was about. Gaudier-Brzeska had the guts to press on in the face of everyone saying 'rubbish.' They don't say 'rubbish' anymore."

"You always seem to me to bring out the blood, sweat, and tears of creation . . ."

"It's with one every day," said Ken. "Making films is one of the hardest occupations I know. We've got a farmer up the road who's up and around at all hours driving himself until he drops; a film director is much different.

"The people who work on the crew do very long hours, not every day but quite a lot. You've got the people, or whatever it is, to inspire with enthusiasm. You have to drag around boxes yourself and move lamps, and it is very, very hard physical work.

"There's an enormous mental responsibility too. I really envy a painter—I wish I could paint or compose—because there is one man sitting down with a canvas or a blank sheet of paper and writing dots, but whether they're good dots or bad dots, bad brushstrokes or good, it depends on *him*—no excuses.

"A film director has to turn eighty-eight people into his paintbrush or into his pen to go with the thoughts in his head, and it's an aggravation that painters or composers don't have. It's also a very stimulating one, though people get upset, people get hurt, people cry . . . people storm and rage off, friendships break up. One lives a lifetime in every film. Since all art comes out of the same sort of passion, I think I know what it's about.

"I've never made a film about someone I've hated, even Richard Strauss. He was misguided. Life is too short to make destructive films about people one doesn't like. My films are meant to be constructive and illuminating."

"Actually, I Love Tchaikovsky"

"A lot of people say of the film I made about Tchaikovsky that I must have hated him to have done it. Actually, I love Tchaikovsky very much. He was the first composer who turned me on to classical music. I wanted to know why he wrote the music he did. He wrote the music he did because he'd led a tortured life. He hurt a lot of people.... If he had to hurt a lot of people to write that music, then it's too bad on those people.

"It's always a question of equating the cost—there's always a cost in any form of creation. I am sometimes investigating what drove a particular artist to produce such wonderful music. They are often pretty awful circumstances. There's a line in my film about Delius, for instance, where someone says, "How can such an awful man have written such wonderful music?" That's a question I like exploring—why there's an immense amount of goodness and beauty in humanity which somehow can come out of the worst of situations.

Note

1. Joseph A. Gomez, *Ken Russell: The Adaptor as Creator* (London: Frederick Muller, 1976).

With Ken Russell on the Set of *Valentino*

Herb A. Lightman / 1977

From *American Cinematographer* 58, no. 11 (November 1977): 1138–41, 1164–65, 1206–12.
Reprinted with permission.

We drive through the curlicue outskirts of London . . . through a fine misty drizzle—what used to be called "typical English weather" . . . until the drought.

We pass the ghostly hulk of what was formerly MGM's Borehamwood Studios, shooting site of many a cinematic triumph . . . now sadly serving as some sort of massive garage . . . but surely still shimmering with the shades of Kubrick's fabulous *2001*.

Off to the left, a higgledy-piggledy complex of sprawling structures . . . the venerable precincts of EMI Elstree Studios . . . more like some monstrous button factory than the sort of place where one might expect the magic of the early silver screen to be in the process of re-creation . . . the magic of Hollywood in the 1920s . . . the magic of Ken Russell and Rudolf Nureyev reincarnating a myth within a legend within an enigma . . . the magic of *Valentino*.

On the soundstage, the hush of the cathedral, despite the fact that hundreds of people are milling about. There is a movie set within a movie set—and two film crews, ancient and modern—for the set is a replica of a Hollywood shooting stage circa 1921, the stage where they are immortalizing Rudolph Valentino, "The Great Lover," in *Monsieur Beaucaire*.

One end of the stage is faced with a huge stylized monochrome set—all grays and black and white—suffused with pink light. Through a maze of pseudo-French courtiers in powder-wigged finery, I spot Ken Russell sitting quietly beside a video monitor. He is ready for a take. The chaos of humanity organizes itself into an ordered pattern of "Places, everyone!" The cameras roll: two sets—the Panavision kind and the hand-cranked kind. An extremely intricate dolly shot develops as Nureyev, all white-face makeup and shimmering wardrobe, strides forward, trailed by an entourage.

As he continues off the set at the tag end of the scene, he brushes within inches of me, and I am surprised to note that he is considerably shorter than I had imagined. He is obviously put together with steel cables, however, and moves like a panther.

After several takes and the one designated as "Print!" there is the inevitable tea break, a civilized British custom, and it's time to meet the people. First there is a pleasant reunion with Peter Suschitzky, the brilliant young director of photography (Lighting Cameraman) whom I had previously met just after he had completed the photography of Russell's *Lisztomania* (see *American Cinematographer*, February 1976).

Next I am introduced to the American coproducer, Robert Chartoff. I had been informed quite emphatically that this was very much a closed set and that my invitation to visit it was on the same plane with having been granted the Keys to the Kingdom, but Chartoff welcomes me aboard cordially enough, asking only that I withhold publication of my stories until a time closer to the release date of the picture. Fair enough.

Then it's time to meet The Man himself, Ken Russell. Having been conditioned by his incredibly flamboyant public relations, I almost expect some sort of foaming-at-the-mouth mad scene, but Russell acknowledges the introduction with polite restraint and says he will be happy to talk with me at length after the day's shooting has been completed. He is quiet, totally understated, not at all what I had expected.

But then I realize that my puzzlement in meeting Russell is only an extension of my ambiguous attitude toward his work. I had been deeply touched by the misty *Women in Love*, impressed by the technically brilliant *The Music Lovers*, alternately fascinated and repelled by *The Devils*, charmed and amused by *The Boy Friend*, profoundly moved by the vastly underrated *Savage Messiah*, put off by the frantic overkill of *Mahler* and *Lisztomania*, and dazzled by the spectacular brilliance of *Tommy*. But I have always been aware that, controversial though he may be, Russell, even at his most excessive low, is probably the most exciting filmmaker of the decade.

After lunch with Peter Suschitzky and his delightful family (visiting him on the set that day), I return to the stage, where a new scene is in rehearsal. This is a re-creation of the famous pink powder puff incident which, I am told, cast such doubts upon the virility of the real-life Valentino that he was forced to engage in a public boxing match to prove his machismo.

Still garbed as the effete Monsieur Beaucaire, Nureyev is sprawled on a settee dallying with a lady. On a catwalk directly above them, two grips of the period are watching the rehearsal. One of them drops a large pink powder puff onto Nureyev. Symbolism!

The scene is a simple one, but it involves much clambering about up high to get the lights set and exquisite timing precisely on cue. Sitting in his chair, Russell checks the action on the Samcinevision video monitor, quietly asking for repeated takes until he gets what he wants. Then it's a wrap, and he invites me to his office.

It is sparsely furnished in early studio drab, with no accoutrements to suggest the creative ferment that must surround the man. On the desk are copies of a new book which has been written about his work, and he tells me that he's very happy with it. "It's really one of the best of its kind that I've ever seen," says he. "Absolutely first rate." He offers me refreshment, pours a glass of white wine for me, but nothing for himself.

I cannot but marvel at how different the man seems from the image that has been built up about him, a seemingly calculated public relations effort which must have come about with his cooperation, reluctant or otherwise. In the press he is almost always depicted in some sort of bizarre gear, clowning it up like a proper buffoon. But the man with whom I am now alone does not jibe with that image, not even slightly. The impression that comes across to me is that of a down-to-earth, keenly intelligent, serious professional, with no affectations, but a dedication to perfectionism in his craft.

Just now he also seems a bit ill at ease. "Do you really want to do this interview?" he asks me.

"I do if you do," I reply.

"Well, I don't really," says he, "but I will."

And he does—most articulately—as follows.

Question: Can you tell me first what visual style you have conceived for *Valentino*?

Ken Russell: I usually find that a visual style imposes itself on a film. In shooting *The Devils*, for example, we worked out very carefully beforehand the idea that we wanted it to look like an antiseptic world, because although it was set in the medieval period, I wanted it to reflect the modern world. So we had all our buildings white and glistening and shining. As I say, it was the sixteenth century, but in most period films the buildings look like ruins, even though they are supposed to be contemporary. You see the people wandering around in new "old-fashioned" clothes, but all the buildings are in a state of decay and crumbling. Bits do fall down in towns, but there are parts of towns which always look new to the inhabitants. So in that film we wanted to create a modern feeling in order to make the audience identify with the protagonists of the drama. They were in the Middle Ages, but, at the same time, there was the feeling that it was all happening then and there, not in dim and distant history.

I try to match the style to the subject. For example, in a film I did for television about Rousseau, the primitive painter, I employed a very primitive style—shot everything dead center, with people just walking through the frame, and no camera movement. *The Boy Friend* was a pastiche of 1930s films, so it had that sort of style. *Tommy* had a definite rough style about it that sort of suited the modern idiom. And now, in *Valentino*, the thing about it is that each sequence has its own style. I have never done a film with so many different stylistic sequences. We go from the black-and-white style of silent films to a sort of sophisticated Russian ballet style, to art deco, mixed up with Edwardian, Hollywood bad taste, Hollywood good taste, and so forth. Really, it's almost too much. It's a very, very rich canvas I'm painting, but the main thing about the film is that every sequence is totally different to any other in the film.

Question: You've made several biographical films in the past, mostly about composers, but while those films dealt with real people, the cinematic treatments were often wildly unrealistic. Just how important is authenticity to you?

Russell: I try to get authenticity into my films. I can't say that I always succeed, but that's what I always try to do. I do it through the use of colors and costumes mainly. Most of the clothes in this film are original, and my wife designed some sort of stunning period costumes for it. We have some very snazzy dresses in our films, and that's true of the clothes worn by Nazimova, the MGM star of the twenties, and Natasha Rambova, who was Valentino's second wife. She was a costume designer, but she didn't design her own clothes. She was dressed by famous French designers. This is a very stylish sort of film, mixed up with the rough hurly-burly of Hollywood. It's a bit of a kaleidoscope. There is a variety of styles and techniques.

Question: Can you give me some specific examples of that variety?

Russell: Well, as Valentino's story unfolds, we show four of his films being made—and that could become boring if they were all treated in the same way. Yet they are important, because they are backgrounds that lead to the dialogue, to the action, to the drama between the protagonists. Each time I felt that I wanted a slightly different look at the film unit, so on one of his film projects the camera goes whizzing by, and you get just an impression of it. On another one, the action is very laid out, almost like a battlefield, with strategic positions for cameras and so forth. Another one is being done by a very arty group, and it's all in the pinewood, with violins playing to give it mood, and everyone dressed in pastels. The one which you've just seen being filmed in the studio has a much more cosmopolitan, sort of "metropolitan" feel to it—and much more hustle and bustle and hurly-burly than the other sequences. It's been interesting devising these different ways of making a film, although they all serve as background to the main film itself. They do not dominate it but almost sort of make a comment on it. All of the films which we show within the main film are staged to make a comment on the action. *Valentino* is about the divergence of the real man from his image. The primary action takes place after he is dead. The film is about flickering shadows. The "real" man is never seen, and nothing is known about him.

Question: You say that the primary action takes place after he is dead. Does that mean that the majority of the film is done in flashback?

Russell: It starts off in a funeral parlor, with the heads of the studio carving up the body, as it were—carving up what's left of him. It then becomes a series of flashbacks throughout his life. The difficulty with this film, as with all biographies, is that there is too much material, really. It's very hard to cut it down and still have a coherent story. Valentino did have an action-packed life, and one always has a problem of condensing such a man's life into two-and-a-quarter hours. You find that you always end up—as I have in this one—with a sort of succession of highlights. We did have a lot of quieter moments of him cooking spaghetti five feet long (which he actually did) and things like that, but if you showed everything of that sort, the film would last six hours. So you say to yourself, "What can I lose and still keep the dramatic thread of the story?" That's what it always comes down to. You find at the end that you have a series of very dramatic moments, but a lot of the warmth and humanity and the simplicity has had to go by the boards, because, although it's important, it's not dramatic and in order to include it you would have to sacrifice something that is dramatic and was a turning point in his life. This man had lots of turning points in his life—at least half a dozen key changes over a period of ten years—and one has to decide either to sacrifice a bit of warmth and domesticity, as it were, which shows his background, or to sacrifice one of the key changes in his life. We've ended up with a very dramatic film, but one which is not quite as relaxed as I would have liked it to be. This is all talking in theory, of course, since we are only a third of the way through the filming. I'm trying to slide little bits of softness into it, but it's difficult.

Question: I understand that you were in Hollywood previously researching this film. Did you originally plan to shoot it there, or were you simply gathering background material?

Russell: We did indeed intend to shoot it in Hollywood. When I first went to Hollywood, however, it was to announce the film, because other films were being planned about Valentino and we felt that if we announced ours it might put the brakes on a few of the others, which it actually seemed to do. At that time, I hadn't quite finished the script, but I knew that it was a Hollywood story and should be shot in Hollywood. While there, I continued working on the script and, at the same time, I was looking at the work of various cinematographers, art directors, and so forth because, naturally, I would need an American crew. The fact is that I didn't see any work of art directors that I liked at all. I may have been unfortunate, but I just didn't see anything which quite suited the way I felt. There was one film with Barbra Streisand, *The Way We Were*, which I took be a 1960s film—and then found that it was supposed to be 1935, then 1943 or something. Well, there was no way you could tell that from the costumes or art direction. I realized that *Valentino* would be a period film and that I would have to get the period exactly right. I know there are lots of art directors in America who would be very good at it, but I didn't happen to see the work of any that I liked.

Question: What about cameramen?

Russell: It was the same with them. Although there are indeed many very competent cameramen in Hollywood, I only met one who I felt would be right for my kind of filming. His name was Jordan Cronenweth, and he could do any style of photography: the ultraromantic, handheld, grainy, rough and tough, anything. He seemed to be one of the few cameramen who could be presented with any kind of exterior and handle it well. I saw a film of his called *Zandy's Bride*, and every shot (which seemed to me that he had very little control over) he was able to invest with an amazing atmosphere that I found to be unique. I would have been quite content to do the film with him, but he was busy on another film. That was before we had a star anyway, and by the time I had completed the script I found that it was almost all interiors. That being the case, it suddenly struck me that I could do the film better in England than in America. For one thing, I didn't actually know the crew people well enough to gather those around me that I would need to do this particular film—whereas, if I were doing a contemporary American film, there would be no problem. (In fact, I nearly did one. I tried to fit it in between that visit and this project, but I didn't have time.) All in all, I thought I could do it better in England, since there were so few exteriors. I had looked for locations around Hollywood, but it's all built up now. I was sure we could find better exteriors in Spain, and we did. They seemed to be more Hollywood than Hollywood itself, but not built up. They were the same as in the 1920s. As far as I'm concerned, it was the right decision.

Question: I noticed on the set that you have one of the original Dead End Kids in the cast, Huntz Hall. Since this was a totally American picture in content, what did you do for actors?

Russell: We have used mostly American actors, and I was amazed at how many of them are working in England full-time. The man who plays the role of the Lighting Cameraman in our film came over as Officer Krupke in *West Side Story* twenty years ago, and he's been here ever since, and a lot of others have, too. There is some very good American talent here, especially for character roles, very good indeed. Then, of course, we brought various people over from America specifically for this film.

Question: Did you do any actual casting while you were in Hollywood?

Russell: What struck me when I held casting sessions in America was that I was disappointed in the people they brought in. They seemed such stereotyped types. If I wanted a business manager, the people they sent over were right off TV and had played nothing but business managers. I got rather tired of seeing sort of typecast characters. There were never any surprises. There was never anyone who walked in and made me think, "Gosh, well, I hadn't quite thought of anyone like you, but you're marvelous!" I finally asked the casting manager if he had the equivalent of the British *Spotlight* (which is the theater guide of all our actors), and he brought out a book that had sort of postage-stamp-size pictures in it. I started flicking through it and found the people I liked, those who struck me as being interesting and cut a bit different from the others. They were mostly people I had seen in 1930 and 1940 and thought were either dead and buried or pensioned off or whatever. I got quite a few of those people and some of them gave me a great laugh. The Ritz Brothers came and did an amazing song-and-dance act which was superb. I wish I could have used them. A case in point was Huntz Hall. I just listened to him speaking and knew he was right. He grew up in Hollywood and said that he'd acted with Nazimova at the age of eighteen months, when she was on the stage. (He was a baby and was brought on in a pram.) He also acted with her when he was six, and she boxed his ears. He seemed to be exactly the right character to play the head of the Lasky-Famous Players Studio, and he brought a great atmosphere of Hollywood along with him when he came here.

Question: You did *Lisztomania* with Peter Suschitzky as Lighting Cameraman. Can you describe your method of working with him on this film, as compared to that one, since they differ so greatly in photographic style?

Russell: We're actually working in much the same way, insofar as we discuss each scene and the effect we want, and then he just goes and does it. Of course, I keep an eye on him, because I'm very photography conscious. I photographed three films myself (amateur films they were, but they got me started profession-ally), and I was also a stills cameraman and all that. I always take a great interest in the lighting. When I first started, I was more interested in the lighting and the camerawork than in the actors, but I think I'm a bit more balanced now, and I realize that the actors can't act by themselves and so need a bit of guidance. I can't make an actor act if he can't act. When he comes in, I can't wave a magic wand and make him act. I think it's a question of creating the right atmosphere for actors and explaining things to them—and hoping for the best. But I think that the whole mise-en-scène, if you like, of the film is that if the lighting is wrong or the camera operating is wrong, the result will be wrong. It's not just down to the acting; it's all the ingredients. It's like when you are doing a painting; it's the pigments and the oils and the brushes and the canvas, not just one thing, that create the final effect. In the same way, I think one's got to have a grasp over the entire film.

Question: Film directors vary greatly in the ways they "cover" the subject mat-ter of the script. Some (like the late George Stevens) shoot a scene in its entirety from every possible angle, while others (like Ford and Hitchcock) shoot only the bits and pieces that will actually be needed in the final cut. How thoroughly do you cover yourself in shooting?

Russell: I shoot my films in a way whereby, generally, each sequence is self-contained, and often there are no cutaways; they are just joined together one shot after another. So the editor just tops and tails them and sticks them together, if you like. Now and again I might take maybe three or four shots which could go in to break up any sort of difficulty, but I am not a believer in long shot, mid-shot, and two closeups. I never do that—ever. I generally conceive a sequence as one flowing sort of choreographic pattern. I suppose that having been a dancer myself (trained as a dancer for five years, and then danced for three or four years with various ballet companies and musicals, including *Annie Get Your Gun*), I do see things in terms of movement. I see my films as sort of ballets of the movements of actors and camera and extras and colors—and I think that this does give the audience a sense of involvement. I don't mean using a busy camera for its own sake; I think it should all be constructed to a definite purpose and build up to a definite end. Some sequences should be very legato and flowing, while others should be very staccato—so that the audience never quite knows what it is getting. That's what I like. *Tommy* was a case in point. There were various moments in that (the Marilyn Monroe sequence, for instance) which I covered a great deal. We cut, cut, cut, cut. It was an editor's dream—or nightmare, depending upon which way you look at it—and the same was true in the Pinball Wizard sequence. But then there were other sequences where there was a sort of flowing thing—a sequence in Tommy's house, for example, which was a very calming sort of number. He just sort of invited people into his home, and the sequence was made up of flowing legato shots.

Question: I notice that you repeatedly use musical terms in describing certain cinematic analogies. How importantly does music enter into your approach to filming?

Russell: I play a lot of music when I write my scripts. I generally write them all myself, but I needed some help with the dialogue on this one, since I'm not an American. Although, oddly enough, the chap who offered to write the American dialogue (and who said I wrote the most atrocious dialogue he'd ever read), when it came to reading what I had written, hardly changed a thing. He was most amazed and so was I. It suddenly struck me (and him) that the reason my dialogue for this film was better than my dialogue for English films was that I was brought up on American films. In the thirties and forties I probably went every day to the cinema, and so I saw almost every "A" and "B" film that was made in America from 1930 to 1946. As a result, I had absorbed the way Americans speak and, since this was a 1920s film, and in the thirties they were still using more or less the same slang as in that period, I was able to write this dialogue. I couldn't possibly write modern American dialogue; it would sound ludicrous.

Question: The casting of Nureyev, a Russian ballet dancer, as Valentino, a Latin screen lover, is unusual, to say the least. Is it working out the way you hoped it would?

Russell: Yes, I think so—because it's sort of a case of a myth playing a myth. We always were up against it in trying to find someone to play this role. We did see Al Pacino, but I didn't think he was quite right, and he didn't like the script anyway, so that was two good reasons why he shouldn't be in it. He was a bit short, really, and while he's a brilliant actor, he didn't quite have the sort of charisma that was needed to play a legend. One could have found an Italian waiter who looked like Valentino, but he would have been just an Italian waiter dressed up, because whereas Italian waiters in 1920 may have had some magic, they don't in this day and age. There are too many of them about, especially in London. There are more Italian waiters than English waiters. So I had to think of something new. First off, since we have Nijinsky in the film, I thought of Nureyev to play that role, and that's all. When we contacted him, he agreed to play Nijinksy. Then we thought, "We're mad; he should be playing the lead!" Actually, he's very similar to Valentino. He's a myth. People don't know a great deal about him. He's before the public every day of his life and no one has heard him speak—and so, he's a living legend whom nobody knows. It seemed too much of a coincidence to let slip by, and, oddly enough, when I spoke to him about it and he said he'd do it, he seemed to know more about Valentino than I would have imagined. I asked him why and he said that he had been asked to play the role a year earlier. I said, "Why didn't you do it?" And he said, "The director died." It was the chap who made *The Bicycle Thief*, the very famous Italian director Vittorio De Sica.

Question: Getting back to the technical side—I have been told that you never look at rushes. Is that true?

Russell: I used to, but I found that there were so many small fiddling details that annoyed me that I kept wishing that I could do them all over again. Also, viewing rushes sort of slightly distracts me from the work in hand, and I find that since there are never enough hours in the day to do what you have to do, it's no good worrying over things that you can't change—so there is no point to it. I'll see it if there is something drastically wrong, and now I have this video thing, as you know, so I see every take that we do. I would rather let my editor cope with it. As I've said, he hasn't got much option; he can only cut the scenes a certain way anyway, although he can fiddle about a bit.

Question: But what about spotting things that may actually be wrong?

Russell: Well, I found with *Tommy* and *Mahler* in particular that if I saw them all put together at the end in a sort of rough fine cut, I could immediately put my finger on what was wrong; whereas, if I had seen rushes over and over again fifteen times, out of context to the filming, and then seen a rough cut, my judgment might have been blunted. Of course, one can easily sort it out, but there is nothing like seeing something brand-new for the first time. Apart from actual disasters, I don't think there is much to be gained from looking at rushes, although, for a time, I thought there was a sort of cowardice about not seeing them. I think seeing the rushes inhibits you, actually, and you also get a slightly false impression, because some things you like very much, but in the finished film they are either cut to ribbons and you have to throw them away, or you get too attached to certain scenes. It's better to let the editor have a pretty free hand and chop things down a bit. You can always put them back in—but you don't, of course. In making *Women in Love*, which was quite a confusing film, we worked on it as we went along and cut and recut and cut and recut, but I think that if I'd just looked at it when I was finished, the first rough cut, I could have put my finger on what was wrong.

Question: You mentioned the "video thing," the Samcinevision device that you've been using on the set. How well has that been serving your purpose?

Russell: Well, I use it mainly to check certain scenes that require intricate camera movement. When you have several hundred extras, plus actors, and lines that have to be in the clear while people are rushing in front of the camera, and you have tricky camera work, and the operator says, "Well, I think I got it, but there may have been a moment when he went behind the lamp when he was walking" . . . when you've got all those variables, you wouldn't know until you saw the rushes next day whether the scene was alright. With the video thing, you simply go to the machine and play it back and there it is. Also, I can play things pretty tight, so if an actor is putting a powder puff up to his face, and it is two inches out of frame, his fingers will be cut off. It's very useful for checking technical things like that. You can just call the actor over and say, "Look, see what you did." It saves quite a bit of time. Also, I'm very meticulous about the way shots are framed. I sort of look through the camera, then let the operator set it and say, "Just let me double check it, because I'm nervous and I saw it move a thousandth of an inch." Now, all I do is look at the video monitor and say, "Pan up a thousandth of an inch." We did a shot yesterday of two electricians right up in the rails. There was this rickety old rostrum swaying about fifty feet in the air—and the less people on it, the better. With the television monitor on the ground, I was able to see the faces of the actors very clearly, so I didn't have to be up on the rostrum, and I didn't have to crawl on my belly and push away the operator and look in the eyepiece and then crawl back. We did it in half the time. So I consider it a labor-saving device. It also lets you sleep at night, because you know exactly what you have got on the screen—providing the film does come out, providing it doesn't get scratched in the lab, providing nobody treads on it, providing it's not stolen—and all those things. But you know what you've got, and that's another reason why I don't see rushes. I've already seen them. The image is bright enough to see the actors' performances. The only thing you can't see is the color, because it's in black-and-white. It offers a slight guide for lighting, but not much, because it's slightly contrasty. When it's in color, it will be fantastic!

Ken Russell: An Interview

Ric Gentry / 1981

From *Post Script: Essays in Film and the Humanities* 2, no. 3 (Spring/Summer 1983): 2–23.
Reprinted with permission.

Flamboyant, primal, laconic, mad—these are some of the adjectives often associated with British director Ken Russell. But the maker of such innovative and controversial films as *Women in Love, The Music Lovers, The Devils, Savage Messiah, Mahler,* and *The Boy Friend* is hardly at all like this in person. In fact, he is quite the opposite—patient, articulate, sensitive, and, quite honestly, even cherubic. Certainly, he does not seem like the same man whose work at different times has elicited official condemnations from both the Vatican and the British Parliament.

Still, as a filmmaker, Russell is a kind of provocateur and visionary. As he discusses here, he is interested in subjects, usually artists, who, in one way or another, are "in touch with some mystery." Or, put another way, who have some unusual oracular power that they channel through creative means. Russell himself may be his own best model for interpreting his protagonists, working as he claims from a subconscious-level inspiration and translating such uncensored and personal images into some of the most unforgettable impressions of "the sacred and profane" ever filmed.

The following interview was conducted at the Beverly-Wilshire Hotel in Beverly Hills several months after *Altered States* had been released.

Ric Gentry: *Altered States* is really your first Hollywood film, in the sense that you shot it here.

Ken Russell: Not all of it was literally done in Hollywood, but you could say that, yes, it was a Hollywood film, shot with Hollywood crews and performers. I was supposed to do *Valentino* here, and I wanted to. While I was finishing the script, I began to look at the work of various cinematographers, art directors, and so forth, because naturally I would need American people. But the fact is, I didn't see any work by art directors here that I liked at all. I may have just been unlucky, but I just didn't see anything which suited the way I felt about the material. There was one film with Barbra Streisand, for example, *The Way We Were*, which I took to be a sixties film and then found out that they were trying to recreate 1935. Well, there was no way that you could discern what they were trying to do by the look of the costumes or the art direction, which are crucial to a period piece. *Valentino* would be a period film that had to be very precise, and so it struck me that I'd be much better off doing the film in England, rather than in America. With *Altered States*, because it was contemporary, I felt less inhibited about accepting it and doing it here. Naturally, I had very little choice since the production was already underway, but the fears I had before did cross my mind.

RG: You seem antagonistic toward Hollywood, and *Valentino* had rather an anti-Hollywood theme. Did *Valentino* represent your feelings toward Hollywood, the institution?

KR: Oh, I suppose. *Valentino* was about the divergence of the real man from his image. The action takes place after he's dead, most of it. The film is about the flickering shadows of a mystery that was a man. The "real" man is never seen, and nothing is known about him. It was also about, however indirectly, the problems of identity in our world today. More and more we are displaced by what we are told we are and what we should be, and motion pictures are very central to that equation of self-alienation. We look in the mirror and see an image which is not really us. It is more often a fabrication of what we think we should be. People are constantly bothered by a sense of need, to *have* things which might placate their own self-image. But things change so quickly that they aren't ever able to feel content with who they are, and they are made to feel this way. People are covered over with the exigencies of modern life, conveyed largely through the media, so that finally a real person disappears underneath. They live their whole lives never knowing that this is what bothered them, urged them on, and that their real poverty is in the imagination. They live vicariously through the stars of the movies and things and some kind of action that always takes place "out there." Well, this is reprehensible to me. And here was Valentino, who was a victim of what people thought he should be, which was this dashing figure of the screen. All he really wanted when he came to California was to have his own orange grove.

RG: Do you blame the cinema for creating illusions and misrepresenting what should be more important goals and values?

KR: In a way, I do, but like everyone who works in this business, I've had my ups and downs with it. In the beginning, when I was a young man, I used to go to the cinema on weekends. I went to a nautical college. I was actually attracted to the college because I had dreams of sailing to the South Seas and meeting up with Dorothy Lamour. But there was nothing romantic about the college or anything else. It was rigid and archaic, and I didn't like it at all.

RG: Did you start to associate the movies with guilt in any way, and did this tie in with your later feelings about Catholicism?

KR: That was later, the Church. From the college, I went on a cargo ship bound for the Pacific. And we had a modern-day Captain Bligh about the ship, and that was horrible, too. I was about to jump ship in Australia, but I quickly found out that I didn't like Australia either. It was hard times, and all that because of the movies.

RG: And so you base part of your conception of Hollywood on that experience?

KR: But movies were a revelation as well, you see. I probably went to the cinema every day in the 1930s and '40s, and so I probably saw every film made in America between 1930 and 1946, all the A and B films. In fact, when I was doing the script for *Valentino*, the chap who was supposed to write the American dialogue hardly changed a thing. He was most surprised, and so was I. But it finally occurred to both of us that my dialogue was so accurate in terms of the American vernacular because I was brought up on these American films, and the period for *Valentino* was actually the appropriate one for the period I knew. I had absorbed the way Americans speak, and since it was a 1920s film, and since in the thirties they used more or less the same patterns of speaking in that period, I was able to write the dialogue. But I couldn't possibly write contemporary American dialogue. It would sound ludicrous.

RG: What about the demythification of the Church you often portray, and one that is not unlike the criticism of Hollywood that was in *Valentino*? It shows up in *Tommy* in another sense, this undoing of popular myths.

KR: I was ripe for conversion [to Catholicism]. I was very moved by a friend's simple but very firm belief that Christ was mystically present in the communion service of the Mass. It was the most mind-shattering thing that ever struck me. I was also very taken with the theatricality of the Mass, the beauty and wonder of it. But when I was very young, I really didn't know where I was going, but as soon as I came into the faith my work, my philosophy, all gained direction. I began to think more clearly, to see much further than I had. The faith taught me that there was no easy road to life, that pain and purgation are very much a part of it. And I was inspired by artists, very much by Gaudier, who you see in *Savage Messiah*. I began to realize that I could survive anything in my quest to fulfill my potential as a person and as an artist. I am a lapsed Catholic now, as you know. I think one of the reasons I left the Church is that I couldn't live up to it. I wasn't good enough to continue. Almost all my films are, nevertheless, Catholic in outlook. Even the most recent. They are films about faith, love, sin, guilt, forgiveness, and redemption.

RG: Do the Church and the cinema have synonymous importance for you? You criticize and defame them, and even more you do it with your artists. It's almost as if you take revenge against these once hallowed subjects to compensate for your own sense of doubt, or even unworthiness.

KR: I don't know. I see what you're getting at, and what you say is very astute, I think. I do so much from an unconscious or subconscious level of inspiration that I would be hard-pressed to give you the answer you're looking for. I tend to deal with the conflict of illusion and reality. The church makes illusions and so do films. So do artists. We tend to obscure what they really are and what they're capable of. And we need to see them clearly so as not to confuse the world of illusion with the world of reality. I think this is something that runs very deep in me, the world of images. When I write a script, and I didn't write *Altered States*, of course, I like to work with music in the background because it stimulates me to think in pictures. Monteverdi and those people. All sorts of things come to the surface, perhaps your true disposition. I don't know.

RG: What about the condemnation of *The Devils* earned from the Vatican when it was released? How did you feel about that?

KR: *The Devils*, as are all my films in one way or another, was based on the facts of the time. It was based on Huxley's book, *The Devils of Loudun*, a study of religious and erotic hysteria that really did take place in that city. All the corruption within the Church, the politics, the King, the methods of torture, the rites of exorcism, they're all there. I took no liberties with what happened. The hero, Grandier, the priest, was no perfect priest. He did have a mixture of good and bad qualities. He knows what his obligations are, but he often fails to observe them. Then he gets the opportunity to stand up against Richelieu in order to preserve the rights of the city, and he does so. In this crisis, his virtues surface, and he dies a Christian martyr. He is regenerated, "saved" if you will, by the suffering he is forced to undergo. It was all pretty much right there in the book, because once I decided to do *The Devils*, I had to go along with the truth as it was reported. I had to show the violent atmosphere created by the plague at the time, for instance, in order to show how ordinary people could allow a man they knew to be innocent to die a hideous death. They had become calloused as a result of the plague. When there is death at every doorstep, the death of a single man like Grandier (not to be confused with Gaudier of *Savage Messiah*) becomes inconsequential, an everyday occurrence. That is why the crowd attending his burning behave as they might at a football match. And it's all a jolly sight less ugly than Huxley's book. When one reads these accounts in Huxley, one can sift the words through one's imagination and filter out as much unpleasantness as one cares to. You can't do that when you're looking at a film. In fact, I was reading another book by Huxley, his antiutopian novel *Ape and Essence*, and I said to myself, this is ugly stuff, and were I to film it people would probably say that I had exaggerated the material.

RG: You did have some stylistic flourishes of your own. You did some astonishing reversals in *The Devils* by using white instead of shadow or chiaroscuro, which is typical of a film set in a Gothic era. You seem to be establishing a leitmotiv of whiteness which resists and dissolves relationships. And there were also modern structures, the almost contemporary architecture.

KR: The architecture was contemporary because I noticed the obvious. And the obvious was that when you're doing an historical film, the scenery is always old moss on the stones, and crumbling masonry everywhere. But there must have been a time when a city went up and it was brand-new. The whole thing about *The Devils* was that the people were proud of their city because it was new, or fairly new, to them. It would have looked as bright as new stone, and I wanted to get that feeling, that it was white and strange and wonderful. I wanted the audience to absorb that feeling, so that if it wasn't a skyscraper, they would still intuit something remarkable about Loudun. Another reason that I had it designed that way was that I took a line from Huxley wherein he describes the exorcism of Sister Jeanne as very similar to a rape in a public lavatory. So I took the public lavatory theme of the white tiles, and we used them as well, and that seemed to tie in with the modern concept of this happening today. We have a different kind of horror today, the mystique of needles and the chill and sterility of hospitals, you see, instead of medieval times, back when cobwebs were falling across the street. The tendency is to view something as old because it is old to us, when it wasn't to them at all.

RG: Another thing about *The Devils* were the fantasy sequences that you used and which occur in many of your films, the "fantasias" as they are called in musical terminology. The hallucinations in *Altered States* are typical, and then there are these kinds of sequences in *Mahler, Lisztomania, The Music Lovers,* and, of course, *The Devils*, where Sister Jeanne identified Grandier with Christ and herself with Mary Magdalene. In a way, she subconsciously disguises her physical attraction to the priest as a spiritual love for Christ.

KR: That's quite true. Very correct. One thing at a time. The "fantasias" to which you allude are, as I said, always about the conflict of illusion with reality. When a priest, who is a kind of artist of spiritual inspiration, devotes himself to the making of ideas and thoughts and conduct in other people, he runs the risk of confusing the world of illusions with the world in which he lives, the human world of which, of course, he is a part. What I do is take the facts and the crisis known to exist in that person's life and present it in such a way that it is certainly imaginary but a summary of his or her predicament. It was something that took years for the BBC to accept, because, for one thing, they weren't ready for some permutation of the traditional documentary or any other kind of story that dealt with historical situations. I had to coax them along, and do it to get closer to the truth which was in the facts but also in and around the facts, the atmosphere, and also the historical perspective, which weren't evident at that time. Another thing is that you have to condense the facts, because screen time is only so long. It's sometimes easier and more expedient to condense the facts by handling things on the level of symbolic occurrence. You enhance the drama as well.

RG: More specifically, though, the fantasias usually have to do with certain erotic and/or violent imaginings on the part of one of the characters, and they usually have to do with some form of repressed energy or anxiety, the grotesque consequences of repression such as Sister Jeanne's deformed spine or Mahler's fascist visions of sex. On the other hand, though not necessarily in the fantasias, you show a healthier life for uninhibited people, such as Ursula and Rupert in *Women in Love*, or that wonderful scene in *Savage Messiah* where the young aristocratic woman meanders down the steps naked, talking to Gaudier as if it were no big deal. My question is, do you feel that you're arguing a point of view, a politics of the body in a way, a "love's body" kind of thing?

KR: What you say is very interesting. I'm not sure, but I think there is a correlation between moral and emotional tyranny, whereby the pressures to behave this way or that can have startling and unhappy consequences. But it is not so simple, and I would not want to say that what is right for one person is right for another person. What I will say with certainty is that I am after anything that will arouse people who have become desensitized. Sex is the common denominator, and it circumscribes our social relations, but it remains with us like a vessel, a nucleus that is very vulnerable. I certainly don't mean that sex constitutes liberation. I don't mean that, not consciously or any way, I don't think.

RG: You don't have a theory of sexuality then, a theory per se?

KR: No, not at all. Such a theory would be a lie, damaging in fact, a terribly destructive thing. I deal with it in my work, but I have no prescription for it, how it should be spooned out. Anyone who thinks he has an answer is dangerous, and a dangerous influence if he or she is in a position to be listened to. You can't deal with sex honestly or intimately with blanket statements. Human behavior is much too complex and fragile for that. It's at the core of us all, like death, and in modern life we deal more and more with sex as we also increase our terror of death, which is a result of our jealousy of the machine. Sex has become the fight against death, and there is no fertility to it any longer. There is no more sex with the intent to procreate, which is—or was—its main function, though it's not meant to be unpleasant, obviously. But our society is filled with a kind of pleasure that in its basis mirrors the convulsions we go through to wipe death from our awareness. You see sex in all of its manifestations, but at the same time we have an anxiety unknown before our time. Emotion is also by the boards, because in emotion a sense for the frailties and despair of our present behavior is too painful to carry around.

RG: Do you think what you're saying may have a certain kind of Catholic ring to it?

KR: I don't believe so. As you said, I'm against certain things it stands for. That would be a gross oversimplification to ascribe that to what I'm saying. It's typical of people to make things into either/or situations, especially now with what the computer does. I'm saying there's a placebo effect, the pornography of our billboards, which puts sex into our cereals and our toast and tea and its use in our day and age to sell things, to distract us from life. Sex is used to control, to manipulate people, like rats in a maze. There's always the promise that if we do something, a bell will ring. The bell never rings. It's Pavlov on a mass scale. . . . But movies, art, music, they can still do their job, which is to counteract the social images that manipulate.

RG: In the early seventies your films were virtually cult items for the youth culture because of their iconoclastic stance. *Altered States* would seem very much again to appeal to that movie constituency, especially since the bulk of filmgoers are between the ages of eighteen to thirty-five.

KR: Well, Jessup's a modern, bright chap. He seems to be fairly normal in most ways, so I imagine that many people identify with him. He's educated. He's American. With most science-fiction films, that's not the case. It's usually too fictional, too incredible. They know it's a mad scientist up there. Well, Jessup may very well be mad, but he is a practicing scientist with somewhat usual relationships. You don't have some kid up there with a ray gun. You have a man who you might know on a real level and not just a fantasy level. I think that's what Chayefsky wanted. It was very, very clear from the start. One reason I don't think he went along with the previous director's concept was that it wasn't realistic enough. It was too overtly sci-fi before we started. I saw the tank room they designed, because it was in fact built, and it was something out of James Bond. It had velour carpets and electric blue walls. It was all unreal to start with, which struck me as a mistake. It was all fantasy and not something to launch the rest of the movie from. God knows how it would have happened had they pursued that approach. I can't imagine. The situation and the characters to me were very believable, and I saw that as a way to carry their concerns into an exploration of the imagination.

RG: You were very faithful to the novel *Altered States* in many respects.

KR: I would say in most respects.

RG: But I nevertheless submit that it was very definitely a Ken Russell film, a quintessential film of yours, in theme, in structure, in all respects we have come to know and expect.

KR: I think that's why I tried Chayefsky's soul. As Gene Phillips was saying, you don't hear about Arthur Hiller's *Hospital* or what's-his-name's *Network*. It's always, "Paddy Chayefsky's *Network*," "Paddy Chayefsky's *Hospital*." And then all of a sudden, he sees that it's going to be "Ken Russell's *Altered States*." I can't say how he reacted, because I would be making it up. But by virtue of the so-called historical precedent they've always been called "Paddy Chayefsky films." I didn't see *Network* and I didn't see *Hospital*, so I don't know what they're like. I saw *Marty* several years ago, but that was about all. I honestly haven't kept up with the others. But his name is always associated with them, that I do know. So that is rather strange. That means that his input must outweigh the director's input, mustn't it? There can't be any other reason. He didn't direct them in theory.

RG: What was your chief discrepancy with Chayefsky? If I understand it correctly, he and yourself had a great deal of conflict.

KR: The only discrepancy that I had with him was that I told him from the start, "I can't be your eyes and ears. I can only direct my own film. And he said, "Yes, of course, I know that. That's what I want you to do. But I'll be around if they say you want to change some of the dialogue, or we think a scene is not working, and I just like to be present while the shooting is going on." Well, if that were the case, that would have been fine. But we'd only gotten so far as shooting a film test when he complained about the color and the angle and lighting. So strike one, that didn't go down very well. If nothing else, I know that one of my fortes as a director is color and lighting, and I think there is a distinguishing consistency in any of my films you wish to look at. But then, after the first day's shooting, he conferred with the actors in private about how they were performing, and I knew why they were calling "Paddy Chayefsky's this" and "Paddy Chayefsky's that." I was still prepared to go along with it as long as it didn't happen again. But the very next time we worked it did happen, and then a very uneasy truce was drawn between us. I just made it known that I couldn't continue directing with somebody constantly interfering. He disappeared and never came back. Later he changed his screen credit to a pseudonym.

RG: I wouldn't call Chayefsky a Jewish writer in the way that, say, Elie Wiesel or Bashevis Singer are Jewish writers, but he is in fact Jewish. And again, it's a Ken Russell film, and there are those very rich Christian tones to *Altered States*. It's mythology—Dante, Faust, the Christ, Mary, and there are many Greek myths as well. But it is Catholic for the most part. I wonder if you would mind discussing some of the specific religious implications.

KR: Yes, it turned out to be. I'm sure it's not written that way, but it is, in my terms, a Catholic film. The imagery, of course, if not specifically so, is from a certain Catholic point of view. Again, though, it is Catholic in the sense that it is about faith and love and soul and eternity, the struggle for meaning in one's life, the religious impetus, which is larger than ethics but what I understand in Catholic terms, or at least in Christian terms.

Jessup is a Christian who is confused, who has rejected Christ. At one time, as he tells Emily in the film (after they've had sex for the first time), he had visions of Christ as a young boy and teenager, and he was thought of as both mad and saintly. But all of this leaves him when his father dies a horrible death, and his faith goes with it, to see such suffering. Later, he endeavors to learn from schizophrenics, and other cultures and mad people, what it is in human nature that knows God. Through science he goes after what he lost.

Now, doing a film like this, unless you're consciously or unconsciously fighting something, your own natural tendencies surface in the film. I didn't feel that when I was preparing the film that I really had to put myself through a chrysalis to discover what kind of crisis, or what kind of hallucinations a man who had rejected his faith might have. From that point of view, he was akin to some of those people you asked about before. There was the genre of reality-fantasy, which is a major thread through all my films. The only thing that struck me as different from the other films, at least my more personal films, like *Mahler*, was that these men were in touch with some mystery. Mahler is a very good example. Mahler was an instrument of the mystery, and he translated it into human terms. But this man, Jessup, he's the antithesis of my other heroes. He is a man not in tune with this mystery, and he rapes and tears it out. He tries to rip the Truth out with his bare hands, mind, mathematics, his intellect, anything and at all costs. It nearly kills him, as it did Orpheus in the old myths. But all that hadn't occurred to me until I'd done it. But I'm sure that's what it is. It *is*.

RG: What would you call that "mystery" of which you speak?

KR: Well, that thing, that harmony or whatever it is that otherwise "passeth all human understanding." It cannot be conveyed, but it is felt. Mystery, mysticism . . . but both degrade what it is. They're words, and words are only as big as the person who says and hears them. Words are highly imperfect communication. Most poets look mad on paper, but from where they are it's something else. It's your job to get where they are.

RG: Is the "mystery" one reason you are particularly fascinated by artists? That they have some intrinsic relation to it that perhaps the ordinary person gets only fleetingly? You have done at least fourteen biographical studies of artists, including the BBC films, and the others all have some unusual powers to unlock secrets, as it were.

KR: Yes, I am fascinated by that. I'm also fascinated by the so-called creative artist with destructive tendencies. Also, the irreconcilable differences between the artists' lives and their work. Many of them were very hideous men, though they were great inventors of forms and musical inventions and sculptural things, like Gaudier, though *Savage Messiah* was a bit different than many of these others. When I do these films, these biographies, I introduce the artist's work almost

casually into the context of the screenplay instead of parading their work rever-
ently for the audience's inspection. Their work is to be made sense of just as their
lives are. Often the relationship is at great odds, the work versus the living. What
is it that gave rise to this great music or poetry? And if they did such great things,
why were they so miserable? It's a pattern that continues ad infinitum almost.
Now here you have Jessup, who is divorced from a very similar power. He wants
it back, if indeed he ever had it. He causes strife all around him because of it. His
wife in particular, but also in transgressing all the medical rules and things. You
can call him a person who almost sells everything, but not his soul, in search of
some knowledge, truth that's final. It's his soul that's at stake.

RG: Did you feel that Jessup's crisis of faith is akin to your own at one time?
You obviously empathize with his lapsed Christian background and the images
you portray as his in alienation from Christ or faith. He then goes into science,
just as you went into the mechanics of filmmaking, to save himself. Am I reading
too much or too far? You do seem to identify with Jessup in such an intimate
way, and for the first time since *Savage Messiah*.

KR: Well, yes. I liked him. I did sympathize with his problems. And I think
that all you said did flash through my mind at one point and then I forgot about
it, but it did strike me that there was a similarity there. But it wasn't conscious. As
I said, nothing in my work is conscious, hardly anything. In retrospect, you can
write papers and interpret it this way and that, as you are doing a very good job
of here, I think, but when I'm actually doing it, that's when the creative process
really works. It happens by itself almost. You have to be very technical, but you
do your best work, or at least I do my best work, on a subconscious level.

For example, he [Jessup] was talking about the Garden of Eden. Well, that
wasn't in the original script. And that's always a very Catholic sort of thing. But
actually, it came out of a great deal of research into pagan religions, because in
the script it read, and we were very faithful to the script, even following the fact
that it said, "Jessup was to experience, in this hallucination, something that was
common to all users." Well, that's a tall order. What is quite like that? Chayefsky's
original description of the incident in Mexico was that it was just a lizard, the
red-hot lizard, that happened to be passing along and so on. To me, that was just
wasting it, not furthering or integrating the story at all. It wasn't using Jessup's
feelings about his wife or anything else. So I brooded over it for months. And
finally, as it was with most situations like that, when you're looking high and low
for the right presentation with the right values, it was already in the essence of
what we were doing. It always struck me as very strange, that certain answers
are already contained in the questions. And it was the mushroom. Mushroom
was the answer to everything. Jessup goes to Mexico to investigate the proper-
ties of the hallucinatory mushroom. He takes the mushroom in the ritual with

the Indians. It so happens that the terrain in the area where the Indians live has a strange formation of rock in the likeness of mushrooms. They're stones, of course, they're monolithic and scattered about, but nevertheless, if you had to describe them, they are very much like huge mushrooms of stone. So there they were, and there they are in the film, as they are in reality. Then, I still had to think of some hallucination that he could experience among this tribe of mushroom worshippers, or something the Indians could, and though it didn't have to look the same, it had to mean the same. It could be a common image, but I didn't think that had to be essential. So what I did was go back to an image of more primitive religions yet. What I found rather amazed me, because I found that a recurring image was that of a man and a woman and a tree and a snake: the Garden of Eden. It cropped up so many times, in so many cultures, that you wondered how it got into the Old Testament as the exclusive property of our culture, of Western civilization proper. It was in the traditions and the roots of many cultures, from Icelandic to Aztec, as some irreducible image of something we call and understand as the Garden of Eden. Now, I don't know about you, but this is a startling thing to me. And there was one image in particular, a reproduction of a cave painting I saw, very crude, of course, and very old, that was of a man and a woman and a serpent. But the serpent wasn't coiled around a tree. It was coiled around a gigantic mushroom. It could only be a mushroom. There were other, smaller mushrooms growing all around it, to the side and underneath it. So the mushroom as an idea of a tree of knowledge is a very interesting one. I don't know if anyone has of yet taken it up. Maybe Jung or someone. They might have. But the point is this mushroom is the code for this hallucinogenic trip of such supposedly incredible psychic proportions, and Huxley and Wasson and all the others who have written about their experiments with it, all refer to it as the "Sacred Mushroom." It wasn't called that for nothing. "Sacred" is the emphatic word. So all of that seemed to tie in. And as all of this was occurring to me, I was in the garden still trying to determine how I would place Jessup in terms of this hallucination and not have him standing around with Emily in furs or a fig leaf. And I found that I had been looking for over three hours at a beach umbrella in the shape of a mushroom, and it was even mushroom colored, sort of a flesh tone. It had elegant Edwardian chairs beneath it, and I thought that might be the right setting, if you could sufficiently distance it from his own time. So I got them Edwardian costumes and the Edwardian chairs under the mushroom umbrella. And instead of an apple, I had them eating ice cream in the form of mushrooms. And then, of course, because he rips knowledge out, which shouldn't be underestimated, that knowledge becomes its own demise and becomes the atomic mushroom, the scientific mushroom. He's driven out of the Garden of Eden by the atomic mushroom and perishes in the desert as the world and he and Emily are reduced to dust. But that was just starting with the mushroom, because it was all contained in the evolution of that one image. But it took months to figure.

RG: And most of the other images in the film, the hallucinations, are yours?

KR: Yes. Originally, as Chayefsky had them, they were very amorphous, without shape. They're not very specific, as you know from reading the book. So all the hallucinations are my devices. Except for the very first one. The very first one has elements which were his. The seven-horned ram, the Bible, the Veronica with the veil, and the impression of Christ on the veil. Those things are from his writing.

RG: Do you think that as the mushroom is called "The Flesh of the Gods," you made some conscious or unconscious connection with that and the Eucharist of the Church that meant so much to you at one time? Perhaps here, no longer a symbol, but the actual fact and the actual results of imbibing God?

KR: Again, I don't think consciously, but there's no denying the likeness, is there? But his hallucinations were fraught with horrors, and in the end he needed to be more human, more emotional, once he reached a certain apex of his search. It's what he realized, somewhat, through Emily.

RG: What about the embroidery of other allusions in the movie, the things we discussed regarding the *Pieta* and Mary and the Orpheus-Eurydice myth?

KR: Up to a point, there is a certain amount of that kind of symbolism. There are some symbols about which no one's asked me, and which are there and no one has seen and no one will ever see. It's there for me. There's no point in explicating what they are, I don't think. I put them there for a reason, and if they're perceived for that reason, okay, but they never will be. But it doesn't matter because they're still effective. I think it's an artist's prerogative to do things and not give a reason. And if what he does entertains, enriches, delights, beguiles or even creates negative feelings, they serve their purpose as long as they have effect. Some in the film are there for very significant religious purposes.

RG: Michel Foucault, a French thinker, once wrote that "madness is either Nature made manifest or Nature restored," meaning that whatever form madness takes, it must have to do with repression, and that oftentimes madness is no more than a result of not obeying physical urges. You have many examples of physical or mental deformity that capture this repression. I was wondering if you didn't take a view toward sanity or madness which *Altered States* challenges, the conventional notion of that schism. And, moreover, how madness might be thought of as closer to God, or how that might work with your own views?

KR: That's all very complex, and I don't know if I can provide an answer for it. What you're asking is highly conceptual, a rarefied kind of thinking. I must admit that it's not my domain. But someone said to me once, "Some of your films are mad, you're mad, and you deal with mad subjects." One of the things that's wrong with film is that it's not used madly enough. It's used academically. It's used as a prop for words. You take a film script . . . I don't have to read any of them. I know they're just words and words and thousands of boring words. There might be some sort of funny old idea mixed up in them, a germ or a notion of something there, you know, but a script, by definition, has to do with the writer's view. And writers, by definition, aren't seers. They aren't visionary by the generic nature of their medium. They aren't really writing words as much as they're writing pictures, or trying to write pictures. We're just using a medium which has fantastic possibilities and which is used as if a blind man were using it. Everybody does it that way, and me, too, but at least I'm conscious of it. I don't think a lot of other people are. I know it, at least. I think with *Altered States* I made an effort to surpass that usual restriction. And so long as one's aware of it, knows it, he might be saved eventually. I do get the feeling that in a hundred years' time—well, I know, I'm sure of it—that people will look back on our films and just scream with laughter. They will think they're just so banal, that the ideas are banal, that the images themselves are banal. They will know that we had the potential for using images to express the ineffable, to express emotions, to express ideas, and we didn't do it. And, of course, there will be no one around to justify what we did and are doing, no matter what the theories are that lie around, because the images will speak for themselves, literally. And that's what makes me so cross with myself and with the medium in general. This arena of pure cinema, whatever that amounts to, has nothing to do with words, isn't explored enough. We're still doing Paddy Chayefsky plays. That's one reason he liked the idea of doing master shots and close-ups, of doing all kinds of coverage, and that's theater. That's what they did thirty, forty, fifty years ago with movies when it was still in its infancy. This is the cinema.

What interests me is the fact that if, say, Gene Phillips and my daughter were to come in that door together, and I see them together, I have in my mind an instantaneous summary of what I know of them, when I saw them last, the most important things they ever said to me, what I've said to them, when I might see them again in the future, everything about them that I know, and this goes through my head in a millisecond, the whole summary without effort or words or rational associations. But it does it, it is arrived at mentally in pictures. It does it in sort of an amalgamated picture—an image, a feeling, if you like. It goes through your mind as a feeling and a picture. You can't have a picture without feeling, but you can have words without feeling, and your feeling toward something like them, coming through the door, is based on known images. Now, that's what we should be exploring in the cinema, that instantaneous encapsulating of someone's entire life, perhaps, or so many crucial years, in images. I mean, that's what it's coming to. That's what it's about. If we can split the atom, we can split a thought in this way. But what we get—it makes me very angry—are silly little instants around silly little stories that are completely forgettable. But the essence of film is something else, and that's what I'm interested in. And here, in *Altered States*, I saw a chance to do it, to do something more, which is another reason, of course, that I was attracted to it.

RG: For a person who works from the subconscious as much as you do, your pictures are still very well crafted.

KR: Well, yes, because that's not to say that the shooting or anything is sloppy or ill considered afterward. It's like a painter—that by whatever process the image comes to him, he has to have a technique to render it. A very precise technique. He might go through all sorts of directions and experiments, but in the end he knows what he wants. Then he must combine the exact blue, and the exact pink on his pallet, to make the exact purple, and put it on the canvas, or there's nothing there. I have a very, very exact technique in filmmaking. It's just that, working backwards, you have to have the image first. I mean, when we came along [on *Altered States*] there were a lot of formless storyboards which were not achieved through logical form. They were originally just talked up out of a committee. But everything has to have a logic, no matter how illogical it seems when it's there on the screen. It also has to mean something to me. Everything I've ever shot on the screen has meant something to me. It's not just put there for an effect. And often the process of arrival is instantaneous, or it's very dredged up and it's difficult to achieve, to finally achieve form. It was difficult for me at first because the story wasn't mine. I would never, never have known how to write it. So it's just that images and the technique of rendering them are very precisely translated, and there's no reason why they shouldn't be. Filmmaking's a craft. And unless you're a craftsman, you're a con man. There are a lot of people around these days who aren't masters of their craft.

RG: Other than the more advanced notions of cinema that you were regarding and that are in the film, the style of *Altered States* is thoroughly yours. You have that scene, for example, where Emily is confessing her feelings to Mason through the open window of the house, and you use her movements in relation to the camera to compensate for cuts, so it's very fluid and maximizes the use of space.

KR: Yes, that is one of my approaches to a scene, very definitely. I shoot my films in a way whereby generally each sequence is self-contained, and often there are no cutaways. They are just joined together, one shot after another, sometimes one scene after another, as you mentioned it might be. So the editor just stops and tails them and puts them together, end to end. Now and again, I might take maybe three or four shots which could go in to break up some sort of difficulty, but I am not a believer in long shot, middle shot, and close-up. I never do that, ever. I generally conceive of a sequence as one flowing pattern. I suppose having been a dancer at one time, I do see things in terms of movement. I see my films as sort of ballets of the movements of the actors and the camera and extras and color, and I think this gives the audience a greater sense of involvement. I don't mean using a "busy" camera for its own sake. It should all be constructed for a definite purpose. Some sequences should be very legato and flowing, and others very staccato, so the audience never quite knows what it's getting.

RG: And you use music to tremendous effect, for great dramatic punctuation. I was again struck by that in *Altered States*.

KR: Well, music obviously is very important to me. I listen to it while I work, and I think of it as almost synonymous with the images. A lot comes to me while I play music, and I suppose it fixes itself to the images when I make them for the screen.

RG: Have you experimented with "altered states" yourself for your preparation on this film?

KR: I have experimented with only one mushroom. I did it specifically for this film. I was very disappointed with what happened. All the plants in the garden looked very threatening and vindictive, but that was about all. It was the same garden that I described with the mushroom-shaped umbrella, but on a different day. But the plants did become very, very threatening indeed, and I did feel as if I was in some danger, even from the rubber mattress in the pool. It was undulating, and it seemed to be doing so against the waves rather than with them. I was in Shelley Winters's back garden in her pool. We rented her house, you see, when we were here making the film. But I never had any hallucinations, so to speak, other than the plants taking on a certain animistic bearing. But I get them all through music anyway. That's my real drug. And there's an amazing variety.

RG: I'm not surprised that it was disappointing for you, in a way. You're probably used to seeing extraordinary things naturally, if your films are any evidence, and a mushroom was very minor by comparison.

KR: Yes, it was, you see. It was a great letdown, because I can do much better with Bruckner and Monteverdi.

RG: Do you take any particular view or responsibility toward what the film might encourage, insofar as a new trend toward drug use?

KR: Tell them it's Bruckner. If they all knew it was Bruckner, they would run to the record shops.

RG: Considering the extent to which *Altered States* has elements of pure cinema, what will you be doing next?

KR: I don't know for certain. *Altered States* had, in those moments, pure cinema as best I've got it, but I hope to do better. It's impossible to say how I would do it, because it would have to grow out of the material. Something totally new, perhaps, that I haven't thought of.

Ken Russell: Looking into Madness

Graham Fuller / 1987

From the *New York City Tribune*, April 10, 1987. Reprinted with permission.

"I don't set out to shock," complains Ken Russell, whose latest movie *Gothic*—which opens at Cinema 1 today—must therefore be calculated to make us laugh or squirm, or both. "If that's the effect my films have, then it's because their subject matter, which is something I don't generally choose, is shocking in itself. I didn't go knocking on people's doors to do *Altered States*, *Crimes of Passion*, or *Gothic*—they came to me. I actually toned *Crimes of Passion* down, because there's a limit to what an audience can take. I censored it for them."

The mildest of Russell's critics might argue that the snowy-haired enfant terrible of the British cinema has never toned anything down, while the notion of him caring for his viewers' moral welfare is more than faintly jarring. But if he's never directed one single tasteful movie, it is equally certain that he has never made a completely dull one or failed to shake up our preconceptions about films with each excessive new offering. Besides, prickly and ironic in the morbid semidarkness of his Fifty-Fourth Street hotel room, he doesn't invite swinging attacks on his oeuvre.

In an era of timid screen artisans and homogenized Hollywood entertainment, the fifty-nine-year-old Russell—nearly a quarter of a century into his directorial career—remains an inflammatory figure, unable or unwilling to rein in his monstrous talent for framing images of teeming corruption, voluptuous decay, and psychedelic disorder—with feverish stylistic abandon.

Gothic is no exception to this rule, and its central theme of diabolical artistic creation has a special relevance to the body of work—including *The Music Lovers*, *The Devils*, *Mahler*, *Tommy*, and *Lisztomania*—of a director frequently damned for its out-of-control pictorial vitality.

Scripted by former copywriter Stephen Volk, it's a phantasmagorical rendering of the fabled night of June 16, 1816, when Percy Bysshe Shelley (Julian Sands), his eighteen-year-old mistress Mary Godwin (Natasha Richardson), and her half-sister Claire Clairmont (Myriam Cyr) gathered at the Villa Diodati, the Swiss lakeside retreat of the exiled Lord Byron (Gabriel Byrne) and his slighted lover/biographer Dr. Polidori (Timothy Spall).

There, inspired by opium, laudanum, and mortal terror, their nightmarish games, orgies, and seances unleash from their tormented psyches their innermost fears and breathe embryonic literary life into the future Mrs. Shelley's *Frankenstein*—galvanized from her dread of a stillborn child—and Polidori's *The Vampire*, a precursor to *Dracula*.

Far removed from James Whale's 1935 horror classic *The Bride of Frankenstein*, which eerily opens with the ghost-story competition that in reality germinated both novels, *Gothic*'s framework gives Russell ample scope to pile image on image from Shelley's and Byron's poems and his own unbridled romantic imagination. Claire with eyes protruding from her breasts, a knight with a huge distended codpiece, a satyr stooped over Mary's spread-eagled body, snakes, skulls, and (patently plastic) cadavers.

Russell had contemplated a film version of these events a decade ago when the actor Robert Powell (who later played Shelley on TV) brought him a script based on the novel *A Single Summer with Lord B.*, but he was more readily attracted to Volk's.

"It reminded me of a script I would have written myself. You don't get many scripts sent to you with which you feel immediate sympathy, where you can see every scene vividly in the mind's eye, and which also flow very well. Often screenwriters put directorial details in, like camera tracks down the platform to close-up of hero's eyes, which is just rubbish. The only other script I've had as good as this one was *Crimes of Passion*.

Not that Russell is always a great respecter of the words in scripts, although "since you've actually got to use them, they've got to be pretty good. But I'd sooner have a script with no words in it at all." His preference for images over verbose dialogue and complex narrative structures—as if in defiance of Steven Spielberg's acknowledgment of the writer's craft at last week's Oscars ceremony—is pushed to the limit in *Gothic* and in his many pop videos, a form of which he is a champion.

"The benefit of pop videos—which *Tommy* and *Mahler* were before pop videos even existed—is that they can cut down the length of films, which are generally far too long and self-indulgent—although that's a word that's often used about me.

"Since people are bombarded with images all day long on TV, they learn from an early age to pick up ideas quickly. Whereas the tempo of films is exactly as it was fifty years ago. I think a pop video—or let's say, a 'musical film'—can make a statement in three and a half minutes that a movie would laboriously make in two and a quarter hours."

Russell's latest "musical film" is a segment of *Aria*, for which producer Don Boyd has assigned ten major directors each to film an operatic aria of their own choice. Inimitably, Russell chose to set the aria for Puccini's *Turandot* against a car crash. "It's about when you pass the threshold of pain and move on to another sensation," he explains. "I did it in a fairly simplistic way, with this girl floating in space and experiencing a transition from pain when a branding iron is put to her lips like a kiss of life."

He has ideas for another shorter film about Byron, set to Berlioz's music; for a Japanese film of *Madama Butterfly*; films about Australian composer Percy Grainger, which he is currently writing, and Russian composer Alexander Scriabin. His projected erotic horror comedy, "Ketchup," which would star himself, is currently without a backer.

"No one's perfect," he admits. "There are a lot of faults in my films, but I think a lot of people take them too seriously. *Gothic*, after all, is a black comedy. But having been brought up making films on art for a mass public for ten years [the BBC's *Monitor*], I find it fun to try to communicate the enthusiasm I feel for certain subjects and at the same time entertain people."

Images of Reality

Anthony Clare / 1988

From *The Listener* (August 11, 1988): 12–13. © 1988 British Broadcasting System. Reprinted with permission of Immediate Media Co.

Anthony Clare: Ken Russell was born on July 3, 1927, in Southampton, where his father ran a boot and shoe business. He went to primary school in that town and then to Pangbourne Nautical College. When he left school he joined the Merchant Navy and then went into the RAF. After his RAF service he was a member of a number of ballet companies and an actor before working as a stills photographer and going to art school, where he met his first wife and began to make films. In 1962 a film he made on Elgar for BBC TV won widespread acclaim. Since then he has become a world-renowned film director, with films which include *The Music Lovers*, *Women in Love*, *The Devils*, *The Boy Friend*, *Valentino*, *Savage Messiah*, and *Gothic*. His latest film, *Salome's Last Dance*, recently opened in London. Ken Russell provokes sharply divergent views among his critics. He has, for example, been dismissed as "a psychologist of the uglier emotions who threads all the foul ditches and sewers of human despair" to quite simply "one of the greatest directors in the world."

Ken Russell, one of the other things I've found out about you is that you have given many interviews and talked quite freely about yourself and your work. I wonder how you feel about talking about yourself.

Ken Russell: I'm always doing biographical movies, so I'm used to the idea of dredging the mind and the psyche and the personality of whomever I'm dealing with. If I dredge up something that's useful to me about myself during this interview, that's a bonus.

Clare: Have you, through your art, learnt about yourself?

Russell: In a subconscious way. I'm not given to analyzing myself too much. I work on emotions rather than on intellect in my work. Like a piece of blotting paper, I absorb things and let it soak through my mind. Then it's sifted and comes out as a film script and eventually a film.

Clare: That reminds me of something Freud said to Dalí: "I don't have to psychoanalyze you, your unconscious is on the canvas."

Russell: Yes, I'm a bad subject for you because I don't like putting into words what I put on the screen. It's like when Freud met Mahler in a café in Vienna and psychoanalyzed him over a cup of coffee and a cream bun. I don't think either of them got much out of the encounter. I imagine Mahler might have said: "Well, you listen to my music."

Clare: You say you mistrust words.

Russell: They mean so many different things to different people. I didn't have a very good education, but, fortunately, I generally make quite visual films and there is less chance of misinterpreting a picture than there is an essay. When you see an image on the screen, it's instantaneous—it goes straight to the retina, straight to the brain—and there's nothing you can do to censor it. Some of my images tend to rape, and critics don't like being raped. They won't lie back and enjoy it, they resist it.

Clare: Are you shocked by some of your images? Do they touch you at all?

Russell: No. I always equate myself to a surgeon operating on a body: it's the difference between murder and surgery, it's a job. You have to have a very clear, cold mind when you're actually bringing it about. You know how to get all the people around the operating table to help you put the knife in the right place and do the operation correctly.

Clare: There are certain recurrent images in your cinema. You're a man who deals with death and rotting and psychological and physical corruption, to some extent sadism and cruelty. Is this because you are a man whose own inner life is preoccupied with those kind of themes?

Russell: Out of decay comes growth, for one thing. Basically, decay is just a process; it's rising above the decay that matters.

Clare: Can you sit and watch horror?

Russell: If there is horror in my films, I try to make it different from the horror that has no effect on people. You can't turn on the news without being washed over with violence, and I think everyone's got used to this. That's why, when I do show it, I try to show it in a way that will shake them up, make them look at it in a different way. I don't necessarily want to shock.

Clare: You are an intensely emotional man. Were you an emotional child?

Russell: I do remember the preschool days when I spent a tremendous amount of time alone in the garden. I had this big horse-chestnut tree, and I think I formulated my own sort of existence there, my own world. Sometimes this conker tree was a galleon, sometimes it was a castle. I just absorbed what I'd seen on the films the day before, and then the tree became part of living my own adventures.

Clare: From the various things I've read about you, I don't form any clear picture of either of your parents. What was your mother like?

Russell: She was a film fan. Before she married, she was a shop assistant in a big store in East Street. I think her one idea was to get out of the shop. When my father proposed to her, she was about twenty-one and he was working for his father, who had a couple of shoe shops. My grandfather gave him a small house, and there was a live-in housemaid. My mother, who was an active person but not educated, did the only thing she could do: take me to the pictures. Sometimes we went twice a day and we saw an endless succession of films. My father didn't like films. He worked hard all day, and when he came home just listened to the radio. They listened to the radio in the evening.

Clare: Were you very close to her?

Russell: Not particularly. I wasn't wanted, I think. Three years before I was born, she had had a little girl who had died at birth. I think she never got over that. She said to me, "If she'd have lived, I wouldn't have had you," which wasn't a nice thing to hear. She seemed to devote more of her love and attention to my brother when he came along. But we saw all those movies, we did have that in common.

Clare: When did she die?

Russell: About seven or eight years ago. She was in a mental institution, her mind totally disintegrated. I think because it had nothing to grasp on to. If you just watch images all the time of beautiful love stories on the screen and your life doesn't reflect it, it must in the end affect you. I think it affected her. She became very bitter and disillusioned with life towards the end and then finally rejected it and went into a sort of haze of the past.

Clare: Your father, what happened to him?

Russell: He's still alive. He's eighty-five or eighty-six, frail, and lives by himself in Southampton. He was very keen on sailing. He was a ship's detective when he was a lad but eventually knuckled down and gave up this job to start in the boot shop with his five brothers.

Clare: Was he like you?

Russell: No, I don't think so. I don't think any of the family are like me. My brother has stayed in Southampton, is very happily married with a couple of children, and runs a car-hire firm. He did for a time join the business my father and his brothers had, which they were always asking me to do, and he had a nervous breakdown. So maybe I had a premonition that that might happen to me.

Clare: You went to Pangbourne, which is slightly odd. I don't sense that you're particularly fond of the sea.

Russell: I hate the sea. I've got a morbid fear of it. It's bloody deep and I can't swim very well. But I never liked the sea much anyway. When I was in the Merchant Navy, the sea was very rough or it was very calm. When you have nothing to look at all day long but the sea and the sky and there's not a ripple on the water for about eight hours a day for weeks on end, you can go completely bananas.

Clare: How would you describe yourself? Do you see yourself as a shocking man?

Russell: When I do slightly ridiculous things at times, it's just a coverup. I do it because it helps, I'm told, to publicize the work I'm doing at the moment. I would be quite happy never to be seen or heard of again and live with my family in the Lake District, going for walks with my wife and kids and listening to music.

Clare: Do you dream?

Russell: I'm sure I dream all the time. There is a subconscious world that I inhabit that is like a shadow world of England. It has its own network of railways, it has its own sort of air flights, it has its shops, it has its network of underground railways. . . . I always get screwed up around Stockwell as to where I should change. And there's a train in the North that I'm planning to get, from the North-West to the Midlands, and there's six minutes to get the train. It's always a steam train. . . . Trains are supposed to be a Freudian sexual image. . . . Then I'm in shops a lot. I was in shops a lot with my mother. We used to go to big stores to tea dances before we went to the pictures. There was always a jazz band playing, and for a shilling you'd get tea with fancy cakes. It's a band all dressed up in green and black—very art deco—and playing the latest things, and I and my mother are dancing.

Clare: Is that a real memory?

Russell: We occasionally danced at these tea dances.

Clare: Was your mother a pretty woman?

Russell: She was rather like Alice Faye. Yes, she was pretty and she dressed prettily.

Clare: Are you something of a loner because of a shyness, or are you because, in general, you're something of an outsider?

Russell: I suppose it's a bit of both. I remember as a child being painfully shy: I'd even hate to meet other members of the family. If my aunts and uncles were coming, I would just seize up and run away and hide. My mother was looked down on by the other members of the family, because my maternal grandfather was a private in the war. I had quite a strong feeling that I was being slightly disapproved of because my mother wasn't quite up to the social level of everyone else.

Clare: I sense you certainly don't feel that Britain values you.

Russell: I'm trash, you know. I'm in good company, though. They trashed Elgar. They took him back into their bosom eventually, but at least I gave him a helping hand.

Clare: But why do they trash you?

Russell: I don't know. I don't feel that I'm particularly English so far as the cinema's concerned. I think that unless you really fit in and conform in this country, you're not popular. In a way, I'm sort of socially exiled: I've been sent to Hollywood. But my heart is still in England.

Clare: Why do you say you're socially exiled?

Russell: I am, as you said at the beginning of the program, considered to be a monster of depravity. Well, they've got that idea, I suppose, from the images in my films.

Clare: You have a very acute sense of death; it's a recurrent theme. Do you think a lot of your own death?

Russell: Occasionally. I often think how I'd like my funeral conducted, what songs to sing around the coffin. To have the coffin painted white and give everyone a Magic Marker to write a message on it before it goes into the flames. I keep saying to my wife that I'm going to write out the directions for my funeral. I staged my second wedding on the *Queen Mary*, and I had Anthony Perkins of *Psycho* as the priest.

Clare: Why did you do that?

Russell: Well, the first ceremony didn't work. . . . My first marriage.

Clare: Though it lasted many years, and there were five children? What broke it up?

Russell: Disillusion. . . . One has a vision of somebody, and I suppose the vision often takes over the reality. One shouldn't look at visions; one should look at reality and keep looking at it. I had a picture of my wife which wasn't the real picture. It was my fault, not her fault, that the picture was a fantasy.

Clare: Is there something you carry around with you that you really want to do?

Russell: I want to finish my autobiography before I die.

Clare: Why not make a movie?

Russell: Because no one would finance it. They're paying me to write the book, and it's cheaper to write a book.

Clare: But you don't like words.

Russell: That's why I have to find a way to do it. It's got to be finished, and it's got to be okay. I owe it to all the people who denigrate me or don't understand me. Maybe they'll understand me even less. But I think it'll contain some sort of truth about me that isn't contained in crude assessments. It's about somebody who doesn't, on the face of it, seem too political, too committed or press his working-class background. I can't be fitted into any of those pigeonholes. The biography's a dismissal of all that crap. It's a picture of imagery and bizarre happening and fun and contradiction and crazy dialogue. It's a montage, it's a happening, but it's not conventional.

Ken Russell's Best Laid Planaria: Wormomania

Karen Jaehne / 1988

This interview first appeared in the December 1988 issue of *Film Comment* and is reprinted with the permission *Film Comment*, Film at Lincoln Center, and the author.

When the ballad "The Lampton Worm" lured Ken Russell into the lair of folk music, we expected the "folk" to come out as deformed as Franz Liszt in *Lisztomania*. Rather, it came out folksy. Not even the worm is outrageous—just big, long, white, and unmistakably phallically witty. The story most resembles a very good episode of *Dr. Who*.

Nothing Russell has done for the last fifteen years prepares us for his spelunking expedition into the folk ballad and primitive music of *The Lair of the White Worm*. Just as *Tommy* surprised us with Russell's witty endorsement of the mystical powers of pop culture through rock 'n' roll (when we had thought he would devote his art and life to classical longhairs), so *Lair* spins out a web drawn from a folktale developed by Bram Stoker in his final novel.

"Stoker was something of an amateur sleuth of the occult and what normal people called mysteries," says Russell. "Local mosaics and coins found in the area of ancient Mercia provided the images, and the folklore contains the themes of the worship of serpents in England at that time, some 1,600 years ago. I wrote the script in about three weeks and decided to bring it up to date and make the characters contemporary, which didn't at all damage the legend. After all, people are far more superstitious now than they were in 1911, when Stoker wrote it.

"And I was just sick and tired of things Victorian," continues Russell. "I've done so many costume dramas, I thought, 'Hell with this!' Apart from *Altered States* and *Crimes of Passion*, I just haven't done modern times. And that's odd, because I really do prefer the times we live in to other eras, musically and in every other way. You know, even fantasy can get in a rut."

To wrap our minds with the music that inspired and shaped *Lair*, Russell wove in a performance by a thigh-slapping group resembling the Irish folk-punk band the Pogues, who bellow ballads to compete with rock groups but continue the tradition of Irish balladeers. Russell mines this vein of popular culture in as enthusiastically speculative a way as his adaptations of high culture. But the folk music is great counterpoint to the baroque of flaming effects, and simplicity for its own sake is a virtue Russell has finally grasped like the Holy Grail. When he's not derailed by the demon worm.

Russell's script for *Lair* owes as much to the folk song "The Lampton Worm" as to Stoker. "For years," he says, "I've known that folk song, and I'm fairly sure Bram Stoker would have known it, for it's obviously based on something that happened in this region five hundred years ago. If our hero, Lord James, had done battle with a local monster, it would have been celebrated in song and carried on still today. There are strange local celebrations all the time, some very weird things that pop up in provincial music—what we would call folk music. George and the Dragon, kindred myths, and then the Lampton Worm, no less, but remember that the worm is not some species of fish bait." Nor could the still-living Lord Lampton, whose ancestors had slain the worm's ancestors, be involved without a new nom de guerre.

The script has Hugh Grant (as the unflappable, rational-but-versed-in-irrational-traditions Lord James D'Ampton) bless us with a bit of etymology. "Don't take the word 'worm' too literally," says he. "It's an adaptation of the Anglo-Saxon 'wyrm,' meaning dragon and snake; from the Gothic 'waurms,' a serpent; or the German 'Vurm' . . . the common worm was not always the lowly creature it is today."

"I took upon myself the task of bringing the good ethnic folk song up to date," explains Russell, "and I gave the ballad to two musicians, Emilio Perez Machado and Stephen Powys. One finds that sort of music by scouring [London's] Cecil Sharp House—where all British folk music is collected—and the guys set about giving it a proper rhythm and ring for the barn-dance number. I rather liked what they dished up . . . suited the knees-up we'd planned."

Knees what?! Shades of rollicking nymphomaniacs imbue Russell's calm and well-modulated British voice.

He laughs roguishly at the expectations he has raised over a twenty-five-year career of feverish essays on the creative juices of famous composers. Russell explains, "A 'knees-up' is a local dance . . . what Americans know as a square dance, you know, like the people perform at the manor house in the celebration hosted by Lord D'Ampton." Included in that scene is a mock slaying of the dragon, where several revelers dress up, Chinese New Year–style, sporting about in a huge white worm costume, which young Lord D'Ampton slices in two before serving up pickled worms in aspic on the groaning boards.

Noblesse oblige among the worm exterminators is only one of the jibes Russell takes at class distinctions maintained so loyally on this hearth. Here two orphaned maidens, Eva (Catherine Oxenberg) and Mary (Sammi Davis) Trent, keep a farmhouse/inn where once a convent stood (that, itself, replaced a pagan village).

Russell's most delightful creature is Lady Sylvia March, who tromps around her Temple House mansion in slinky bas couture and spike heels and becomes progressively toothsome, as it were, until she wears little more than fangs, blue paint, and an enormous sacrificial ivory and silver dildo to tickle the farm girls' . . . uh, fancy for her beloved deity, Dionin. If he's the worm, she's the lair, and sensuous Amanda Donohoe brings both her Old Vic training and her drop-dead-gorgeous body to bear on the subject of pagans versus Christians. (Pagans win.)

Lady Sylvia is surrounded by saxophone music and, once, is lured out of a straw basket by Lord D'Ampton playing Turkish belly dancing music on his outdoor loudspeaker system. The requisite butler (Central Casting outdid itself with Stratford Johns) reminds the young lord of "one of the belly dancers your father encountered in Istanbul. I recall his Lordship's very words: 'That would charm the D'Ampton Worm itself from its home. . . . I remember it worked extremely well with a king cobra.'" The cobra has little on this serpentine sex bomb, whose first appearance in the night fog assures us that vamp derives from vampire.

A stylish sangfroid unites Lady Sylvia and Lord D'Ampton. He is the keeper of the legend; she is the keeper of the power. Every time Lady Sylvia bares her teeth at the Trent wenches, or once at a crucifix in their farmhouse, she inspires delirious visions of Roman soldiers ravishing bare-breasted nuns or a supple white worm tangled around a crucified Lord D'Ampton.

With mad departures from terra firma, it's significant that the power of simple ethnic music can control monstrous forces. A young Scottish archaeologist who is digging up the Trent girls' farm once gets himself up in full kilt to blow his bagpipes at a vampire constable—a truly comic scene as they sway around the sundial in Lady Sylvia's courtyard. (She'll nibble the Scottish knee before it's over.) In another hilarious triumph, Amanda Donohoe pulls together the world-weariness of Mae West as she brings home a Boy Scout for tea and crumpets and a game of Snakes and Ladders. When the swain pulls out his mouth organ and starts to pipe up, Lady Sylvia undulates unwillingly but manages to quell him with, "Stoppit! That kind of music freaks me out." Then she emasculates him.

"Well, of course, music played on simple instruments reinforces the idea that good is guileless, unsophisticated, and unadorned," argues Russell. "But don't forget that the score includes some organ music and the usual range. I was quite pleased with Stanislas Syrewicz's uniting all this material, because I can't remember having harmonicas or bagpipes to deal with before. But I think they give a certain propriety to the Christian side of the struggle against paganism. Perhaps because pagan forces are traditionally under the sway of ritualistic music? I don't know, but it felt right, and it also has the feeling that it's based on fact. If I believe there is a factual basis for something, I can enter into the spirit more readily and embroider what would otherwise remain dreary data."

The Derbyshire countryside holds enormous fascination for Russell, who has happily returned to make films in England after fifteen years and an arduous bout with Hollywood, where his work had mixed reception. "Working in culture this rich is an enormous challenge," he says. "For example, part of the decision to make *The White Worm* was that it was set right here in the heart of foggy, sloggy England, not on some Transylvanian ridge. England made it potentially more alarming—and, of course, absurdly comical.

"It was also for that reason that we decided to play it absolutely straight. Look at these lines! We looked at each other and quickly knew we could camp it up, but if the characters lived right down the road, it gave us more power to invent a psychic monster, as well. Stoker drew on things everyone in England knows. Local witchcraft abounds.

"Oh, did you know that Dick Bush, a cinematographer on *White Worm*, has seen the Loch Ness monster? Shortly after shooting something in Scotland, he and his crew were driving over a hill, and there it was, steaming up. Five bumps and a big wake—ten to fifteen knots, but by the time they loaded the mag to photograph it, it had immersed itself. There's still the odd monster swimming around England."

Not the least of them, London critics. Russell seems to have become relatively philosophical about the way critics deride his work while forgetting that this eccentric Englishman has arguably paved the way stylistically for the Coen Brothers, Tim Burton, John Waters, David Cronenberg, and the Pythons, not necessarily by direct inspiration but by priming the pump for visual and thematic outrage.

"The critics, at least, are always outraged," admits Russell, "except for Derek Malcolm [of *The Guardian*]. If Mel Brooks or Fellini had done what I do, they'd like it, but one of their own is expected to respond to their very favorite word—*restraint*. If I were American, who would want restraint? But it's not for that reason that I tamed *The Worm*, but for the contrast in the humor.

"Now having stretched my fingers, I'm doing *The Rainbow* [an adaptation of D. H. Lawrence's novel preceding *Women in Love*] with a return to rhapsodic realism. It takes place in the English countryside and is dialogue oriented. Glenda Jackson is playing her own mother, Anna Brangwen, from her role in *Women in Love*. It is a film about her and her child, a sixteen-year-old dying to spread her wings, and people who won't let her."

Russell is extremely critical of the films that constitute the British Renaissance. Their spasmodic nihilism strikes him as too downbeat. He says, "Even fine directors like Stephen Frears are responsible for more harm than good. When you reflect on what goes on beyond London, you realize that people outside don't recognize his England. My neighbors here in the Lake District find his films totally fantastic and ostentatiously anti-English. I see it as a destructive element in British cinema. Mike Leigh is very astute and perceptive, but he's mean-spirited.

"What they lack is eroticism. They want to deny the spirit and the flesh, and I think our job is to unite them. I've shown that through music written by people who experienced that union. And music is the most visually inspiring way to portray that. My films are not biopics or social tracts. They're about the union of the spirit and flesh, body and soul."

Will there always be an England?

"Well, as long as people like John Boorman keep making *Hope and Glory*," says the repatriated Russell, "England will always be somewhere . . . I don't know where. On the *screen*."

And Russell has made his contribution.

Next of Ken

Graham Fuller / 1989

This interview first appeared in the May–June 1989 issue of *Film Comment* and is reprinted with the permission of *Film Comment*, Film at Lincoln Center, and the author.

At the foot of a wooded slope, just outside the village of Nettlebed in Oxfordshire, a rubicund Ken Russell is stroking his chin and mentally felling the magnificent elms that shelter *The Rainbow*'s camera crew from the persistent August drizzle. "Which of them shall we cut down?" the director half-jokes, dissatisfied with the terrain. This from a man who, through lunch, has proffered his love of pastoral England as the prime reason for filming D. H. Lawrence's once-suppressed novel—twenty years after Russell's movie of its sequel, *Women in Love*, earned him his biggest critical success and only Oscar nomination.

"Lawrence is my favorite author, and the Brangwens are my favorite family," Russell says. "The only two people who have written about England and understood it are Lawrence and Shakespeare, and I'm not ready for Shakespeare. To me, England is the most mysterious place I've ever been—it feels better here than anywhere else. You only have to think of *The Tempest*: Shakespeare's magic island *is* England. Most British films these days are about people hitting each other over the head with bottles in Brixton. You can get caught up in that kind of nonsense to the exclusion of the mystical, spiritual, and, above all, physical beauty of the place."

Half an hour later, however, the buzz saws have buzzed, and six twelve-foot saplings have been shorn from their roots and "replanted" under the elms, creating a makeshift avenue in the glade for lovestruck Ursula Brangwen (Sammi Davis) and uniformed Anton Skrebensky (Paul McGann). Already plagued by midges, McGann is wondering if he will have to finish the scene nude; six weeks into the seven-and-a-half-week shoot, Davis is not only physically exhausted but nursing a black eye she sustained tumbling from her bicycle during Russell's recreation of Ursula's phallocentric vision of the charging horses. But, fully clad, they do the scene and fall kissing to the forest floor several times; a few months later, this particular climax ends up on the cutting-room floor.

Lawrence's narrative about Ursula and Gudrun, protofeminist daughters of Nottinghamshire yeoman stock, was originally to comprise one novel, *The Sisters*, but grew into two. The first half of *The Rainbow* (1915) follows the two preceding Brangwen generations and culminates in the drowning of the patriarch; the second half is Ursula's cathartic quest for sexual and spiritual fulfillment. *Women in Love* (1916, published 1920) allows her to achieve her "paradisal union" with Rupert Birkin, even as Gudrun presides over the "snow-abstract annihilation" of the industrialist Gerald Crich. Russell's 1969 movie of the latter was nothing if not indelible: Rupert (Alan Bates) fucking Ursula (Jennie Linden) in the undergrowth, with the camera also prostrated; Rupert and Gerald (Oliver Reed) nude-wrestling by firelight; Gerald's rape of Gudrun (Oscar-winning Glenda Jackson) from her POV.

"At once fascinated and horrified by physical passion, he paraded his disgust and fear in the trappings of a showy masculinity," moralized the *Times* obituary of Lawrence in 1930. The words might once have suited Russell, too, except that *The Rainbow* shoot finds the snowy-haired enfant terrible of the British cinema in a positively mellow mood.

Scripted in the early eighties by Russell and his second wife, Vivian, and finally financed by Vestron after David Puttnam ("He thought it was a bit of a downer") and others had passed on it, the movie has accumulated its own mythology. Given her first lead role by Russell (she appeared in his *The Lair of the White Worm*), Davis had been turned down for Ursula for the BBC's own three-part version of the novel, adapted by Anne Devlin, directed by Stuart Burge, and due on PBS this August. The parents of Glenda McKay, cast as the adolescent Gudrun by Russell, who apparently named her for Jackson, returns here as the girls' mother, Anna, along with another *Women* alumnus, Christopher Gable, as her husband. "I like the continuity," Russell observes. "I believe in the cycle of the seasons, of birth, death, and rejuvenation. My children by my first wife were in *Women in Love*, and my children by my second wife are in this, and there's a certain satisfaction in that."

Women in Love cinematographer Billy Williams and production designer Luciana Arrighi also returned to the fold, enabling Russell to revel again in Lawrence's empurpled lyricism and fecund sexual imagery. *The Rainbow*, though, proves to be the more strident half of Russell's diptych, its screenplay raw and terse compared with Devlin's, which includes a number of Potteresque flashbacks.

Following the camp-horror pastiches of *Gothic*, *Salome's Last Dance*, and *Lair*, Russell has broken from his relentless pictorialism. "The film's got strong images in it, but they're less explosive than in *Women in Love*. I think this is even more glowingly beautiful and evocative of England, it's a crisper story as well. I couldn't really do justice to *Women in Love* in two hours, so it wasn't as good as it could have been. Here, two hours is more than ample to evoke the soul of this girl searching for freedom, breaking free from the bonds of family, and going where her spirit guides her—over the rainbow." Perhaps inevitably, given the film's long gestation, Davis's theatrical protestations against entrapment will cut no ice with the school of postfeminist thought.

Unrepentant in his disdain for the political rhetoric of the Sammy and Rosie school of British cinema, Russell meanwhile contends—with a certain opportunistic zeal—that Lawrence's England endures in the current cinema. "That's what appealed to me the most. When Sammi and Paul were rehearsing lines about the English attitude to sex, India, God, democracy, and money, I thought, 'Well, that's Thatcherite England today.' Ursula is the free spirit who recognizes that 'England has become meagre and paltry [and] . . . unspiritual.' It's Lawrence's vision but it's more relevant than any other contemporary play or film I've seen."

Morning, Mr. Grumpy!

Lola Borg / 1989

From *Empire* no. 5 (November 1989): 58–61. Reprinted with permission.

Ken Russell's London pied-à-terre is a small mews house in a quiet lane not far from the bustle of the Marylebone Road. There's a shabby black front door next to a rather inauspicious car showroom (new and used but with definitely more of the latter). The assistant in the showroom pokes his head out from behind a door. "Are you looking for Ken? Well, I haven't seen much of him today. But if he said he'll meet you at three o'clock, he'll be here—dead on three." Ken, it seems, is a complete stickler for punctuality. "If he orders a car for two-thirty," continues the assistant, "and it's not here on the button, well . . ." He draws air through his front teeth to suggest the most awesomely severe displeasure.

A few minutes later, at precisely three o'clock, a portly gray-haired figure in a lurid pink and orange baggy shirt and off-white trousers comes shuffling around the corner at the top of the road, plastic bag full of shopping in hand, creaking towards the house. From a distance, it could be Mr. Benny Hill, or any old codger out on a trip—to the local Tesco's to get in the groceries or, perhaps, judging by the florid complexion, a trip down the local boozer for a couple of light ales— but no, this is the man who once engaged the wrath of one Mary Whitehouse and shocked cinemagoers in the seventies with such controversial scenes in his films as, say, a bevy of masturbating nuns, the sixty-two-year-old enfant terrible of the British cinema, ladies and gentlemen . . . Ken Russell.

Given that Henry Kenneth Alfred Russell is a director famed for his love of the grotesque and extravagant in his art, one would perhaps expect his abode to be some sort of gothic monstrosity, or at the very least boast a theatrical interior of relentless black or midnight blue with plush velvet curtains and a few crucifixes here and there for light relief. In fact, it's nothing of the sort. Having changed into something more comfortable (worn leather slippers), Ken Russell leads the way up olive-green carpeted stairs (after issuing strict instructions that feet must be wiped so that the oil from the garage doesn't soil the carpet) and shuffles, Steptoe-like in his backless slippers, across polished woodened floors across a corridor from which a spotlessly ordered wooden kitchen can be glimpsed and into a light airy living room. It could be a page from a Habitat catalogue. There is a working table at one end (papers and books neatly stacked), sofas at the other and ordered shelves stuffed with his collection of classical music and CDs, large-format books (Bram Stoker or vampire cinema), and a collection of videos (*Abigail's Party*, *The Best of Iron Maiden*), photographs of his two youngest children, and a portrait in oils, set near to the area he lives in the Lake District.

"There are a lot of stupid people in the world," he remarks apropos of nothing as he lowers himself deliberately into a large pink sofa. "And most of them are critics. It's not *my* fault they're stupid. I just think they're pathetic."

Oh, dear. It is immediately apparent that Ken Russell is not exactly enamored with the extractions of the press ("Where are you from? *Empire*? Hmmmm"), but he does have rather a lot to promote right now—hence, the grudging hospitality. After being rather quiet on the work front for the past few years (his last film, *Lair of the White Worm*, slid quietly into oblivion), he is suddenly busy again. There is now an autobiography out in hardback, *Ken Russell: A British Picture*, with the wonderfully bitter sleeve notes by Ken. "I owe my autobiography to all the people who denigrate or don't understand me," they read. "I think it'll contain some truth about me that isn't contained in crude assessments. It's about somebody who doesn't on the face of it seem too political, too committed, or press his working-class background. I can't be fitted into any of those pigeonholes. My autobiography's a dismissal of all that crap."

There's a *South Bank Show* on his life and work to coincide with the book, commissioned by friend and neighbor Melvyn Bragg, and made, in "impressionistic style," by Russell, "which gave me more pleasure than more or less anything I've ever done." It stars Ken's four-and-a-half-year-old son Rupert as his father up until the age of sixty-one, and his eleven-year-old daughter Molly as Russell's second wife, Vivian. "This little fantasy," as he describes it, also has a couple of cameos by Russell as a sadistic flight sergeant in the Royal Air Force, Captain Bligh of the *Bounty*, and a crazed Austrian film critic.

And then there's the latest film, his twenty-first in a twenty-six-year career. Released this month, *The Rainbow* is based on the D. H. Lawrence novel about the Brangwyn family, stars Russell stalwart Glenda Jackson, and is a modest film for him in terms of budget and style (only one fantasy nude scene). It is also, he has claimed, his best ever.

"Oh, I always say that about the last one," he says dismissively. "It is a good film. But my best? Well, there are less things wrong with it, let us say, than some of my other films."

Almost twenty-six years ago, Russell's first, and very (possibly most) successful feature film, *Women in Love*, again based on a Lawrence novel, starred Glenda Jackson and featured the now-notorious nude wrestling scene between Alan Bates and Oliver Reed (incidentally, the first male full-frontal scenes ever shown in British cinema). Lawrence is a writer Russell has always professed to have sympathy with.

"I identify with him quite a bit," he sighs. "I have mixed feelings about England, the way he did. A love/hate relationship—well. I don't hate it. I like it very much. But it's a funny old place. It's become fashionable to hate England, and everyone jumps on the bandwagon. Mostly the media and angry young film directors who work for Channel Four. They would all do a lot better if they lived in the country and looked at a sheep or a farmer now and again."

"My life has been funny," he pronounces wearily. He is not wrong. Born in Shirley, Southampton, in 1927, Russell is the son of a ship's detective who turned to retailing shoes. The young Russell was raised on the cinema by a mother and aunt who were rabid fans. He was a graduate of the Nautical College, Pangbourne (caned for booking off to see Dorothy Lamour films), a cadet in the Royal Navy (discharged for anxiety neurosis), an electrician in the air force, a graduate in evening ballet classes with the International Ballet Company (his only performance being in *Annie Get Your Gun*), an actor with the Garrick Players of Newton Poppleford, South Devon (only performance, a ghost in a suit of armor in *When Knights Were Bold*), took up photography and made amateur films (one of his first being about Lourdes and its pilgrimage). He married his first wife, Shirley, a costume designer, who bore him five children. He converted to Catholicism "when I was young and impressionable" and mislaid his faith during the making of *The Devils* in 1971. "You have to be in a state of perpetual grace, and I wasn't."

He got his first major break at thirty-two when he was employed by (now Sir) Huw Wheldon to replace John Schlesinger on the influential BBC arts program *Monitor*. Russell was given a relatively free hand by Wheldon but advised not to get the "dressing up basket out" and "not too many bloody crucifixes, Ken." He made a series of films—*Betjeman's London* to a film on Elgar's *Enigma Variations*, voted the best single program of the sixties by TV viewers, which, he recalls, "certainly put me on the map."

The first feature film he was offered was *Summer Holiday*. "But Ken," his mother said at the time, "Cliff's going to look silly driving a London bus in a toga." He wisely turned it down, instead making a series of films for the BBC, personal interpretations of the lives of favorite musicians such as Delius (*Song of Summer*, 1968), Richard Strauss (*Dance of the Seven Veils*, 1970), and the poet Dante Gabriel Rossetti (*Dante's Inferno*, 1967), which were all a bit strong for the BBC then, featuring as they did the inevitable fantasy sequences such as

Strauss being besieged by a melee of lust-filled nuns. Then followed his string of ever more outrageous films of the seventies: *Women in Love*, the biopics (*The Music Lovers, Mahler, Lisztomania*, etc., etc.), the rock opera (*Tommy*), the Busby Berkeley pastiche (*The Boy Friend*)—each one successively dubbed "the most excessive and obscene of all this director's works."

"I've always believed in what I've done," he now says, still slumped on the sofa and appearing somewhat disinterested in the proceedings (except to tell the photographer not to scratch the floor with his tripod). "It's been disturbing, but it's disturbed me more than the audience. I don't regret anything I ever did. I'm proud of them all. They are all me and they're all rather unique. I don't think anyone else could have done them—for better or worse."

Even his later two Hollywood projects—the most commercial of all his films, *Altered States* ("the most difficult film I've ever made") and *Crimes of Passion*, although not personal Russell projects, were, he feels, turned into personal statements. "I wouldn't have done them in the first place if I didn't think they could be." The same is true of his now-abandoned video projects. Cliff Richard's *Time* (banned by the BBC), and two for Elton John, *Nikita* and *Cry to Heaven*. "I thought *Cry to Heaven* was a tragedy, so I made it about Northern Ireland. People getting shot and killed." He giggles. "I realized I wasn't really cut out for videos then."

The time to write the autobiography was snatched at five in the morning in bed, when as an insomnia sufferer, Russell gets up, makes a cup of tea and writes. This he finds "an early morning therapy in a way. I like writing in bed. It gets your mind ticking over. I actually listen to the news and celebrate the fact that I am still alive and all those poor dead people aren't. There's always death. You wake up and there's one hundred dead, one thousand dead, four thousand dead, and feel slightly at an advantage."

The reason he's written the autobiography at this point in his life is because he was asked.

"Good reason, isn't it? I'm asked to do films, I'm asked to do interviews, I *obey*! He barks, looking for a moment as though he may just spontaneously combust. "I do as I'm told! At the drop of a hat!" He has just been asked to act alongside Michelle Pfeiffer and Sean Connery, playing a "poofy" MI5 spy in the film version of John le Carré's *The Russia House*. Will he do it? He thinks so.

Yesterday he made a pop video (probably his last, he admits) for Jim Steinman, who wrote *Bat out of Hell* for Meat Loaf. Tomorrow he meets a producer about a possible project called *The Eleventh Commandment*, about Moses. This morning he's been editing his *South Bank Show*—this afternoon, he's going shopping to choose some shirt fabrics in Regent Street.

"I have a very good Greek man who made about twenty shirts for me ten years ago, and they've all just fallen to pieces. So I shall go to Liberty's and get about ninety meters of different fabrics. That should see me out. I won't be going again. It should last me the rest of my life. It's very good cotton."

Mainly, though, Ken Russell prefers to sit at home with his large Sony TV, hi-fi, and surround sound unit.

"There's very little point in going to the cinema when someone with the last Afro hairdo in London is going to sit in front of you. He always does—he follows me around. Also, you can't go at nine times the speed at the cinema. Most films are nine times too slow."

So what *does* Ken Russell enjoy? *A Fish Called Wanda*, it seems. *Withnail and I* ("Bruce Robinson is an old friend and had a part in *The Music Lovers*"), *Raising Arizona* ("but in the last ten minutes it copped out and became sentimental claptrap"), *Robocop* ("The machine had more soul than the humans, and I thought that was good"), and *The Hitcher.* "Have you seen it? He asks. "It's wonderful." Blockbusters are "OK" as long as they are entertaining, but mention the word "Spielberg" and Ken Russell makes no effort to disguise his disgust.

"I really don't like Spielberg's films. I think they are sadistic and fascist and the worst possible influence on children. There's usually a fifteen-minute sequence where someone gets beaten bloody with hammers or propellers and they're usually Oriental—never American—and the women are made to seem totally stupid. He uses all the worst elements, and I dislike the way he generates everyone's worst prejudices. I think he's quite sick. I wouldn't encourage my children to see his films—I'd turn it off, probably, if it was on, but I don't think they'd want to see it anyway, frankly. They're more sophisticated."

But surely *The Devils*, say, is just as "sadistic" as good old *Indiana Jones and the Temple of Doom*. Russell rolls his eyes.

"I don't *care*," he barks. "It's not important. *I* know and I don't care how they are taken. . . . My films are about something. His films are about making money. My films are about events that happened, or apocryphal events or ideas—he has no ideas. They are all comic strip. Nothing wrong with that, but they prey on everyone's worst instincts. And when he tries to be serious—I mean, *Empire of the Sun*! I've never seen a better-turned-out prison camp in my life. Everyone was beautifully made up with not a hair out of place. They all looked lovely, everyone sunbathing in deck chairs . . ."

He's off and running, so perhaps it is time to make one's excuses and leave. As we do, Ken is going into detail about how he has just been the only guest of honor at the Helsinki Film Festival and how he is about to get the Director of the Year award at the San Remo Film Festival. He blows a loud raspberry. "So the old saying about a prophet not being without honor except in his own country—I'm afraid it's an old cliché, but in my case it happens to be true."

The Impossible Romantic

Lynn Barber / 1991

From *The Independent* (London), July 14, 1991. Reprinted with permission.

Ken Russell's new film is called *Whore*, and there is a certain resonance in the title. Of course, the subject of prostitution is just up his street, but one might also argue that Russell has been whoring his own talent of late. At sixty-four he is a director-for-hire and a cheap one, too (around $200,000 a film); his recent Hollywood work has all been low-budget destined-for-video stuff—a very long way from the sensitive *Monitor* documentaries (Elgar, Delius, Vaughan Williams) which made his name. It doesn't help that he has rows with producers, though he would say the alternative is to lie down and be a doormat. Bob Guccione, who hired him to direct *Moll Flanders*, sued him for breach of contract; he is now at war with his latest producer, Richard Dreyfuss.

His troubles began in 1977 with *Valentino*. His early feature films, *Women in Love* and *Billion Dollar Brain*, won critical acclaim, but then he went increasingly over the top in *The Music Lovers, The Devils, Mahler, Lisztomania*, and finally sank on the reef of Nureyev's unintelligible accent in *Valentino*. It was a very public and expensive flop, and for many years Russell carried the kiss-of-death label "unbankable"—he was conspicuously omitted from the Goldcrest/Attenborough "British Film Renaissance" of the 1980s. Fortunately, he was able to build a successful secondary career as an opera director. But his 1985 film, *Crimes of Passion*, which did good business in the video shops, marked something of a comeback and led to a three-film deal with Vestron. *Whore* is a horse from the same stable, and no doubt film buffs will admire the camerawork and music (as they usually do with Russell's films), while wankers will buy it for the title.

Russell is a really complicated character and one I can't pretend to understand, though I've interviewed him before (in 1985) and followed his career and read his autobiography. We met for lunch at the Ivy, and, again, I was struck by the odd dichotomy between how he looks and how he sounds. He looks flamboyant, extrovert, jolly—in fact, he looks like his favorite actor, Oliver Reed—and is exotically dressed in clown's striped trousers held up with braces. He has snow-white hair and a bright red face, with a newly grown Father Christmas moustache, which he apologizes for not having waxed for me—"With Hungarian pigs' wax it sets like cement." But then he starts talking and all the jollity is erased—his flat, dreary voice makes him sound like some old misery in the bus queue grumbling about her bunions. Actually, what he says isn't dreary, but one wishes one could hire another actor to dub him. Even when he is enthusing, for instance, about a new film composer he has discovered called Barry Kirsch, he still sounds glum. His wife once told him, "There's so little joy in you," and I'd second that.

One sure way of cheering him up is to ask him about things he hates—he is an almost Swiftian master of the denunciatory tirade. His current hates include *The Godfather*, *Twin Peaks*, the Mafia, and Richard Dreyfuss, plus all the old favorites like Bob Guccione, Meryl Streep ("an android"), Harrison Ford ("just an extra with a big hat"), Richard Gere ("smallest eyes in Hollywood"), Al Pacino ("all those serious faces") and, of course, Elaine Paige ("face like a potato"). It was his failure to admire Elaine Paige that lost him the job of directing *Evita*, although he worked on it for years. When describing one of his pet hates, his voice rises from its normal monotone and takes on animation. The absolute number one hate at present is Richard Dreyfuss, for whom he has just made a film.

"It's called *Prisoner of Honor*, but it's about the most dishonorable film I was ever involved in. It's about the Dreyfus case, and apparently Richard Dreyfuss has nurtured this project for years—he identifies with Dreyfus—and he saw my biographical films and liked them and asked me to direct it. Well, of course, when the star is the producer and more concerned with his hair than any other aspect of the story, you're in trouble: in fact, the last day was spent reshooting scenes where he felt his hair looked a bit thin, so we had to rebuild sets and redo them. Then he felt he should have a close-up in the dueling scene, so he actually shot it himself in America without telling me—the fact that there are two completely different actors playing seconds and palm trees in the background didn't seem to worry him. I kept getting all these faxes from him saying 'I look terrible in that scene, can't you drop it?' and I'd say, 'Well, it is rather important to the story.' And the Home Box Office people kept ringing up and saying, 'Where are the close-ups?' I said, "I made a film on Elgar in the sixties that didn't have a single close-up—that seemed to go down all right.' They said, 'Oh, well, these days you must have close-ups.' But I knew if they had close-ups, they could cut. I shot scenes in master shot and without any cutaways so they'd got nothing to cut to. Anyway, one day a lorry came and just took the film away. And Dreyfuss had the cheek to say, 'I know you're very good on music, so I'll send the film back when I've cut it my way and you can supervise the music.' That's a bit like someone asking you to hold your sister down and spray her with perfume while he rapes her!"

Why does he put up with it? Basically, because he has to. He is broke; he owes a lot of back taxes; he may have to sell his London flat to pay them; he has to take whatever work he can get. He has been in financial trouble ever since he tangled with Bob Guccione of *Penthouse* over the film of *Moll Flanders* in 1986. I interviewed him just before he signed to direct it and warned him not to—I worked for *Penthouse* for seven years and saw grown men cry—but Russell wouldn't be deterred. Eventually Guccione sued him for every penny he owned. "It went on for about two years; it seemed a lifetime. That, I think, was the low point in my life, when I was going to the trial in New York and feeling it was hopeless." In fact, he won the case, but it left him a quarter of a million poorer: he also had to make a promo video for his lawyer, who fancied himself a pop singer, as part of his fee. The loss of time and money means he is still running to catch up.

I remind him that he is supposed to be plugging *Whore*, and he goes into a long PR-y rigmarole about how a taxi driver handed him the script one day, but we both find it boring. When I ask if he knows any real whores, he jumps with alarm, looks over his shoulder and lowers his voice. "Ah, well, I have to draw a veil over certain subjects . . . I've talked to them, yes. I used to be rather frightened of them and thought they were ladies of mystery, sort of semicriminal types, but they're just working girls, some richer than others. I know one who works the grand hotels and has a mobile phone. She makes a lot of money."

Last time I met him, he was at the height of his love affair with the Lake District, living in a little cottage in Borrowdale with his wife Viv and their two small children. The Lake District, he said, had replaced Roman Catholicism as his spiritual sustenance. But this time he seems reluctant to talk about it—his wife still lives there, but he doesn't—and wants to talk about Southampton instead. In fact, he orders a fishcake for lunch because, he says, "it's a very Sotonian thing to have" and then calls for some Lea & Perrins to drown it, which is presumably Sotonian too. He was born and brought up in Southampton and has just shot a film there for TVS. It is called *The Road to Mandalay*, and he made it in five days with no script and a total budget of 76,000 pounds—he likes what he calls "home movies." It consists of himself, his son Rupert, his aunt Moo, and cousin June driving round Southampton trying to reach a restaurant called the Mandalay but never being able to turn right and ending up at the ferry terminal and then on the Isle of Wight.

In his autobiography, *A British Picture*, he describes Southampton with almost hallucinatory vividness—the drab suburban street where he grew up and nobody ever came; the boating trips with his father, who ran a shoe shop but really yearned for the sea; the heady exoticism of the docks and the Kasbah cafe; the glamorous department stores and picture palaces where his mother took him every day to dream their separate dreams. As a child, he said, "Films were my world. Every day. With my mother. In the dark. I never saw daylight till I was ten."

It was escape from an unhappy home. His parents bickered continually, and his mother went mad at the end, may have been a bit mad all along; she told Ken as a child that she wouldn't have bothered to have him if the daughter born before him had lived. Both parents are now dead (his eyes fill with tears at mention of his father), but he still goes back to Southampton to see Auntie Moo, eighty-five, and Cousin June. They were furious about his autobiography, as was everyone in the book (and the ones he left out were furious at being left out): June wouldn't speak to him for two years. "She said, 'You intimated we were poor and couldn't afford coal. We could have fires whenever we wanted to. And to say we had candles in the bedroom . . .' I said, 'But, look, your father was dying; you're Catholic; you burn candles. I didn't mean you couldn't afford to put the light on.'" Anyway, June has now forgiven him and consented to star in *The Road to Mandalay*, where, he says, she is "absolutely fantastic, sort of like Rita Hayworth." Auntie Moo said nothing for most of the shoot, then, suddenly realizing they were really on the Isle of Wight, screeched, "What about the cat? I've got bread on the doorstep."

It sounds a gem—maybe as good as the enchanting film he made for *The South Bank Show* a couple of years ago called *A British Picture* (to go with his autobiography), in which his son Rupert, then four, played him. He says that's his own favorite, too, "because it takes all the grandiose nonsense out of filming. Films are just films. Things are written about them and they're blown up to be greater than they are, but I really thought that was a good film. It said lots of things."

For one who claims he is so unfashionable as to be almost unemployable, he has an impressively booked-up diary. He is doing a BBC film this autumn on the Czech composer Martinu and is waiting for the go-ahead on an Italian-BBC coproduction of *Lady Chatterley's Lover*. He is directing two operas next year—Strauss's *Salome* in Bonn, and Gilbert and Sullivan's *Princess Ida* for the English National Opera—and writing a book on British cinema to be called *Fire over England*, which means watching all those smug little Ealing comedies he so detests. Then there is his great project, his dream project, Sacher-Masoch's bondage classic, *Venus in Furs*. Amazingly, he says he only came across the book recently: "My agent put me on to it and it was a revelation. Because it's based on the guy's real-life story, and it gives all the reasons why he likes being beaten, likes women in furs; that's the good thing about it, and totally credible. It's about the balance of power in a relationship because, to start with, she doesn't want to whip him, doesn't want to do all these things, but then she gets into it and the tables are turned—she is the one who gets the kicks out of it, and he is beginning to suffer a bit too much. It's a question of who is in the ascendancy at any given moment, and it shifts all the time, so you never quite know where you are, and I think that's true of any relationship."

Was it true of his own two marriages? The first was to Shirley Kingdon, a fellow student at Walthamstow Tech, whom he married in 1958, the same year he became a film director. He was a keen Roman Catholic at that time, and they had five children very quickly, "like spots before the eyes." Their careers rose in tandem; he made films and she dressed the actors; she is now one of the top film costume designers in the world and, he says, earns more than him. But on the morning of their twentieth anniversary, he upped and left her. In his autobiography, he made it sound her fault, but now he says he thinks he was "too hard on her" in the book. They are on cautiously friendly terms again.

He met his second wife, the American photographer Vivian Jolly, when she turned up on the set of *Savage Messiah* and he hired her as his runner. She rejoined him when he left his wife. (Not having a flat at the time, they moved into the Elizabeth Taylor suite at Elstree.) He finally married her in 1984, when they already had two children, aboard the *Queen Mary* at Long Beach, with Tony Perkins as officiating priest. Vivian, he said then, "kicked me out of the dour, middle-aged path I was travelling and made me enjoy life." But now, he says sadly, "our lives are going in totally different directions."

Does he like to suffer in a relationship? "No, I hate it. I really hate it. I hate, hate, hate it. I really don't like it at all. No, I have nothing of that in my nature. I hate it . . . but I seem to be doing it. I seem to opt for it." He could perfectly easily find a nice little wifey who would cosset him, but he evidently prefers strong women. His book gives plenty of ammunition to those who would say he is a masochist. But perhaps it is just that he is unusually honest. He doesn't bother to gloss over his mistakes, or his humiliations, the way most people do; he talks about himself impartially, the good and bad alike. I thought his autobiography was one of the best and most honest books I'd ever read and told him so, whereupon he assured me it wasn't honest at all. He'd tried to write a straightforward factual autobiography and got nowhere, until a publisher asked him if he'd ever read Isadora Duncan's autobiography, and he said, "Of course. It's a marvelous book." "Yes," said the publisher, "and you know the most marvelous thing about it? There's not a word of truth in it." "So, then," says Russell, "I went home and started writing. I felt released."

One theme of his autobiography which surely can't be faked is his love of music. When he was invalided out of the navy with a nervous breakdown, aged nineteen, he heard Tchaikovsky's Piano Concerto no. 1 in B-flat minor on the radio and was henceforward hooked. He collects records obsessively—he claims he can go through albums in a secondhand record shop at the rate of one hundred a minute, and one of the happiest events of his life was finding a stereo recording of Martinu's Sixth Symphony, which he believed was unobtainable. For five years after national service he struggled to become a ballet dancer before finally conceding that his roly-poly shape and short legs were against him. Then he was briefly an actor, and a student of photography, before Huw Wheldon hired him for *Monitor* on the basis of a couple of homemade shorts. It seems, in retrospect, that he wasted his twenties, but he says no, on the contrary: "I think the things I had to go through to become a film director served me well. That was my apprentice-ship—years of doing those funny things like dancing, acting, choreography, and photography—all that experience is absolutely central to my work. And then to find Huw Wheldon! *Monitor* was, I think, the greatest experimental film school of the twentieth century anywhere in the world, and I was fortunate enough to slip into it. That was my bit of luck." His autobiography is dedicated to Wheldon; he hero-worships his memory. When I asked if he ever wished he'd stayed at the BBC, his eyes filled with tears and he said yes, but "I couldn't afford it. I need to do feature films. But, yes, it was nice."

He probably loves music more than he loves the cinema; indeed, he says he seldom watches new films. He makes a great point of forgetting the names of actors and directors and claims he won't bother to watch *The Silence of the Lambs*, because "everyone tells me it's the worst film ever made, all close-ups and no point-of-view shots at the end." I agree it did rather collapse at the end, and he snarls: "Best not to collapse at the end, I would say. Lesson number one of filmmaking: do not collapse your film at the end."

He says—although I'm not sure if this is him being "controversial"—that he hates the cinema and hopes that soon everyone will only watch films at home on video. He says the sound on video is ninety times better than on film because it is encoded at the rate of ninety feet a minute; with the right equipment—a big video screen, hi-fi speakers, surround sound—you can see and hear more than you ever can from film. "And you don't have to queue, and you don't have the last Afro haircut in London sitting in front of you, and you don't have to watch a print that's scratched or cut and patched or out of focus. You know you have to watch a projector the whole time because as it vibrates, it goes out of focus, but nowadays they have just one projectionist covering eight screens in these multiplex places. I've seen my films soft; I've seen the sound coming out the sides when it should be out the front; I've seen the framing go wrong, and once watched a whole reel of *Billion Dollar Brain* with half Michael Caine's head off the screen. I just wanted to die, you know?" The only cinema he feels he can trust is The Screen on Baker Street, which has the old projectionist from Elstree studios in charge, "so the picture is always pin sharp."

He concedes there are occasional advantages in going to the cinema, as, for instance, when he saw *Godfather III*. "The director has his daughter in it. What's his name? Coppola, yeah. And she's the ugliest girl you've ever seen—not her fault, but she shouldn't be exposed in close-ups. And at the end there's this scene where they're watching *Cavalleria Rusticana*, and everyone starts killing everyone else, and then the Godfather comes out with the director's boring daughter, who's bored everyone to death by not being able to act or even walk properly, and suddenly she's blown apart with a shotgun and everyone in the audience shouts "Hooray!" Now that was good. I wouldn't have got that in my sitting room. That was worth turning out and paying good money to go to the cinema for."

He admits to watching a couple of episodes of *Twin Peaks*, but "I thought the last episode was so bad, it was absolute crap, absolute bullshit, and really conning the audience. It wasn't even entertaining; it was boring beyond belief." But, although it pains him to say so, he loved David Lynch's early films, especially *Blue Velvet* and *Eraserhead*. "But you see, he's like Fellini, like a lot of filmmakers—they start off well, but they deteriorate because they use the same old gimmicks over and over." Surely, I think at this point, he must realize critics have often said the same of him? But, no, he carries on apparently unaware. "I do like good films—I'm glad they've revived the greatest film ever made, *Citizen Kane*, and also *L'Atalante*, which I love—but there are so many bad films about. There's this cult of the Mafia, and all the critics seem to be taken in by it—they're all sentimental, they're all abysmal, they're all crap, and they all have the same actor in, what's his name, De Niro, yeah, they daren't make a film without him." He must love film very deeply, or he wouldn't get so steamed up about it.

Derek Jarman (who worked as his set designer at one stage and reveres him) explained: "Ken is a romantic who sees the world in vivid black-and white. His vision of the artist is pure nineteenth century." In other words, he isn't meant to be accepted—the true artist must starve in a garret rather than receive a Lifetime Achievement Award. Russell recently gave a talk at the Museum of the Moving Image in which he startled his audience of eager film buffs by telling them, "Forget all this stuff about Art: we're working for gangsters, and sometimes the gangsters don't like what you do, so they stop you doing it. Everybody still thinks film directors are these magical, all-powerful figures—and I suppose some are, like Spielberg. But usually it comes down to bargaining, and in the end, if you've got nothing to bargain with, you're in trouble. I'm not complaining. We're all grown up. I hate people who complain." And so he goes off back to his cutting room, still complaining in his Eeyore voice about how broke and neglected and unemployed and unfashionable he is—and still, at sixty-four, one of the busiest film directors around.

Ken Russell: The Victorian Dreamer

George Hickenlooper / 1991

From *Reel Conversations: Candid Interviews with Film's Foremost Directors and Critics* (New York: Citadel Press, 1991): 243–53. Copyright © 1991 by George Hickenlooper. All rights reserved. Reprinted by arrangement with Kensington Publishing Corp, www.kensingtonbooks.com.

If Ken Russell weren't one of Britain's most respected and controversial film-makers, one could easily envision him as a character in a Lewis Carroll novel. While I spoke to him by telephone, I couldn't help but picture myself as Alice lost in Wonderland, sitting under a giant mushroom, listening to the benevolent caterpillar laconically throwing out riddles and answers that jumped around my questions like fish swimming up the stream of consciousness. Russell is a tough director to interview, but in the end one can't help but get a sense of the passion he has for his work—an artist's passion that is difficult to articulate but easy to feel.

His films convey the same kind of ardor. Critics who scrutinize his movies, many of which are biographical accounts of other artists' lives, often find themselves outraged and condemn Russell for his sensationalistic portrayals and often fantastic historical inaccuracies. In Genoa, Italy, where he was directing opera for the first time, his interpretation of Mephistopheles infuriated the Italians so much that a riot broke out during the performance. But Russell dismisses this particular attack as being very Italian, choosing to see himself as a director led only by his love for the subject he renders, not by the politics it may breed.

Born July 3, 1927, in Southampton, England, Russell worked in the British Merchant Navy and served with the RAF before joining the Ny Norsk Ballet as a dancer in 1950. The following year he moved into acting, and, after some training in photography, became a freelance still photographer, contributing to *Picture Post* and other illustrated magazines. In the late fifties he directed a number of amateur short films, the quality of which opened doors for him at the BBC. There he embarked on a series of fictionalized biographies of such famous composers as Elgar, Prokofiev, Debussy, Bartók, Delius, and Richard Strauss, and of the dancer Isadora Duncan. These TV films, which were praised for their imagination, extravagance, [and] mixture of fact and fantasy, and criticized for their self-indulgence and lack of traditional form, paved the way to feature filmmaking.

For the past twenty-five years Russell has dedicated most of his work to portraying other artists on film. With the exception of a brief but tumultuous working career in the United States, culminating in the making of Paddy Chayefsky's science-fiction script *Altered States*, in addition to the less successful thriller *Crimes of Passion*, Russell has lavished most of his genius on biographical films about the lives of composers. Whether it's Tchaikovsky in *The Music Lovers* (1971), Mahler in *Mahler* (1974), or the portrayal of such literary figures as Byron and Shelley in *Gothic* (1987), or films based on the work of great literary figures, like D. H. Lawrence's *Women in Love* (1969) and *The Rainbow* (1989), Aldous Huxley's *The Devils* [of Loudun] (1971), and Bram Stoker's *Lair of the White Worm* (1988), Russell continues to outrage and delight with his flamboyance and unpredictable excesses.

George Hickenlooper: Back during your days with the BBC you delighted, stunned, and upset television audiences with a number of documentaries about the lives of Strauss, Duncan, Prokofiev, and Bartók.

Ken Russell: They were fictionalized.

GH: Your work has been called sensationalistic. For you, what are the differences between documentary and feature filmmaking?

KR: I don't like to categorize like that. Every film has its own unique approach. Each film has its own special requirements, so I never like to differentiate between documentary and fiction. To me they are films, whether they're about Mahler or a D. H. Lawrence novel.

GH: But you've been criticized for treating history cavalierly.

KR: What is history but a group of assumptions? I work intuitively.

GH: So you don't believe that a filmmaker can be historically accurate?

KR: There is no such thing as historical accuracy. I'm currently working on my next film, which is more or less an autobiography, and there's no way on earth it will be historically accurate. It's impossible. It's all so subjective. If someone were going to make a film about my life or write a biography of me and they referred to information that had been printed in books, magazines, and newspapers, the whole thing would be a tissue of lies. Nobody knows the real me, and I've never seen the real me written about. So there is no such thing as historical accuracy. What is most important as a filmmaker is to get to the spirit of what you're trying to put on the screen. The spirit of music, the spirit of Mahler, the spirit of D. H. Lawrence, that's what I'm into. That's the truth, the artistic truth, not the mundane. Who cares about whether he got up at nine o'clock in the morning and went to bed at eleven? That tells you absolutely nothing about anyone. If you want to get the whole truth, you would have to know them every day of their lives, every hour, second by second, every tenth of a second by tenth of a second. You see, people usually equate the truth with dullness. If it's dull and boring, then it's likely to be true. Well, that's not the way I think.

GH: When critics berate a film like *The Music Lovers* for its sensationalistic portrayal of Tchaikovsky, while music professionals like conductor André Previn praise it as being the greatest film ever made about music, who do you listen to and how do you gauge your own work?

KR: Well, who needs it? I get accused all the time of distorting history, that I'm untrue to these people, that I loathe all of them. But then someone comes along, like Shostakovich, and says it was the best film about a composer he'd ever seen. He thought it was a great tribute. I prefer to go with that rather than with the critics who hated me for showing the Gestapo throw Mahler into an incinerator. But then Klaus Tinstead, who I think is the greatest Mahler conductor alive today, thinks not only that *Mahler* is the best film about a composer he's ever seen, but that it's one of the best films he's ever seen, period. He said I'd captured the essence of Mahler's prophecy in the march movement, the allegro of the *Sixth Symphony*. One is usually criticized by people who know little about the subject. I make these films because I love these people. Consequently, it's always the aficionados, the people who fully understand the subjects I am portraying, who praise my films. For instance, when *The Devils* was released, the only people who objected to it were the irreligious. The fact that it's on the curriculum of Loyola Marymount University as a good example of a truthful and imaginative representation of a real event says something, I'm sure. The Catholics know their own business.

GH: Why do you like making films about artists?

KR: I think they deal in mysteries just the way I think life is a mystery. Artists somehow make mysteries concrete, make them more tangible. They interpret the ineffable for the rest of us.

GH: In *Gothic* you're once again courting the Romantics. Would you explain your attraction to Shelley and Byron and the other artists of that period?

KR: Well, I suppose it's like getting together to have drinks with some old friends—Shelley, Tchaikovsky, and Byron. I look at them all as my contemporaries. In my social life I've always mixed with artists and musicians, and they're all sort of a crazy lot. So I'm sure there's nothing profound about Shelley or Byron just because they're "Romantics." An art movement is one entity despite what epoch it's from.

GH: But you have faith in them and their work?

KR: That entirely depends on whether we're talking about artists or *artists*. And just because I may believe in them doesn't mean I wear blinkers and they're all wonderful. They're like anyone else, and their relation to their work fascinates me.

GH: As a director, what do you think an artist's relationship to his work should be?

KR: It should be pure dedication to the work. Filmmaking is a very difficult art form. You've got to convince sixty other people of your vision, your point of view, whereas if you're a painter you've just got a pot of paint and a canvas. It's up to you. Filmmaking is a difficult job. It's from morning to night. And you think about it maybe a year before you actually do the film. In the case of my latest project, *The Rainbow*, which is a prequel to *Women in Love*, it took eight years before I actually did it. A piece of art, whether it's a film, a painting, or a story, is not something to be undertaken lightly, at least not by me anyway.

GH: When you're directing a biographical film like *The Music Lovers*, *Mahler*, or *Gothic*, who are you making the film for? Is it for a general audience or scholars?

KR: First of all, I don't think there's any such thing as a general audience. I mean, I make it for myself, and I hope that if it entertains me, it will entertain someone else.

GH: You've been called a director who tries to bridge highbrow art with popular art. Do you agree with that?

KR: I worked at the BBC for ten years, and we were told we had to communicate. I was working on this arts program, and we were dealing with esoteric subjects but were also dealing with a mass audience who'd never heard of Debussy, Bartók, or Strauss. And we weren't supposed to talk down to this television audience; instead, we tried to fire them up with our own enthusiasm for these artists. And on this program there were half a dozen directors who all had backgrounds in music, painting, or literature. It was like doing your own hobby. It was like making a film just for the sheer excitement, the exuberance, of seeing it on the screen. And the trick of it was to try and communicate that.

GH: You think high art and popular culture can mix with success?

KR: Yeah, I'm sure they can.

GH: At one time you said you never made your films for commercial purposes. Do you ever feel pressure from the studio to make your films more mainstream, and, if you do, how do you continue to make films that are very original?

KR: I don't know if I exactly said that, but, you know, one hopes that people are going to see the film. I suppose by commercial I meant *Friday the 13th*–type films, which are totally cynical.

GH: Do you ever feel pressure from the studio to control your work?

KR: Well, they have an input on the casting, so from that perspective there is a certain amount of studio influence.

GH: Many of your films have English casts. Is this something that you prefer?

KR: No, not really. Frequently, it just turns out that way. *Lair of the White Worm* had an English cast because it was an English film with English people, except maybe [Catherine] Oxenberg. I still don't know what she is. But in general, I think that a good actor is a good actor. I suppose that some Americans take themselves a bit too seriously.

GH: In England your success has been fabulous, whereas in the US it has not. What do you think the differences are between English audiences and American audiences?

KR: Well, they speak different languages.

GH: Could you be more specific?

KR: Well, I think that is an English statement.

GH: *Altered States* was a very American film, with an American cast and an American writer. How was the experience of making this film different from some of your others?

KR: Well, it was the only film on which I ever had an unlimited budget. That was nice, and it was American, too.

GH: You mentioned *Lair of the White Worm*. What attracted you to Bram Stoker's novel, and why did you make that film?

KR: Vestron, with whom I had a three-picture deal, were keen for me to make a film about Dracula. I had written a script on *Dracula* several years ago which they read and liked, but there were problems with the rights, because they were held by another company that had become extinct. There was also the problem of there already being 338 films based on *Dracula*, so I thought it might be a better idea to make some changes, you know, retain the fangs but get rid of the bat. Coincidentally, at that time, someone asked me what I thought of *Lair of the White Worm*, and I was ashamed to admit that I had never read it. I didn't know of its existence, so I immediately read it and found myself quite taken by it. I didn't think it was as good as *Dracula*, but I certainly felt that it had potential. At the same time, I was getting a little tired of the Victorian Gothic period, so I updated the story and wrote it on spec for Vestron. They liked it, so they asked me to do it.

GH: The film has a lot of humor in it. Were you parodying the novel?

KR: No, no, it's not a parody of the novel, but it is a parody of horror films in general. You see, I couldn't be entirely faithful to the tone of the novel, because it isn't very good, certainly not as well constructed as *Dracula*. I mean, Stoker must have been ill when he wrote it. I felt all I could take was the basic premise, and it had a good basic premise. It's nice to get out of Transylvania.

GH: When you updated the novel, what kind of changes did you make?

KR: Very little apart from the sports cars. The setting already worked because I put it in a kind of primitive society, a feudal society. I had a lord of the manor, and not much had changed except the uniform in the five hundred years since the life of his ancestor, one of the knights who slew the dragon. I mean, the country girls were still country girls who were terribly simple. It was pretty primitive to begin with, so there was really no need to update it that much.

GH: *Women in Love* is still praised as one of your best films. Why do you think it stands above the others?

KR: To me it doesn't, but we probably shouldn't say that. It may be okay in itself, but trying to get a six-hundred-page novel into two hours is a real problem. It has some very good performances in it, and it was very outspoken about relationships. I hope that I went into them in depth much more than most other films had done by that time.

GH: You once said, "All good entertainment shocks people." Someone like Bertolt Brecht may have done this for political reasons, to make an audience aware that they were watching theater, and Jean-Luc Godard might do this to break the illusion of reality that film creates. Why do you believe this? Why do you think films should shock people?

KR: I think they should be shocked into an awareness, a kind of awareness of enjoyment, to liven them up and show that they can actually share in the excitement.

GH: Do you think your films are manipulative, or are you working against that?

KR: I don't know what they are. I just make them. I don't analyze my films. I've been making them for thirty years. That's just how I do them. They just present themselves in their own way. Of course, they have to communicate, they have to be cinematic, they have to flow, they have to do all sorts of things.

GH: Over the past few years you've directed a number of operas. What was it like for you to come out of feature filmmaking and go into another form of drama that didn't require cameras?

KR: Well, it's a totally different approach to film. There aren't many films where you can shoot in chronological order, scene by scene. But when you rehearse an opera, that's generally what you do. This enables the actors to watch their characters grow as they develop onstage. In film you've always got to make an inspired guess because you often shoot the last scene first and the first scene last. Everything in between is like a jigsaw puzzle. So from that point of view, directing an opera is much more interesting. It's like having the soundtrack already finished. You just set the action to the soundtrack and watch it happen. It's totally different from film, but it's similar enough that when you do go back to directing movies, you can look at it with a fresh eye. I would imagine that each benefits from the other.

GH: Specifically, what did you enjoy the most about directing opera?

KR: The fact that it's out of your hand, it's live. On the first night of a film, you know exactly what you're going to see—though if you see it in a cinema theater, it most likely won't be in focus, so you probably won't see anything! You know you'll see the door open and in will come Glenda Jackson, and you'll know she'll close the door all on cue because it was filmed that way. But in opera you never know what's going to happen. You're a captive audience on the first night. You don't know if the orchestra will play badly or inspiringly. At the same time, when it works, there's a certain magic which you don't get in film. And that's due to the fact that film is obviously a mechanical process. It's done with electricity, with amps, watts, and volts, whereas opera is done with just sheer vocal power.

GH: You mentioned that you often don't know what's going to happen onstage. That seems to be true for the audience, too. I understand one of your operas caused a riot in Genoa.

KR: I don't know what's going to happen, but whatever it is I always hope that it will be exciting because the opera company has asked me there for that very reason.

GH: In 1986 you started Sitting Duck Productions, which focused its energies on making music videos. How did that come about?

KR: Dick Clark rang me up and asked me to make a music video for him.

GH: Are you still making music videos?

KR: No, I'm too busy now. I've sort of phased it out.

GH: At the time you seemed rather excited about it.

KR: Well, I was, but like everything else you always find that there are snags. I discovered that I was being a bit too literary with the lyrics. My approach only suited certain songs. It didn't suit them all, and I began to feel that I didn't know what people wanted. I felt that we were talking different languages, so I stopped.

GH: At the time you felt that the music video would have a great impact on narrative feature filmmaking.

KR: I think that it has and it hasn't. It has, but at a cost. A lot of music video directors are brilliant on the two-minute or four-minute format, but you can't keep up that bombardment of images for over an hour and a half and not expect the audience to get punch-drunk. So I think it has diminishing returns. Not many promo directors have bridged the gap to feature filmmaking.

GH: I read that you constructed your films like symphonies.

KR: If it suits the film, yes. Despite the fact that I can't read a note of music, I try to start with the soundtrack first—you see, that's the most difficult part. Because once you have the soundtrack, you have the movie. Music is architecture to me, so I always try to get a musical or architectural sense for the film. In the opening scenes there's the development section: first, second subject, etc. I'm really conscious of it. For example, I did *Mahler* in rondo form. There was a statement, the sections in the railway train, then variations with episodes interlinking the journey. In *Lair of the White Worm*, and nobody's noticed it yet, I've done something that I don't think anyone else has ever done since Hitchcock—I never cut away from the actuality. You never cut away from somebody who's not immediately involved with what you're seeing on the screen, so time is continuous in the film. I don't think that's been done too much. Also, nobody has seemed to figure out the dream sequence. In Freudian hindsight, if you understand the dream, you understand the mystery, which is why the hero of the film gets the solution. He doesn't consciously analyze his dream or even remember it actively, but he subconsciously remembers it and acts upon it. And the audience can do that. I certainly didn't mean for the dream sequence to be just a series of pretty pictures. It tells the whole of what happened. It tells who everyone is and what they're up to. It's a mystery, but it's solvable. I haven't read a review that says the dream is interesting because it meant this. Nobody said that. Now, whether the critics are too lazy to bother or just think it's an obsession doesn't matter. If you look, the whole mystery of the story is there.

GH: Is the dream sequence in the novel?

KR: No.

GH: To me, it was a collective flashback of what had happened in that exact place when the Romans were in Britain.

KR: Yes, absolutely—memory, hallucinations, all that was part of it, but the dream was a dream as such. And the dream as a dream we are told has a meaning.

God and Monsters

Sally Vincent / 1999

From *The Guardian*, June 5, 1999. Reprinted with permission.

He called the shots: train times, restaurant location, duration of encounter, date of next meeting (groan groan), responsibility for bill ("This is on *The Guardian*!"). Fair enough, I suppose. I'd hoped an hour and a half of South West Trains entitled me to a backdrop of seaside, or New Forest, or both, but, hey, who am I to choreograph this? Directors direct.

After half a century of knowing what he wants and getting his own way, even if it means shooting himself in both feet, Ken Russell has today chosen to lunch in this unappetizing shack across from the railway-station car park, against which sad edifice the gay colorways of his Tweedledee costume, tomato face, and white hair shout hallelujahs to a drab world. Clearly a big man in this chapel, Mr. Russell knows to advise against the fish and has it in his gift to cause the Muzak to be turned down should the tape recorder require. He has only to say "the usual" and the maitre d', who calls him "Chief," brings a veal escalope with side order of spaghetti bolognese. Down the little red tunnel with every last crumb and a bottle or two of house white, voice pitched against yammer of Clayderman and grizzling kiddies, blue eyes peering through a lacework of down-curling white eyebrows, it matters not that I miss three words in four. The gist is this: hereabouts, there are bridges. Many bridges. Many old, defunct bridges built who knows when and who knows why. They go nowhere. They never did go anywhere. What he finds fascinating, what he's been doing with his time of late, is to seek out bridges and go over them to check they really don't go anywhere. And they really don't. On my way home, I must be sure to look out of the train window to affirm for myself the plurality of said bridges. Should I be particularly vigilant, I will observe that they do, indeed and in fact, go absolutely nowhere.

Is this metaphor? It is not. There are bridges and there are trees, great trees with thousands of twigs, feeling the wind, dancing, touching each other, being alive. They are alive and they know he's there, he can walk among them and not be alone. He's living in a magic world, all alone but not alone. In conversation with himself now, part of the living landscape. Not for nothing, he says, do nuns and monks go into retreat. Eight children, three wives, there's self-indulgence for you: all that laughing, crying, babies, and washing-up, it wears a man out. Of course, there's the occasional non-nookie drawback, but who wants the nonsense that goes with it? There are other things in life.

Living alone for the first time is a commonplace experience in terms of the realization, and acceptance, of unopposed selfishness. You do what you like when you like, de-da-de-da-de-da. Without the responsibility of responsiveness, you come upon your own self without the relief of distraction. Your life flashes before your eyes, your mind coasts, you freewheel until it seems as though another person is there. Someone else or something else. For Russell, it might be a guardian angel. More likely, it's God.

As I say, he's not being remotely portentous. His tone is throwaway, a little bored, banal as the ambience of this eatery, his desire to impress or endear himself on a par with the chef's pretensions towards haute cuisine. In the light of the violent religious and sexual imagery of his more notorious contributions to cinematic art, I might have urged him to more metaphysical flights, but it all sounded perfectly prosaic at the time. What I could hear of it.

Russell converted to Catholicism at twenty-eight. Before that, he'd been brought up C of E, so didn't know what religion was. As you don't. This is what happened: he was a penniless student of photography sharing a big Victorian house in London's Notting Hill Gate with a lot of other part-time vagrants. Since no one had much money, whoever possessed a shilling for the gas ignited the fire in his or her room, and everyone else assembled for the warmth and whatever else was on offer.

It was in the course of one such soiree that Russell tuned in to the enthusiasm of one Norman Dewhurst, a trainee tax inspector from Bradford, who was improving the shining hours of his leisure by taking instruction from the Jesuit priests of Farm Street. The really knockout thing about Catholics, Norman said one night, is we eat God. "We eat God." It was the most extraordinary thing Kenneth had ever heard. Like science fiction. Naturally, good old Norman was challenged on the ecclesiastical niceties of his assertion, but he stuck to the point. No, we don't believe we eat God. No, we don't imbibe the symbol of his holiness. We eat God. Literally. It was the willful certitude that got our Kenneth by the throat. He wanted to belong. Norm had won a convert.

It was a bit of a bummer to be turned down by the intellectuals of Farm Street and palmed off on Poor Clares down Portobello Road, as though they thought he was a bit simple, but Sister Rose turned out to be about seventeen and a half years old and fantastically beautiful.

He went to her for chats, and after six months she reckoned he was about as ready as he'd ever be to join up and sent him to a Farm Street egghead for the final brush-up. Confiding a few agnostic niggles along the lines of not really believing, he was reassured by the priest, who said airily that he didn't actually believe, either. So he joined immediately. And ate God. And has continued to do so on a regular basis. It's much like eating a wafer without the ice cream, since I ask. And no, it wasn't a spiritual awakening at all, just a complete change of attitude. All that happened was he stopped thinking about making films and went out and made one.

The first Ken Russell film, as described by himself, was about a little angel who lost her wings. No self-mockery here, just the facts of the matter. A little girl has a bit part in the school nativity play. The third angel on the left. The teacher tells her to take great care of her wings, not to play with them, not to take them home, not to lose them. But she takes her wings home to show Mummy, and her little brother breaks them, and she has to find another pair of angel wings before the show that very night. She finds them in London. Through prayer and hard work. The end. "And that is the story of my life, sweetie," said Russell. "Prayer and hard work." Russell survived, if that is the word, the usual lower-middle-class nightmare of familial interaction. His dad ran a boot-and-shoe emporium, Mum went to the pictures. She'd been a shopgirl, a cut below, as it were. The normality of their union was that they didn't get on. She was like a Chinese water torture, nagging away. "I saw you look at this woman, I saw you look at that woman," and he'd fetch her one across the mouth as he drove the family saloon on some unthrilling outing, so there'd be blood all over the upholstery.

There was always the threat of his belt coming off; the belt with H, his initial, H for Henry, on the buckle, to hit one or other of them. For the most part, though, they ignored each other. By default, then, Ken accompanied his mum on her daily sojourn in the ninepenny stalls. They chummed along because there wasn't anyone else. "I'd never have had you, our Kenneth," she'd bawl at him, "if my little girl had lived." Not that she ever made a big deal of it.

He wasn't hurt or anything. He just took it as a sad fact of her life that she had lost a child. He didn't so much realize he was some kind of stop-gap as feel it in his bones as some kind of personal lack that he might, if he tried really hard, overcome. When his brother, Raymond, came along, he suffered the usual older-sibling displacement miseries with the best he could manage by way of fortitude. Once, when Raymond broke a window in the greenhouse, Kenneth belted straight out to buy his mum a quarter of chocolate Brazils because he knew he'd get the blame.

For reasons that are largely unfathomable, young Kenneth put up no fight when they sent him to Pangbourne Naval College. He hated the sea. It frightened him. On the other hand, he was madly in love with Dorothy Lamour, whose South Sea island, saronged persona had charged his loins in countless ninepenny-worths. He had some vague idea that one day a ship might take him to her. With his crappy forename and unpleasant diction, he aroused the contempt of his more aristocratic peers, who left him in no doubt of the full horror of bullies' victim-hood until he grew tall enough and spoke posh enough to join the Merchant Navy and be driven still further round the bend.

Life on the ocean wave was not a success. For one thing, he never met Dorothy Lamour, and for another, the captain of his ship was completely bonkers, who caused his crewmen to stand bolt upright and stationary for four-hour stretches, staring lamely into the Pacific Ocean in case a postwar Japanese midget subma-rine was still lurking about.

And that was all there was to it. He stood stock still, with the tropical sun beating on his skull, and endlessly watched the rise and fall of the ship, the haze, the empty horizon, until it got the better of him.

The official discharge called it anxiety neurosis. What happened was he went home and sat in a chair for six months. Moping. His dad would come and tell him to pull himself together and join him in the boot and shoe business; his mum reckoned the Royal Air Force would take him out of himself. But no. He got up, sat in the chair all day, went to bed. People said, "Don't just sit there," and he sat there. Until, one day, he heard on the radio the slow movement of Tchaikovsky's B-flat minor Piano Concerto and was galvanized. "I didn't know," he says now, "there were so many tunes. . . ." He got up out of the chair. He had to do his National Service, anyway.

They put him on an electronics course in the RAF. They had a defunct cinema on his camp, and he wired up the old projection room so as to play Tchaikovsky very loud for all the other erks. His little music circle became quite popular among the more cultured defenders of Her Majesty's skies, and there was one lad who was drunk enough one evening to leap and pirouette around the place when they played the "Sugar Plum Fairy." Twenty-two years old, Ken Russell had never heard of ballet. What's this? he cried. What are you doing? And before the night was out, he was doing a pas de deux to Swan Lake. He was the swan queen, the other guy was the prince. He thought he'd found his métier, and, since nobody thought to mention that ballet dancers begin as soon as they can walk if they're ever going to amount to anything, devoted five years to studying and practicing ballet until he'd sprained his ankles so many times they said it was time he pranced off.

Ken's mum and dad were fairly bemused by this turn in his career. They thought it was a pansy activity; his mum said ballet was men wearing stockings, and his dad said what will they say in St. Mary's Street, which was where he sold his boots and shoes. But when he got a job as a chorus boy in *Annie Get Your Gun*, they were quite impressed. His dad would have gone to see him but had a thing about germs, though his mum went all the way to Sheffield. "Hello, Ken," she bawled across the auditorium. "Look, there's our Ken!" When he took up acting, she followed the company for the full three weeks of its existence. He was only playing a suit of armor in *When Knights Were Bold*, but she recognized their Ken, pointing him out to whoever was within her voice range. She was a good old soul, his mum. At least she had a bit of fun before she ended her days in Fareham nuthouse, no longer knowing who she was, let alone their Ken.

Not many people know this, but in the fifties and sixties the BBC really was the cultural heart of the nation. I don't want to draw attention to myself in this regard, but BBC television used to be very, very good indeed. Intelligent people used to watch it. Not only that, they'd earmark their favorite programs and stay home to see them in confident expectation of their continued excellence and inspiration. Towards the end of the fifties, it occurred to Russell that if he was ever to make something of himself, he must make a film for *Monitor*, the BBC's most prestigious arts program of that time, and any other time.

Moved, perhaps, by innate good taste, and certainly by naked ambition and gall, he dispatched three reels of amateur film to Huw Weldon, *Monitor*'s most formidable editor. A week later, they shared a cheese sandwich and a pork pie in the Red Lion pub on Ealing Common, and Russell made his pitch. Albert Schweitzer playing the organ in his leper colony, Edward Elgar tobogganing down Hampstead Hill on a tin tray, or John Betjeman's London: take your pick.

Weldon circumspectly chose the Betjeman and, all unknowing, launched the career of Britain's most gut-wrenchingly dangerous filmmaker. They used to call him the "enfant terrible" while he dominated the sixties. God knows why. He had pink, cherubic chops and a petulant pout, but he was thirty-two years old before anyone had heard of him. Plus, he wasn't all that terrible, to start with. He engendered the odd frisson of controversy in devout or prudish circles, but nothing untoward. Those were the days.

Before I got back on the London train that day, I asked Russell to write in my notebook the titles of four films from the 130 or so he has made. Films he felt it was important for me to see. He thought for a few moments, wrote slowly and neatly, snapped the book shut and handed it back with a businesslike little frown. Two days later, I knew I had to see him again, if only to ask why he had elected to violate my delicate sensibilities with these outward and visible manifestations of his disgusting preoccupations. *Whore* (1991) came first, then *Crimes of Passion* (1984), *Altered States* (1980), and an ill-fated load of old toffee called *Lair of the White Worm* (1988), which sent me to sleep. No mention of his early adaptation of D. H. Lawrence's *Women in Love* (1969), or even *The Devils* (1971), his notorious screen version of Aldous Huxley's *The Devils of Loudun*. It was a mistake to watch them end to end, but the relentless battering of desperately joyless sexual images is something I could have done without. It is all so pointlessly energetic: frantic masturbations, mountings, jerkings, throbbings, pumpings, suckings, gruntings, stocking tops and brassieres, stiletto heels and suspender belts and crotches and yogurt-smeared lippy and jeroboam-cork nipples and dildos and truncheons and nuns and air hostesses and laps and Oh Dear, Oh Lord, Oh Me! Put it this way, at the end of it all I didn't feel elevated.

He purported not to comprehend my misgivings. First, he couldn't remember which films he'd recommended, then he couldn't recall their detail on account of it being a long time since he made them. And suddenly he's shouting, "Everyone's masturbating in an audience. Why do you think they're there? They had them in *Annie Get Your Gun*, for pity's sake. Jerking away in the front row, they didn't think we could see them. Enjoying the show! An audience is a conglomeration of two thousand masturbators," he roars, punching himself in the side of the head. "Mental. In the head! What's the difference?" His fascination for the power-game inherent in prostitution, it seems, is purely allegorical. Tart as metaphor. At face value, he thought it was worth conveying the truth about what tarts thought about men and, through that, to expose something more universal, more endemic in Western society. If I insist on there being a moral to films such as *Whore* and *Crimes of Passion*, he has to say they are about domination, power, and money. Not about sex. They are, in fact, about America, exposures of the corruption, lies, and hypocrisy of the land of the free. Especially Hollywood.

"Nobody means a word they say," he says, more in sorrow than anger. "All the producers I've ever met are acting a part; all the studio bosses, the agents, everyone. Nothing is real. It's all fantasy, all false. The great passion is only a rat race. Acquisition has taken over from connection. People are masks. I've made a couple of all-American shows. Bugger America." A hymn of hate to America, then? No, he says, and he's knuckling the top of his head, crack, crack, crack. "A hymn of exposure. Of looking in the mirror wiping away the mist and looking. Take off the blinkers, take off the dark glasses, see the reality underneath." Crack, crack, crack. "I can't tell you," he concludes. "I'm not an intellectual. I don't do these things. I feel them. I can't explain why, I can't rationalize them, I can't give you the answers. I don't know, that's the answer. I can't penetrate this thick skull." Crack, crack. My thick skull, more like, I'm thinking.

I imagine Ken Russell has had more kicks than ha'pence in his profession. He has no money—he doesn't even bother to answer the question, just allows an expression of wonderment to flit across his face that I could be fool enough to ask such a thing. Britain rejected him, he went to Hollywood, they rejected him. He's hardly about to frolic through his later years with a gilt-edged pension plan. Does he regret? Of course he does, though he's sparing with the details. He shouldn't have made *Valentino* (1977), should have made *The Rose*, should have done more sci-fi, should have done *Evita*. The Hollywood monsters thwarted him. He thwarted himself. So what? What concerns him now is the really big mistake. It took him a quarter of a century to realize it, and it's only just hit home this past year. He should never have divorced his first wife. Maybe his problem was only that he never had any friends. Well, one perhaps. No, two. But they're in America. So there was never anybody to confide in when he stood on the brink of doing something daft. Nobody to kick his problems around with.

He was in a cheery mood and a salmon-pink jacket when he swanned into London to promote his first novel.[1] His publisher has given him the boardroom to hold court in, and a pretty girl brings wine and an aura of optimism. Everyone'll be outraged, he says chirpily, everyone'll call it sacrilegious. If I want to know the truth, he wrote it as a film script twenty-five years ago, and nobody would put the money up. Hollywood's idea of Christianity has always been a lot of Bible-speak kowtowing to the Bible Belt: in truth, this is the "Sarn of Gard" crap. They didn't want the Ken Russell Jesus Christ. Sod 'em. Hence, he's been tinkering with his vision of God, the Universe, Jesus, et al., for all this time, and now it's a book. A Very Devout Book, too, in his opinion.

"Look," he says, "There is no way I'd trash Jesus and co. On the other hand, they were human beings. Some were gay, some weren't. They got drunk, went to brothels, made mistakes. They were teenagers. Some people think Jesus ran off with Mary Magdalene in the end. Think about it: he was only on the cross for three hours, and it usually took six to kill you. The other guys were put up at dawn, so they were really well dead. But Jesus had a foot support, he went up late, and they had to get him down by three because nobody was allowed to be up there when the Sabbath was on. So when they took him down, Simon of Gonorrhea, or whoever he was, patched him up, and although he was in a bad way, he recovered. A lot of people think that." It makes sense, I say. "The thing of God being a woman is interesting," he goes on. "You need a positive and a negative, a male and a female. My theory is the Big Bang did go off, but before that the universe was a huge womb, waiting to be fertilized by Big Bang. I like that idea. I don't understand about the Holy Ghost. It's supposed to mean "the spirit of love between God and the son." I don't get it. But I do believe in the Virgin Mary, as the female force. And, if I believe in her, I naturally believe in her son. I have experienced her beneficence," he adds mischievously. Go on, then.

"Have I told you about the miracle of the snuff? No? Are you sure?" The wine is going into my empty stomach. I might as well take in the miracle of the snuff while I'm at it.

Many years ago, when Ken Russell was a young Catholic convert, he was a hopeless nicotine addict. It was a grotesque habit, eternally poking snuff up his nose like his life depended on it. He tried to give up many times. One day, he saw a statue of the Madonna in a shop in Victoria. He had to have her. She cost twenty pounds and, though he had only twenty-two pounds in the world, he bought her. They parceled her up, and he boarded his bus to Notting Hill Gate, holding her carefully.

So there he was, trundling down Artillery Row on the top of a number 19, and he found he couldn't get the lid off his snuff tin. He was dying for a pinch. DYING, DYING, DYING for one. He tried to find a coin in his pocket to prise the lid off, but he only had a pound note. He tried to get change from the conductor, but no dice, and he was going MAD MAD MAD. He was shouting, "For fuck's sake, let me give up this fucking habit," and the lid still wouldn't come off. He got home, put his Virgin on the mantelpiece, laid a crown of flowers on her head, and never touched snuff again. The craving had gone. Just gone. And it never came back.

I would have thought this would suffice by way of miracles, but apparently not. A couple of years back, alone in bed, he suffered a wee stroke. He thought his number was up. "You can't believe the noise when you're dying," he says. "It's like a thousand volts of electricity shorting out in your head." So there he was, with just enough time to register the inevitability of his demise, and what does he see, up in the corner, but the Virgin Mary, the one with the child in her arms, looking down on him. He knew he was going to be all right. He was. Aha. She's all over his house, he says. He's got more Virgin Marys than you can shake a stick at. But only on the top floor. On the ground floor he's got the fourth Mrs. Russell. She's a shop mannequin. Naked. She's not allowed upstairs.

Note

1. Ken Russell, *Mike and Gaby's Space Gospel: A Novel* (Little, Brown, 1999).

Savage Messiah: An Interview with Ken Russell

Nik Huggins / 2002

From *Future Movies*, www.futuremovies.co.uk/filmmaking/savage-messiah-an-interview-
with-ken-russell/nik-huggins, November 1, 2002. Copyright © 2002 *Future Movies*.
Used with permission of *Future Movies*.

Someone once said that you should always decline the chance to meet your heroes face to face, you'll only be disappointed with what you find. I have always felt that such words of deterrence, whilst reductive, were well worth bearing in mind. Nevertheless, when I was offered the chance to meet a man whom I consider to be one of the most visionary filmmakers this country has produced in the last forty years, I was, despite the nerves, more than willing to take the chance.

Ken Russell has carved out a remarkable career in film, and prior to that television, that displays a vociferous interrogation of the visual and aural parameters of filmmaking. Constantly testing the boundaries of style, taste, and onscreen complexity, Russell's work at its best aspires to all that is great in cinema; at its worst, amidst moments of unbridled visual bombast, it is never less than interesting. Always willing to pursue his personal interests on screen, Russell's films are almost all self-evident labors of love. Crafted with a flair for the elaborate that manifests itself in every facet of his work, the cinema of Ken Russell speaks of a characteristic style that transcends genre and subject matter.

Equally at home with horror (*The Devils, Lair of the White Worm*), family musicals (*The Boy Friend*, which I am reliably informed "works on so many levels"), character-driven period pieces (*Women in Love, Savage Messiah, The Rainbow*), science fiction (*Altered States*), or a riveting generic blend, Russell has continued to confound expectation and invigorate even pedestrian material with an injection of wit and excess.

Constantly seeking, in his own words, a perfect "wedding of image and music," Russell continues to work in his own home, despite a virtual absence of financial or logistical support from the UK filmmaking community. His personal projects feed a still-strong desire to keep creating. Despite his advancing years, Ken Russell's appetite for the problem-solving challenge of filmmaking has in no way diminished.

Future Movies met Mr. Russell for lunch, where we gained an insight into a career devoted to keeping people hooked to the screen by any means necessary. Along the way we discussed past projects, present preoccupations, and future ambitions.

Future Movies: So tell us about your latest project, a biography of the nineteenth-century scientist Nicola Tesla?

Ken Russell: That's now been postponed. It was all set to go, and then the president of Serbia was shot, and the country's been in turmoil ever since. They were due to put in a chunk of the financing. Hopefully it will be made one day but not at the moment. At the moment I have a feature film coming out after Christmas called *Jonathan Tooley*. It's a strange name and will probably be changed. It's based on a children's bestseller in America. It's a very charming fantasy, primarily a children's film but with lots for adults as well.

I am also working on a project of my own called *The Revenge of the Elephant Man and Other Tails* [Ken assures me that T-A-I-L-S is the intended spelling]. I have just started shooting it in my back garden on digital video, and hopefully it will be released on DVD eventually.

FM: You mentioned the DVD format. How is it that most of your best-known feature films are not available on DVD in the UK?

KR: Search me! I guess they don't appear to be commercial. Of course, most of my stuff is available in America, just not here. Over there, most of the shops have shelves devoted to my films alone, but that's not the case here.

FM: What attracts you to biography in your films?

KR: Well, it started when I joined the BBC *Monitor* program, which was the first arts program in the world. It was about artists, and the various directors and producers on the program were encouraged to make programs about their particular hobbyhorses. Mine was music, so I started on the classical composers: Elgar, Delius, Bartók, Prokofiev, and so on. I loved their music, and that led me into discovering about their lives and throwing light on them as individuals.

FM: So you threw yourself into the work?

KR: Yeah, it was like a paid hobby. It started off as very simple twenty-minute documentaries, which soon developed into drama documentaries that lasted over an hour, essentially mini feature films.

FM: Do you feel that as you moved into making features your approach to onscreen biographies changed?

KR: Not really. One had more money to spend, and so one could afford to be more spectacular, such as in *The Music Lovers* [about Russian composer Tchaikovsky], that had a big budget. All of the work done for the *Monitor* program was, in contrast, very low budget, so you had to think about the subject in a different sort of way.

FM: When watching your films, it becomes evident that they are trying to transcend reality.

KR: "Reality" is a dirty word for me, I know it isn't for most people, but I am not interested. There's too much of it about.

FM: Do you see film as some sort of transcendental experience?

KR: Music I do, but not films very often.

FM: Were you not trying to strive for that in your work at any time?

KR: Well, my films do rely on music and imagery. I soon realized that a certain image with the right music creates something "other." I discovered that when I used to show films during the war in my dad's garage. I had a 9.5-millimeter Ace projector. I showed a lot of Charlie Chaplin, Felix the Cat, and Betty Boop, but the only films available that weren't shorts were German Expressionist films. So I was showing *Siegfried* by Fritz Lang, and as he was slaying the fire-breathing dragon, sons of Siegfried were dropping firebombs on us, and the irony never struck me. I also showed *Metropolis*, and I had one classical record to accompany it, and I found that when the march from *Things to Come* by Arthur Bliss happened to coincide with a scene from *Metropolis*, it fitted just perfectly. On the other side of the record, a much more romantic march by Edvard Grieg fitted the epic hero of Siegfried slaying the dragon. It made a huge difference on the audience too, I could tell, and so from that moment on I really appreciated the wedding of image and music.

FM: It's interesting that you mention German Expressionism as a formative influence. It certainly emerges in your mature work.

KR: Yeah, that and Jean Cocteau. His films (*La belle et la bête, Orpheus*) made a big impact on me. The third amateur movie I made, *Amelia and the Angel*, was heavily influenced by Cocteau. It was the one that got me into the BBC.

FM: You have begun to shoot films at home now; do you also edit them at home and do all the postproduction there?

KR: Yes, I edit my so-called home movies on a machine called the Casablanca; it's nothing to do with Humphrey Bogart. It's a rather unique editing machine, because it has Victorian picture frames around the images, and it's as though Thomas Edison invented this electronic editing machine; it works along very basic picturebook terms. It is very simple to operate. I have edited a couple of movies on it so far. Alongside these home movies I am writing a series of books on composers. The first one is concerned with Brahms; it's called "Brahms Gets

Laid," and it's a new look at someone who is usually associated with the three B's—beard, belly, and beer—but was a honky-tonk pianist in the red-light district of Hamburg until the age of twelve, and he therefore probably knew a good deal about sex. Having made a film on Elgar for the BFI in 2002 [*Elgar: Fantasy of a Composer on a Bicycle*], I have written one on Elgar called *Elgar: The Erotic Variations*, as opposed to the *Enigma Variations*, and am now working on one about Delius.

FM: When you started making features, were you surprised at the freedom you could enjoy, in contrast to the more restrictive nature of television?

KR: With the first big feature film I made, *Billion Dollar Brain*, I could afford to have an army on an expanse of ice and have the army fall through the ice; well, of course, you couldn't do that on TV. Feature filmmaking was far freer, and pictorially the sky was the limit, but the budgetary limitations of TV didn't bother me; it meant you were forced to use your imagination even more. When I did a TV film on Claude Debussy, I couldn't afford to re-create turn-of-the-century Paris, so I thought of another way of doing it, which was equally imaginative and possibly added another dimension. I set it in Eastbourne, where he wrote one of his greatest pieces, *La mer*. I combined this with a modern allegory of another of his pieces, a cantata about St. Sebastian, as the center of the drama. I soon realized that although we were an arts program, we came on at 9:30 on a Sunday evening and I had to keep the father of the house from getting up and changing the channel, so before he could get up I wanted to pin him to his seat. So my film about Debussy opens with a girl in a T-shirt crucified, being shot full of arrows by a bunch of other beautiful young girls in T-shirts.

FM: So I am guessing that Dad liked that?

KR: Yes, Dad sat back down and was too tired to get up to change the channel again, so he watched the entire thing. That was my theory anyway, and to a large extent it worked.

FM: Very pragmatic.

KR: There was always a reason for the impacting opening, and that would be explained later in the program. Again, that was just the use of imagination with one idea following on from the other. Whereas, if I had a lot of money at my disposal, I would have probably shot it in Paris and would have not come up with that sequence. However, when I did start making feature films, there was a lot more money to play around with. You have to remember that in the sixties England had the "swinging" reputation in Hollywood, and for almost any idea that you could come up with the sky was the limit. This was not just true for me but also for John Schlesinger or Karel Reisz or any number of filmmakers at that time. You only had to convince two or three people; nowadays you have to convince two or three hundred. Also, it's not just one company these days making the films; it's part of the budget from here, another part from there. You could have ten investors and they could all have a say about what you do with their money, so the limitations today are extraordinary.

FM: Recently you have talked about censorship, particularly in relation to *The Devils*. Given the somewhat protracted tussle with the censor, especially in the seventies, do you feel a sense of satisfaction that the restrictions in relation to film are finally being relaxed, or do you not feel they are being relaxed enough?

KR: I'm not one to talk with any sort of authority on that. In relation to *The Devils*, recently some censored footage from the film was found and incorporated into a documentary. Well, there's quite a reasonable chance that it will be reinstated into the movie and reissued. It's not definite but they are having talks, which is very promising. It had to go before the censor before it was shown on Channel 4 anyway, so there is no problem with the material now appearing in a feature film. I was always fairly lucky with the censors. John Trevelyan [head of the British Board of Film Classification in the late sixties and early seventies] was very good; he stuck his neck out to keep the nude wrestling scene in *Women in Love*. He argued that it wasn't me who put the scene in, it was the author, D. H. Lawrence, so it wasn't for pure sensationalism; it was an integral part of the novel.

FM: Definitely. It was an integral point for the relationship between Oliver Reed and Alan Bates's characters in the film. It's where their friendship really takes off. Do you feel filmmakers should always indulge themselves?

KR: I don't quite know what that means. Films are hard to make, and I think the word "indulge" really leads one to believe that it's an easy sort of business, and it's really extremely difficult. You'll be standing out there in the rain thinking that it's not an easy job being a film director. But the director is the director, and if he feels, for whatever reason, perhaps under great delusion, that he wants that scene and he can get away with it even though it might be questionable in terms of taste, then he should be allowed to do it. It's his movie. But if the committee steps in and says you can't do that because we're going to cut it out, then it's a waste of time.

FM: Do you feel you were always able to make the films you wanted to make in the way you wanted to make them?

KR: I've been pretty lucky in that regard, but as I said, with *The Devils* a very important, climactic scene was cut out. I have had other little scenes cut out here and there, but on the whole I've been pretty fortunate.

FM: How do you feel about being labeled as an iconoclast?

KR: Wasn't Jesus Christ an iconoclast? Oliver Reed used to call me Jesus, so I'm in good company!

FM: It's funny, because when people use the term "iconoclast," they often mean something derogatory, but I think it can sometimes be a positive thing.

KR: Well, I don't believe in sacred cows.

FM: Do you feel you are still learning?

KR: Oh, yes. All the time, and that's the exciting thing. Filmmaking still requires you to be very inventive. I was shooting a scene in my garden last Sunday, and I got my neighbor to turn off his chainsaw, but I hadn't asked him to stop his children playing football. The endless sound of the ball being kicked made it impossible for me to shoot the scene in the way that I had envisaged it. So suddenly I had to think of a new location, move all the equipment, reorganize the whole idea, and start again. It's tiring and it's frustrating, but you have to solve those problems. It's easy to give up, but you have to press on. There's always another way, and you have to use your brain to think what that way is.

FM: Do you have any advice to pass on to young filmmakers?

KR: Just make films. Everyone can do it. Even if young filmmakers don't have a camera of their own, they will know someone who has one. Every other person in the country has got one. For the price of a pint of beer you can buy a tape and shoot a half-hour movie. You can get your friends to help you and end up shooting it for next to nothing.

You do need drive and you must believe in your subject and have no illusions. It's a trial-and-error thing, but once you've shot something, if it hasn't worked, wipe the tape and start over again, but keep at it. There is no excuse these days for someone who wants to make movies; you just need yourself, one tape, and a borrowed camera. Good luck to everyone who has a go; you'll be surprised at the results.

Old Devil: Stephen Armstrong Finds Ken Russell Back among His Muses

Stephen Armstrong / 2005

From *The Guardian* (London), October 1, 2005. Reprinted with permission.

Ken Russell looks out on to the ruffled waters of Coniston. He's sitting on a stone pier beside a granite tombstone commemorating the death of the land speed record breaker Donald Campbell. In front of us, a ramshackle group of artists and local eccentrics seem hell-bent on joining Campbell at the bottom of the lake as they push out a collection of bizarrely decorated boats.

The boats might have floated from one of the more fevered segments of a Russell film. One is draped in tattered gothic mourning robes, another is powered by men with giant, grinning heads. They are part of the Coniston Water Festival's Boat Dressing competition—an event of quaint rural charm until it curled up and died at the end of the 1980s. This year it's been revived by Grizedale Arts, one of the most significant arts organizations in Europe. As a result, the kind of people dressing their watercraft are more inclined to, so to speak, push the boat out.

Russell smiles at the madness. He clearly feels very much at home. Indeed, this once was his home. His Lake District period included the years in the late seventies and early eighties when he dominated British cinema, and although he's not superstitious, his exile from the region coincided with a slump in his fortunes. As it was an acrimonious divorce that forced him out, he's not been back for more than ten years. Today, then, he's keen to reminisce.

"In 1968 I was coming up to scout for locations for a film with Oliver Reed called *Dante's Inferno* about the pre-Raphaelite founder Rossetti's personal crisis," he says. "I drove my Morris up three hundred miles from Notting Hill to Keswick. I got there after dark and when I woke up in the morning and opened the curtains, I looked across the lake and saw God made manifest: Skiddaw mountain. That's what Coleridge said when he first saw it—God made manifest. Of course, he was on opiates at the time."

Russell was so stunned by Skiddaw that he bought a place in the Lake District almost on the spot, paying £10,000 for Coombe Cottage at an auction. At first, he used it as a holiday home with his first wife, Shirley, and his three children. Later, after they divorced, he moved there with his second wife, Vivian. It was at Coombe Cottage that the Catholic faith he had acquired at college began to melt and merge into a sort of animist paganism.

"You look at Skiddaw when the mist is a certain way, and it looks like a vast pair of wings and you think it might actually just fly away." He leans back and sips tea from a Styrofoam beaker. "It's like an impassive god, not caring what you do. You realize you are fortunate just to be in its presence. To see it properly you need to go over to Borrowdale. You could pop into Coombe Cottage and see Vivian while you're there. Knock on the door, say I sent you, and you'll get a nice thick ear."

The landscape had such a hold on him that he shot there whenever he could— putting Cumbrian vistas into *The Devils*, *Women in Love*, and even the rock opera *Tommy*. Roger Daltrey's hang-gliding sequence and a woodland fight between Hells Angels were both filmed around Coniston, although all that's visible in the final cut is the sort of sky and trees you could find near Pinewood Studios.

"I would climb a hill every day," he says. "It's a magic area. I never took drugs here, but Coleridge did. Imagine the impact. Kubla Khan's pleasure-dome wherever you look. I did a program on him while I was here, and one on Wordsworth. I'd found love and I just wanted to show it off."

At the same time, he was losing Vivian. "I spent our time there teaching her how to become a photographer," he grunts. "As soon as she was a master, she said, right, I don't need you anymore, you can fuck off." It's not been as tough to come back as he thought it would, and his fear that he'd feel her presence everywhere has vanished. "I send her a check every month, so you could say we correspond," he quips, finishing his tea.

Later that night, Russell is holding forth in the kitchen of a semiderelict farmhouse high on the hills overlooking Coniston Water. The farmhouse is at the end of a dirt track so perilous that 4 × 4 vehicles need a Forestry Commission license to attempt it. Most people climb up to the property, but Russell gets the 4 × 4 treatment. There's no electricity so, seated in a canvas director's chair, his face is only lit by the orange glow of a roaring fire.

He sips at a glass of red wine and tells his tales to a group of young artists camping out in the house as they prepare to convert it to an arts center. Many of them are in their twenties, and few of them are old enough to have seen his films at the cinema. Nonetheless, they hang on his words, their rapt eyes shining in the firelight.

Russell is at a curious stage in his life. He is struggling with a collapsing career. His scripts are constantly turned down; he is making films with handheld digital cameras, using his garage as a studio; his sci-fi novel *Violation* has been rejected by so many publishers that he's been forced to publish it himself, and his last big movie project—*The Fall of the Louse of Usher*—has been described as unwatchable even by fans.

On the other hand, he is suddenly incredibly influential—especially with today's young artists. Grizedale Arts have been trying to work with him for a couple of years because three of their artists—Jeremy Deller, Lali Chetwynd, and Olivia Plender—cite his films as major sources of inspiration. Deller says *Tommy* is his favorite film.

This is why the artists sit at his feet laughing with glee as he recounts his disastrous marriages, his parlous finances, and his film-set hijinks. They only start to shift uneasily when he talks about a woman he'd spotted that day; a woman he'd been convinced was a prostitute, but who was probably the wife of someone there. Even after the atmosphere cools and Russell has departed, they refuse to condemn his curious erotic imagination. "He's quite a character," the woman's husband says carefully.

The following day we have lunch as Russell prepares for the afternoon's event. He will represent a pioneer of the outdoor movement, Millican Dalton, in a mock contest against an equally eccentric environmental movement called Kibbo Kift, founded by suffragettes, socialists, and the cooperative movement. Dressed in Dalton's typical knee-length shorts and Dumbledore-style hat, he plows through a plate of roast beef with a hefty glass of Shiraz. He used to go into Dalton's cave in Borrowdale to commune with his spirit and identifies with the man's main ideals—romance, freedom, escapism, simplicity, pacifism, and truth. "I'm not sure what he meant by romance, though," he muses. "I don't think it was sexual. Perhaps you had more chance of getting laid in the Kibbo Kift."

Although he's famous for his prickly encounters with the media, today he seems jovial. He puts it down to the drugs he was prescribed after catching MRSA while in hospital for back pain. "They're wonderful," he enthuses, "I don't care about anything anymore. Now I can walk into a room and I'm not intimidated." He doesn't have a reputation as someone who's easily intimidated, I say. "Well, no one likes to let people know they're intimidated, but I always was. The only man who didn't intimidate me was Huw Weldon."

This triggers memories. He has to stop for a few minutes to fight back tears as he talks about Reed. "He was a beautiful man. Everyone who knew him will always defend him. I wish I could say the same thing about myself." But, unlike many seventy-eight-year-olds, discussing the dead brings no thoughts of his own mortality. Even if his body deteriorates so that he can no longer make films, he plans to keep writing—"Maybe I'll be a famous novelist"—and he boasts that he has a jewel-encrusted phone that allows him to talk to God so his path to the afterlife, if there is one, should be smooth.

Later, the Kibbo Kift march to an Elizabethan hunting lodge in curious futuristic costumes. Russell hears their arguments, then praises Millican in a simple, humorous lecture. His team wins the tug of war with ease, spilling Kifters into bales of straw, then it's time for him to show *Dante's Inferno*, the film that started his affair with the lakes.

"What's it like?" someone shouts. "It's a masterpiece!" he cries. And all the young artists roar with laughter, standing about three feet away, as though they're scared to get too close.

Elgar's Ear: A Conversation with Ken Russell

John C. Tibbetts / 2005

From *Quarterly Review of Film Studies* 22, no. 1 (2005): 37–49. Reprinted with permission of Taylor & Francis, Ltd., http://www.tandfonline.com.

"I've used this location many times in my films," Ken Russell says, looking appreciatively about him at the rolling, green meadows of the New Forest. "Somehow, some way, I keep coming back. Look at *The Music Lovers, Valentino, Arnold Bax, The Strange Affliction of Anton Bruckner*, and my new Elgar film, and you can see the wheat fields, the birch trees, the lakes and pine trees that have served me so well."[1]

Ken Russell is on home ground. He and his wife, Lisi, have brought me to their favorite pub, Turfcutters, just a few miles from their home in East Boldre, Brockenhurst. The surrounding verdant fields whisper gently under the westering light of a mild July afternoon. The nicker of several horses reaches our ears from a distant meadow. We are on the edge of the New Forest, a region just above the Isle of Wight, east of Bournemouth and fifteen miles from his native Southampton. The seventy-six-year-old filmmaker was born near here; and after frequent trips back on film projects, he decided in 1972 to settle for good into a rambling, four-hundred-year-old thatched-roof cottage comfortably tucked away off the main roads.

We are talking about Russell's latest film, *Elgar: Fantasy of a Composer on a Bicycle*, which had been recently telecast on London Weekend Television (LWT).[2] Commissioned by old friend and colleague Melvyn Bragg, on the occasion of the twenty-fifth anniversary of Bragg's *South Bank Show*, and narrated by Russell himself, *Elgar: Fantasy of a Composer on a Bicycle* is a delicious Russellian *divertissement*, far removed from the extravagant posturings of his years as the enfant terrible of the British cinema.[3] Yet in many ways it marks a homecoming for Russell. It renews his lifelong association with Bragg.[4] It brings full circle a career distinguished for a series of popular (and frequently controversial) composer films that had been initiated in 1962 by his first *Elgar*, a breakthrough documentary essay that virtually revolutionized the modern British documentary. Since then, Russell had always wanted to return to Elgar and to the Malvern Hills of Elgar Country, just as Elgar himself in middle age had been drawn back to the land of his youth.[5] "Yes, I guess you could say my new film is like coming home," Russell muses, "but it's quite a different film, in its way. The first one was a straight documentary; this is more of a *pointilliste* picture, with episodes organized around Elgar's *Enigma Variations*. And this time I didn't have to skirt some things about his love life." Resembling nothing so much as a charming, albeit quirky home movie, the new Elgar film was shot with digital equipment on a minimal budget, edited by Russell's son Xavier, set in locations familiar to Russell buffs, performed by a cast drawn from neighbors, family, and friends, and fraught with references to scenes and music from his earlier pictures.[6]

The new Elgar film displays a superb economy that both betrays and transcends its obviously limited budget. It has always been an irony that the flamboyant Russell always rose to the occasion when constrained by budgetary and logistical limitations. What could be more charming than the "Fairies and Giants" episode, where music from Elgar's *Wand of Youth* accompanies a procession of children dressed in toy-soldier costumes as they march around the tiny houses and streets of a miniature town? What could be more starkly eloquent of the sweetly collaborative nature of Elgar's relationship with his wife Alice than hearing the words and music of the "In Haven" song from the *Sea Pictures* while in a prolonged shot Elgar and Alice gaze out at us from behind a rainswept window? The film's epilogue is pure Russell in its highly idiosyncratic commentary about Elgar's posthumous celebrity status. Against the setting of the Elgar Birthplace Museum at Broadheath, Russell himself is seen at frame right, silently conversing with a statue of the composer. Panning left, the camera picks up the young, fiercely mustachioed Elgar, in period dress, trundling on his bicycle toward the Museum. As the music from the "Nimrod" episode, the No. 9 of the *Enigma Variations* (which Russell here dubs "Elgar's Ghost"), wells up on the soundtrack, Elgar cycles *through* Worcester Cathedral, gliding down the nave, the pews whipping by in the foreground like so many riffled playing cards. On and on he goes, out the church and back onto the country roads (where, you suspect, he really belongs). "And if you visit Elgar Country today," Russell's narrative voice is saying, "you'll most certainly make contact with Elgar's ghost, should the mood take you, that is. But don't worry, his spirit is benign; though I can't guarantee that his music won't haunt you for the rest of your life."

Clearly, Elgar's music has haunted Russell all *his* life. His new Elgar film reminds us how important music has always been for him.[7] "I heard classical music throughout my childhood," he recalls. "And I first realized at the age of eleven what power there could be when the right music went with the right image. A few years later, I used to give film shows in my dad's garage on a little hand-cranked Pathéscope Ace 9.5-millimeter projector. They generally were Felix the Cat and Charlie Chaplin shorts. Then I realized you could get extension arms for the projector and show feature films. So, one Christmas I looked around for feature movies and found some German Expressionist films, *Metropolis* and *Siegfried*. The one gramophone record I possessed had a march by Grieg on one side and a march by Sir Arthur Bliss from *Things to Come* on the other. I discovered quite by accident that when the modern march by Bliss coincided with *Metropolis*, that the whole screen came alive. And similarly, when Siegfried was slaying the dragon, the Grieg trumpets absolutely brought the scene to life. With the War just starting, it was rather strange that I was showing these films in my dad's garage while we were being bombed by the Hun.[8] But art knows no frontiers, so it didn't worry me too much. But it was ironic that while Siegfried was slaying the fire-breathing dragon on the screen, the sons of Siegfried were raining down incendiary bombs all around us!

"My next big discovery about music came when I was recovering after the War from a nervous breakdown. Back home, I just sat like a vegetable in the armchair. My mother did the vacuuming around me, and the radio would be on, for week after week. One day, something began to impinge on my consciousness. Lo and behold, it was a piece of music. It was such music that I had never heard in my life, and it brought me to. It made me wake up. I thought, I have to find out what this is called! It turned out to be an extract from Tchaikovsky's B-flat minor Piano Concerto. After pumping up the flat tires to my bicycle, which had lain dormant for several months, I pedaled like mad to the nearest record shop and bought the record. And that was the beginning of my 'vision'—hearing music and seeing pictures at the same time. And I suddenly realized that Tchaikovsky's symphonic poems could be minimovies. For instance, when I heard *Romeo and Juliet*, the whole thing flashed before my eyes. Tchaikovsky himself once said that he put his whole life into his *Pathétique* symphony."

Russell came to the BBC in the late 1950s after making a few amateur short films that attracted the attention of Norman Swallow, BBC's assistant head of films. Between 1959 and 1961, working under the tutelage of Swallow and two producers in the BBC's Department of Music and Arts Programmes, Humphrey Burton and Huw Wheldon, Russell made a series of well-received fifteen-minute documentaries about a variety of subjects, including portraits of poets, architects, and the composer Gordon Jacob. But it was his forty-five-minute *Prokofiev: Portrait of a Soviet Composer* (1961), followed by *Elgar* (1962) and *Bartok* (1964), that launched his signature series of composer biopics. He insists they owed nothing to the cycle of composer films that had been coming out of Hollywood in the 1940s and early 1950s.

"I didn't think too much about the big Hollywood movies about composers that were coming out at the time, like that thing about Chopin, *A Song to Remember*.⁹ They seemed like nothing more than nonsense to me. I didn't associate them with art or music. You hear the word 'biopic' used a lot these days. It's become a clichéd term. I think some filmmakers think it's an easy thing to do, but it's not. Too often you never got a sense of the *art*, just people in costumes doddering around. I'm not so interested in the physicality of it all, but the *spiritual* and *poetic* and *creative* side of the subject.

"Later, with Huw Wheldon at the BBC, I was looking to do something quite different. The first music documentary I made for the BBC was on Prokofiev. For my visuals, I used mostly USSR documentaries and movies by Eisenstein. That was all I was allowed to do. I did say to Huw that it would be wonderful to show Prokofiev walking around in exile, very lonely and very disconsolate. Huw said, 'He's dead!' I said, 'Yes, I know he's dead!' He asked me if I had any moving pictures of him; and I said no, no movies. He said, 'It's impossible! We make documentaries here, we want the truth. We can't dress somebody up and pretend he's Prokofiev!' I said, 'I don't see why not; but could I just show his reflection in a pond?' He said, 'Only if it's a muddy pond, and you stir it up!' So, that was that. He did also let me show hands on the piano, because that was almost an abstract kind of image." From here on, with each succeeding project, Russell continued to win a series of small concessions, but always after contending with the formidable Huw Wheldon.¹⁰

"In the next film I did, *Elgar*, he allowed me to show people impersonating Elgar from his boyhood to old age. They could only be seen in medium to medium-long shot, and they weren't allowed to speak. I pushed it further in my next film on Bartók, where I was allowed to show a closeup of someone who purported to be Bartók, the actor Boris Ranevsky; and Boris really did look like him (he was unknown at the time, which helped). But he still wasn't allowed to speak. I allowed myself license to re-create events in Bartók's life, such as when he prowled through the woods with a flashlight looking for insects, and when he took the underground in New York (which he hated). That subway sequence is pretty scary—it scared *me* while I was doing it! And I had fun with the *Bluebeard's Castle* sequence, with the rocket launch and all of that. I was just adding some of my own impressions to what I knew about Bartók. A lot of people ask me where I found those wonderful images of Hungarian peasants on horseback. They were from a famous Hungarian film called *Hortobágy*, which I had seen in London when I was a young lad. It was made by the man who used to run the Academy Cinema in Oxford Street. I like the Bartók film a lot. It had a lot of drama. And the music—well, the music from *The Miraculous Mandarin* is the most sensual, erotic music that I know. That clarinet that comes in three times is pure sex. Bartók was in reality a very sexy dude. The film got really close to the man, I think."[11]

By now, according to colleague Melvyn Bragg, Russell was already garnering considerable attention at the BBC and with the critics.[12]

"Critics were already noticing what I was doing," confirms Russell. "At first, the comments were generally favorable. In fact, the Elgar film proved to be the most popular British television program of the 1960s. It seemed to touch a chord in the English people. It revived Elgar's reputation, since by the 1960s he had been totally neglected or dismissed as a bombastic, Colonel Blimp–type character. I did take care, however, to put right Elgar's feelings about the Great War. His Pomp and Circumstance March, no. 1 had been appropriated for propaganda purposes under the title 'The Land of Hope and Glory.' Jingoistic words were put to it, and he didn't approve of that. He hated that, in fact.[13] But after the appearance of my film, new recordings started to be issued from the record companies, with images from my film on the jackets."

Russell's fourth composer biopic, *The Debussy Film*, holds a particularly important place in his oeuvre, although, unfortunately, it is unavailable for screening.

"My real breakthrough, I suppose, was *The Debussy Film*. I made it clear that it wasn't a biography of Debussy but was about a film company making a *film* about Debussy. So actors were involved, and were identified as such. So, it wasn't merely somebody like Oliver Reed pretending to be Debussy, it was Oliver Reed *acting the part of an actor acting the part of Debussy*. This conceit allowed me to interpret, or 'conduct' the subject of Debussy. Any one of a number of interpretations of the subject can be just as valid as another, I suppose."[14]

Many commentators agree that *Song of Summer*, an imaginative portrait of Frederick Delius, telecast in 1968, is Russell's masterpiece. It relies heavily on the memoirs of Delius' amanuensis, Eric Fenby.[15]

"When I first took on the Delius film, *Song of Summer*, I tried to do it without Eric Fenby, who had been Delius' secretary and amanuensis in the last years of his life. But I couldn't come up with a satisfactory script. It was always too sentimental, hopeless. But when I read Fenby's wonderful book about his association with Delius, I knew he had to be a part of the project, somehow. It was so revealing. While in his early twenties he learned that Delius was blind and paralyzed and still had several works locked in his brain. So Fenby wrote to Delius and offered his services. Delius readily accepted. So this rather naïve fellow from Yorkshire went to France and lived in the Delius house in Grez for four or five years and managed with great difficulty to wrestle three or four masterpieces out of Delius's tortured brain. I spoke to Fenby and got permission to use the book; and he told me some things that weren't in the book, like the fact that Delius had died of syphilis. We went together to Delius' old house, and it became obvious to me that he was very divided in his feelings about Delius, that he loved the music but that he felt his life had been ruined by the man. What was fascinating to me was their method of working. It afforded me a chance to dramatize the very process of composition.

"Fenby never forgot those dictation sessions with Delius. It was a weird process. They would argue and taunt each other and all that. Delius would begin by teasing him—'Well, come along, Fenby; what are we going to do today? Let's take up that piece that you thought we *might* do.' Fenby would reply with the taunt, 'No, Delius, I didn't think it was up to your usual standard.' 'What!?' Delius would splutter, 'you didn't think it was up to my usual standard!—What are you saying?' 'Well, I have to be honest, Delius, though there are some fine things—.' Delius would then try to sing some of the notes and Fenby would exclaim, 'Delius, you're going too fast—I can't keep up!—.' And so on. So I was able to write out in the script this kind of banter and the kind of collaborative process that Fenby described. The actors were able to really get into those scenes.

"I told Fenby he must come along to the shoot, but he said no, he didn't want to interfere with Chris Gable, the actor playing him. But when I told him he was welcome to show up anytime without announcing himself in advance, he did come. He came when we were shooting the scene where Delius is in his chair welcoming the newly arrived Fenby. I remember that scene: Delius demands to know what Fenby's musical background was. And Fenby innocently replies, 'I play for the films, Laurel and Hardy.' Delius explodes, 'LAUREL AND HARDY!?' 'Yes,' says Fenby, not realizing what he was getting into, 'and then I go down to the beach and I listen to the bands playing British music.' Of course, Delius explodes again—'British music!? I don't know British music! There's no such thing! Trust in the Lord! That was the ruin of Elgar, poor man!' At that point in the scene, as I was saying 'Cut!' I heard sobbing. Fenby had arrived, unbeknownst to anyone. He was moved to tears. He said, 'That was exactly how it was—and it was *horrible!*' After the film, Fenby developed a skin complaint of some kind, probably something psychological. He recovered after a year. Then, he came around and asked me for a loan of a hundred pounds. 'I've been asked to come to America to a university close to where I used to work,' he said, 'and I can't afford the fare.' I never saw him again. I did admire the man tremendously, and it was a privilege to meet him. He did feel that his life had been ruined by Delius; that his own composing career had been sacrificed. Who knows how good a composer he might have been? But he did write some good music for a Charles Laughton film, *Jamaica Inn*. He felt that he could have been as good as Benjamin Britten."

If *Song of Summer* marks the apogee of Russell's success and popularity, his next film, the controversial *Dance of the Seven Veils* (1970), aroused such bitter hostilities that his tenure at the BBC was terminated for more than twenty years. The disclaimer issued before the telecast of February 15, 1970, was revealing: "It's been described as a harsh, sometimes violent caricature of the life of the composer, Richard Strauss. This is a personal interpretation by Ken Russell of certain real and many imaginary events in the composer's life. Among them are dramatized sequences about the war and the Nazi persecution of the Jews, which include scenes of considerable violence and horror." Three days before the telecast, Russell was quoted in *Radio Times*: "It's a *comic* strip; it's not a profound, serious, dramatic reconstruction of Strauss' life. I felt it was time to get up off our knees and take a lighter view of someone as an artist. He seemed to lend himself to this sort of treatment."[16] But critics and public alike did not take lightly this depiction of Strauss as a narcissistic, greedy, opportunistic anti-Semite; rather, as critic James Thomas in the *Daily Express* opined: "It was as if a man was being destroyed before the eyes of millions."[17]

"Not since its first broadcast has my *Dance of the Seven Veils* been seen," says Russell, "was it ever shown again, from that day to this. The music publishers freaked out. Maybe it was coincidental, but the next week the BBC held a program of pundits saying that my film was rubbish; that Strauss was never a Nazi; and so forth.[18] There was a huge outcry. Mary Whitehouse wanted to sue me. She found she could only sue the land cable transmitting the program. Then Huw Wheldon made a speech in the Houses of Parliament defending the film and my right to say what I felt. That was a great moment. I have no bitterness about that—if it rains, you get wet. You have to remember that artists like Strauss can be dogmatic and pig-headed, and they override people. Most of the people I've dealt with in films have quite dispassionately sacrificed someone in their way who misunderstood them. It's not nice, but that's how it works."

Yet critical attacks and controversies surrounding Russell's work were just beginning.[19] His theatrical releases, the Tchaikovsky biopic, *The Music Lovers* (1971), *Mahler* (1974), and *Lisztomania* (1975), aroused harsh critical attacks for their free-form, interpretative erotically violent fantasies. Branded by critics as "semiporno," "hyper-Hollywood," and "a monstrosity," Russell offered his own half-mocking assessment of *The Music Lovers*: "It's about a homosexual who falls in love with a nymphomaniac."[20] More than any of his previous films, *The Music Lovers* portrays the artist as an unstable compound of hopelessly Romantic ideals and privately destructive tendencies. "To me, Tchaikovsky [played by Richard Chamberlain] personified nineteenth-century Romanticism," Russell said at the time, "which is based on a death wish. People call me self-indulgent, but he was the most self-indulgent man who ever lived, insofar as all his problems and hang-ups are stated in his music"[22] *Mahler* contains sequences resembling the comic-book caricaturing of *Dance of the Seven Veils*, including images of Mahler as a Jewish Siegfried, his wife Alma as a high-kicking can-can dancer clad in Nazi S.S. leather, and Cosima Wagner as a Storm Trooper in drag. "Elgar apart, Mahler is my favorite composer," Russell wrote in his autobiography, "and I feel we have a lot in common, apart from both being Cancerians and living near a lake surrounded by mighty hills."[22] *Lisztomania* may be the best known, if not the most notorious (even condemned) of all composer biopics. Russell pursued perhaps too zealously the special empathy he felt with Franz Liszt's famous assertion, "Truly great men are those who combine contrary qualities within themselves." Russell conceived the nineteenth-century piano virtuoso, Liszt, as the prototype of today's rock star, confirming the identification by casting Roger Daltrey of the Who as Liszt and bringing in rocker Rick Wakeman to give the musical arrangements a 1970s rock idiom. Writing in *Newsweek*, Jack Kroll dismissed it as a "mad discord of ideas and images" and a "freaked out charade";[23] while Kevin Thomas in the *Los Angeles Times* saw it as "an exhilarating and pleasant wonderment [. . .] *Lisztomania* suggests that it is far more effective for Russell to present the fantasy inspired by the music of his beloved composers as his rather than theirs."[24]

For the last two decades, in between stints in Hollywood for feature films like the science fiction fable *Altered States* (1980), the thriller *Crimes of Passion* (1984), and the erotic *Whore* (1991), Russell has returned to the BBC and to Melvyn Bragg's *South Bank Show* with a new series of composer films—*Portrait of a Composer: Ralph Vaughan Williams* (1984), *The Strange Affliction of Anton Bruckner* (1990), *Arnold Bax* (1992), *The Mystery of Dr. Martinu* (1992)—that mark a return to the subtle, spare style and small-budgeted films of his early years. Far from hindering his concepts and execution, these restrictions have encouraged a kind of imaginative intimacy, whimsy, and personalized expression that had been absent from his more extravagant efforts. "Ken is a brilliant talent," Melvyn Bragg has told the present writer, "and I don't buy in to the idea that late in life he has become some sort of Icarus who, at his height, had suddenly plunged back to earth. When I took over *The South Bank Show*, I welcomed him back. And he's done some cracking films for me."

Russell confirms the highly personal quality of these late films. "All of my recent composer films are like home movies," he confesses, "autobiographical in one way or another. I guess it's fair to say the obvious, that these portraits of composers are in a way self-portraits. It would be pretty fantastic if I didn't have something in common with these artists. I don't stop to analyze myself too much; I just work basically on emotions, not intellect. If an idea comes to me, it comes to me for reasons that I just accept and don't delve into. And didn't Tchaikovsky and Mahler say that their music is autobiographical, too? Anything happens to me, I find a way of getting it into my films. I can't just depend on historical truth, whatever that is. History is bunk.

"For my Vaughan Williams movie I took my family along with me, my wife Viv, and daughter Molly. And I brought with us Vaughan Williams's widow, Ursula. We went on a musical tour of the places that inspired his music—the streets of London, London Bridge, the hills around Lulworth Cove, Stonehenge, the coast of Cornwall—and even argued a little about the meanings behind his music."[25]

Among all his composer biopics, the subject of Arnold Bax, the English composer who at midcentury became Master of the King's Music, is perhaps least familiar to general viewers. There is an elegiac quality to this portrait of a man facing a mid-life crisis, who seeks to recapture the "proud sunlit tumult" of his youth by revisiting—and re-creating—the scene, circumstances, and significance of his 1916 composition, *The Garden of Fand*, based on a Celtic legend. It is likely, suggests Russell, that this music represented for Bax more than just a musical interpretation of a Celtic legend. It may have memorialized a youthful idyll of love with a woman, probably the pianist Harriet Cohen, with whom Bax would have a lifelong relationship. "When I came to make a movie about Sir Arnold Bax, I decided to play him myself. I felt that I *knew* Bax, absolutely.[26] I'm a great fan of his. I financed recordings of his symphonies myself. I also look like him; and I was the same age when I played him. Glenda Jackson got an Emmy for that, I hear. Before I do any artist, I soak myself for maybe ten years in music and research. So, I knew a lot about what was going on in Bax's life when he was writing. I shot some of it at Highcliff, on the beach, and in Hampshire. I used some of the same locations I had used in the Bruckner film to stand in for Austrian landscapes.

"My film about Anton Bruckner caused a lot of comment. People asked me what I think was really wrong with Bruckner; what the hell was this 'numero-mania,' this mania for counting things?[27] I suggest in the film that it was a sexual thing; that he had been 'set up' in some pub with a loose woman, everybody got drunk, and he was ill prepared to deal with the situation. It was a distasteful encounter for him, and it didn't do him any good. The only way he could connect with reality was to treat it as a mass of data, as something to list and count and itemize."

The Mystery of Dr. Martinu is another portrait of an artist suffering from a debilitating psychological trauma. Bohuslav Martinu was a Czech composer who grew up in a tower overlooking his village of Politcka, achieved his first success in the surrealist camp of Paris in the 1920s, fled the Nazis in World War II, and subsequently enjoyed a brief creative resurgence in America when he returned to France before his death in 1959. He often confessed to never feeling "at home" since leaving Czechoslovakia: "I am sick for home and yearn for our hills!" He once said, "My work is that of a Czech tied to my homeland by a cord nothing can cut."[28] Russell clearly found affinities with this classic example of the dispossessed artist. "My film on Bohuslav Martinu was a challenge because I think in many ways his music is very confrontational. I think it's amazingly powerful and evocative and full of hidden imagery. I thought to make out of it a visual psychological study. I did go to his hometown and went inside the tower, where as a boy he and his family lived. He spent most of his childhood in that tower, you know, looking down at the world. And if you go to the top of the tower and look down, as he obviously did every day, the people are just tiny dots. His music sounds like ants busily scurrying around. It also sounds like all the things you see in my film, trains, sewing machines, and machinery, and naked women waving flags. So I just put it all in the film.[29] I'm still not sure about including the film's second half, where the dreams are analyzed. People think I was trying to make my own version of Hitchcock's *Spellbound*, where you lay dreams out on the psychoanalyst's couch and *explain* everything. Well, I don't presume to *explain* Martinu's problems and creative energies, just make some suggestions. You can't take all of that seriously, you know. But he did have a very mixed-up life, with his weird childhood, his wife and various ladies.

"Taking on subjects like this demands I do a lot of research and a lot of listening. If I decide I want to do a film on someone, I become a kind of detective. It's thrilling. I especially remember a moment during the making of *The Music Lovers* where I was trying to re-create something that happened between Tchaikovsky and his wife. I didn't understand just why whatever it was had happened; I couldn't quite fathom it. But when we rehearsed a scene, I suddenly knew what it was. Sometimes if you re-create events, the answer—or *an* answer—just naturally comes out of it. You can't necessarily know it beforehand."

After a sturdy lunch of pork and potatoes at Turfcutters, Russell and his wife bring me back to his cottage, where he had promised to screen for me his own print of *The Debussy Film*. Watching it again after many years released a flood of comments and reminiscences from Russell—particularly at the sight of his daughter, who appears briefly in the role of Debussy's daughter, Chouchou; and of the vital and unpredictable Oliver Reed, who played the composer. "It was a good choice, Oliver as Debussy," Russell remarks quietly. "His performance holds up well today; even when he's calm, there's always that promise of *threat*." Russell pauses a moment; and then—"It was a good way to bring off Debussy. You look at somebody like Debussy, and you see one of the few total geniuses of music. Yet he had faults as a human being. Like all of the composers I've made films about, he had these two sides to him. It's not a tragedy that they can't be reconciled; it's just a fact of existence; there's no reason why they should be reconciled."

Russell admits to many composer projects that so far have proven unworkable for the screen. "There's my Percy Grainger project," he says. "I've written a script about Grainger, but it has never been filmed. You remember that Grainger, Delius's good friend, shows up in *Song of Summer*. He literally drops into the frame. What a character. If you ever get to Melbourne, visit the Percy Grainger Museum, where you'll find drawers full of whips and canes! Think about that for a moment! Another project I've been thinking about is Dvořák —that time he spent in New York. Imagine him there, near the Bowery, surrounded by black jazz musicians; or at Carnegie Hall; or with Buffalo Bill; or visiting Niagara Falls and Iowa farm country.

"The film medium sometimes just won't work for this sort of thing," he continues. "There's radio. I once wrote a script about Alexander Scriabin that started out as a film script. Scriabin always said he was going to write a symphony to end the world, you know. He envisioned thousands of performers and dancers and loving couples and scents and God knows what else. Bells would be suspended from clouds in the Himalayas. The symphony would end with him making love to the most beautiful girl in the world, atop the tallest pile of cushions in the world. And at the very moment he was going to climax with the girl, the orchestra would reach the greatest crescendo any orchestra had ever achieved—and then the world would come to an end![30] Well. I thought, 'That's pretty good stuff! Big budget!' I was talking to a producer about it, and he suggested I not do it for the movies but for *radio*. 'You can do all that just by suggestion,' he told me. 'If you want a thousand mountain peaks, and thousands of bells, and thousands of Russian cavalrymen galloping across the steppes—whatever you want—we just get out the old coconuts and it's no problem.' So, I changed the Scriabin script into a radio piece. I did one other piece like that, on the composer Kelèbey (you know, the guy who wrote 'In a Persian Market'). He had a terribly interesting life; but it was a lightweight affair."

The late thinning afternoon light slants across the tree line, outlining each branch and leaf with a pale, golden glow. I have a train to catch. Russell backs his car out of the garage and gestures me inside for the trip to the Brockenhurst station. As he drives, Russell suddenly remembers something about his new Elgar film.

"I'm always thinking, how in hell do you visualize a moment of musical creativity? Inspiration comes only in flashes, I suppose; and I've been trying all my life to get that on film. You know, the location of the Malvern Hills played an important part in Elgar's creative spark. So I knew I had to show these hills in *Elgar: Fantasy of a Composer on a Bicycle*. But what do you do? Just photograph hills? It's so boring! I did manage to come up with one idea that I thought would look great on film: Elgar was a great kite flyer, and in my first film, I showed him and his daughter flying a kite. Now, after all these years, I thought, I can show a scene like that in color. It struck me how wonderful it would be to show a kite in the shape of an *ear*, and it would be *Elgar's* ear, 10,000 feet up in the sky, listening to the birds, to the hills, absorbing everything. But I was told the aerodynamics of an ear would not be conducive to flight! Pity."

Indeed, no such scene can be found in the new Elgar film. But as I boarded the train back to London, I was intrigued to think that somewhere, high above the Malvern Hills there floats an enormous ear, Elgar's ear, tethered by the slimmest thread to the head of the listening Ken Russell.

Notes

1. Unless otherwise indicated, all remarks by Ken Russell are from the present author's interview, July 13, 2003, East Boldre, Brockenhurst, England.

2. A recent discussion of the film can be found in John Gardiner, "Variations on a Theme of Elgar: Ken Russell, the Great War, and the Television 'Life' of a Composer," *Historical Journal of Film, Radio and Television* 23, no. 3 (August 2003): 195–209.

3. Useful overviews and commentaries on Russell's biopics can be found in the following books and articles: John Baxter, *An Appalling Talent: Ken Russell* (London: Michael Joseph, 1973); Stephen Farber, "Russellmania," *Film Comment* 11, no. 6 (November–December 1975): 40–47; Joseph Gomez, *Ken Russell* (London: Frederick Muller, 1976); Joseph Gomez, "*Mahler* and the Methods of Ken Russell's Films on Composers," *Velvet Light Trap* 4 (1975): 45–50; Ken Hanke, *Ken Russell's Films* (Metuchen, NJ: Scarecrow Press, 1984); Robert Phillip Kolker, "Ken Russell's Biopics," *Film Comment* 9, no. 3 (May–June 1973): 42–45; Gene D. Phillips, *Ken Russell* (Boston: Twayne, 1979). See also Diane Rosenfeldt, *Ken Russell: A Guide to References and Resources* (Boston: G. K. Hall, 1978). Russell himself has written about his work in several volumes: *Altered States: The Autobiography of Ken Russell* (New York: Bantam, 1991); *The Lion Roars: Ken Russell on Film* (Boston: Faber and Faber, 1993); and *Directing Film: From Pitch to Premiere* (London: B. T. Batsford, 2000).

   The following is a chronological listing of Ken Russell's composer biopics: *Prokofiev: Portrait of a Soviet Composer* (1961), *Elgar* (1962), *Bartok* (1964), *The Debussy Film* (1965), *Song of Summer* [Delius] (1968), *The Dance of the Seven Veils* [Richard Strauss] (1970), *The Music Lovers* [Tchaikovsky] (1971), *Mahler* (1974), *Lisztomania* (1975), *Ralph Vaughan Williams* (1984), *The Strange Affliction of Anton Bruckner* (1990), *Arnold Bax* (1992), *The Mystery of Dr. Martinu* (1992), *Classic Widows* [William Walton, Bernard George Stevens, Benjamin Frankel, Humphrey Searle] (1995), and *Elgar: Fantasy of a Composer on a Bicycle* (2002). Russell has also produced *The ABC of British Music*, an overview of classical and pop British composers and musicians. At this writing, Russell has entered negotiations with Melvyn Bragg concerning a possible project about Antonin Dvořák.

4. Unless otherwise noted, all quotations from Melvyn Bragg are taken from two interviews with the present author, conducted at Television Center, London, in 1977 and on July 21, 2003. Melvyn Bragg (Lord Bragg of Wigton) is controller of arts for London Weekend Television (LWT), and he supervises arts programming for four channels in British broadcasting, ITV, BBC1, BBC2, and Channel 4. His association with Ken Russell began in 1965 at the BBC, where they cowrote the script of *The Debussy Film*

(1965). Their next project was a biopic about Tchaikovsky, *The Music Lovers*. Another script, *Nijinsky*, was begun but never completed. Bragg worked as a script consultant for Russell's *Women in Love*: "What I did on that was to go through the Lawrence book with Ken and indicate the things in it that seemed absolutely essential, the key scenes," recalls Bragg. "We talked it over in detail." As producer/editor of *The South Bank Show* for London Weekend Television, Bragg has commissioned and broadcast many of Russell's composer-related productions, including *Ralph Vaughan Williams*, *The Strange Affliction of Anton Bruckner*, *Arnold Bax*, and, most recently, *Elgar: Fantasy of a Composer on a Bicycle* (2002).

5. Despite the success of *Elgar*, Russell purportedly was not satisfied. "The film was all too lovely, like a TV commercial for the Malvern Hills! I was perhaps too much in love with the man's music to see what really produced it." Fifteen years later, in 1977, Russell was talking of a remake, in which he promised to show "the darker side of his life as well as the lyrical, colorful side . . . this time I would want to depict the complete man, 'warts and all,' as they say" (quoted in Phillips, 39).

6. There are many allusions to Russell's 1962 Elgar film—the affectionately gentle tone, recurring images of the composer (James Johnston) bicycling through the Malverns to the music of the "Introduction and Allegro for Strings," the kite flying with his daughter Carice, the ironic juxtaposition of images of wounded soldiers to the "Pomp and Circumstance" music; and the quotations from *The Dream of Gerontius*, to name just a few. Other scenes bring us some new thoughts about Elgar, rendered in the chamber style of Russell's later composer films. For example, unlike the first film, there are now hints, derived from the musical portraits in the *Enigma Variations* (that most frankly programmatic of Elgar's symphonic works) that Elgar enjoyed relationships (probably platonic) with other women in his life besides the dutiful and loyal Alice (portrayed here by Elize Russell and musically evoked by No. 1, "C.A.E."). Excerpts from the No. 10 ("Dorabella") enhance romantic scenes with Dora Penny, a young student whose stutter is cleverly captured in the tripping patterns of the notes; and the No. 13 ("Romanza") evokes the ill-fated romance with Helen Weaver, Elgar's first love, whose premature death is visualized a la Millais's painting "Ophelia" (itself a reference to Russell's biopic about the Rossetti circle, *Dante's Inferno*). Other source music, excerpts from *Falstaff* and the cadenza of the Violin Concerto, accompany, respectively, a picnic scene with Rosa Burley, one of Carice's school teachers, and a fantasy image of a gossamer-clad young female dancing along a beach (so reminiscent of the *Garden of Fand* episode from the Bax film). Russell suggests these women—like the dreamlike figures that haunted Tchaikovsky, Martinu, and Bax—represented the youthful ideals of love that had been thwarted by Elgar's thoroughly respectable, if not entirely romantic, marriage.

7. Russell has recounted events from his childhood in several autobiographical publications. See the aforementioned *Altered States: The Autobiography of Ken Russell*, *The Lion Roars*, and *Directing Film*.

8. Russell recreates these childhood memories in amusing fashion in his film *Russell on Russell*, telecast on Melvyn Bragg's *The South Bank Show*.

9. *A Song to Remember* was a Columbia picture, directed by Charles Vidor and starring Cornel Wilde as Frederic Chopin and Merle Oberon as George Sand. Released in 1945, it garnered many favorable reviews. However, writing in the New York *Herald Tribune* on January 26, 1945, critic Otis L. Guernsey voiced serious objections: "*A Song to Remember* is not a motion picture to remember. Its two-hour Technicolor contemplation of Frederic Chopin's life is a gilded screen biography whose hero conforms

to all the Hollywood conventions governing historical celebrities. . . . Such liberties may be taken with historical details if the cause of drama is served thereby—but fiction has not turned out to be more stimulating than truth in the glossy monotone of *A Song to Remember*."

10. Quaint as it might seem nowadays, producers Norman Swallow, Humphrey Burton, and Huw Wheldon followed BBC strictures of the 1950s in strongly objecting to Russell's desire to use actors to impersonate composers. "This kind of thing would be much more effective if the people concerned were *suggested* rather than literally seen," wrote Swallow in a memo to the head of films, dated April 7, 1959 (BBC Written Archives, Reading, File T32/1, 001/1). Wheldon, likewise, warned that such dramatizations could result in a product that "will seem hollow, like cardboard, as most of them do" (quoted in John Baxter, 122). However, Russell gradually won concessions. In his *Prokofiev* (1961), for example, he was allowed to photograph an actor's reflection in a pool of water; next, for *Elgar* (1962) he was permitted to use several actors in long shot (but without dialogue) to impersonate the composer as a youth, a young man, and in middle age; and for his third composer film, *Bartok* (1964), he photographed actor Boris Ranevsky in closeup (but again, without dialogue). Melvyn Bragg recalls: "All this must sound silly now, but it was a very real problem for us to overcome in those days. The BBC's argument was, 'You'll break the faith with the audience, how can they believe any of it?'" *The Debussy Film* (1965) marked the first time an actor (Oliver Reed) impersonated a composer and spoke lines.

11. In the present writer's opinion, *Bartok*, while little known or remembered today, is one of Russell's finest achievements. It deals primarily with Bartók's years as an émigré in New York City, from 1940 through 1945.

12. When Bragg came to the BBC, Russell was already its "star turn." "He had made lots of acclaimed films," Bragg says, "particularly the *Elgar*, which was already regarded as a landmark. He was considered the man who could make *films* at the BBC, as opposed to the standard 'programmes,' which were heavily influenced by radio. Having a man who could make *films* was rather unexpected for them." Indeed, according to an audience research report conducted by *Monitor* on June 25, 1964, the telecast of *Bartok* "aroused plenty of active interest (to some degree hostile, but chiefly of a very appreciative kind) among viewers in the sample audience. Although the eroticism of some scenes, like the "Mandarin" scene, was singled out as "very distasteful to some viewers," the report concluded that "the quality of Ken Russell's film-making was the subject of very warm praise and, indeed, the photography throughout was noted as most expressive of atmosphere and mood" (BBC Written Archives, Reading. File VR/64/296).

13. In the wartime scenes of *Elgar*, newsreel footage of cheering crowds and proud military processions is accompanied by the music of Elgar's *Land of Hope and Glory*. The film argues, however, that Elgar's patriotic fervor turns to disillusionment with the carnage of war. Accordingly, as the music continues, these jingoistic images are succeeded by shots of slaughter and mutilation (including a procession of blinded and wounded soldiers, marching in a tragically ironic counterpoint to the march music). Protests were raised in the press and by Carice Elgar Blake, Elgar's daughter, insisting this was a distortion of her father's patriotism. Producer Huw Wheldon forced Russell to curtail the length of this sequence, declaring: "It is Elgar's beliefs that counted, not Ken's or mine. And on this Ken and I, as we frequently did, had what you might call an editorial row" (quoted in Baxter, 122).

14. *The Debussy Film* is the first of Russell's many self-reflexive interrogations into the ambiguity of histori-cal fact and artistic interpretation. The director and actors of the film-within-a-film debate issues concerning biographical fact and dramatic interpretation. By extension, this reflects Russell's own struggles to make *his* Debussy film. Thus, in both the film and the film-within-a-film, historical fact, dramatic reenactment, and production history overlap and interpenetrate to the extent that one is sometimes indistinguishable from the other. Any confusion in identifying which is which is entirely to the point.

15. For Eric Fenby's accounts of his association with Delius, see his *Delius as I Knew Him* (first published in 1936; revised in 1981). He supplemented the book with the aforementioned *Delius* (1971) and an article, "Delius," in *Music and Musicians*, 22, no. 262 (June 1974), 26–28.

16. BBC Written Archives, Reading. File T53/159/1.

17. BBC Written Archives, Reading. File T53/159/1.

18. The debate over the degree to which Strauss subscribed to and promoted Nazi ideology continues to this day. Indeed, at a 1992 Bard Festival devoted to Strauss, several biographers and commentators gathered to sift through the arguments, pro and con. Although Strauss never officially became a Nazi, he occupied under Goebbels the post of director of the Reich Music Chamber from 1934 to 1935; and unlike his colleagues Kurt Weill, Arnold Schoenberg, Ernst Krenek, and Hanns Eisler, he chose to remain in Germany throughout the war. An assessment by Leon Botstein at Bard concludes that Strauss was guilty more of personal, rather than political, accommodation: "Here was a man who, on the one hand, was very wise, very profound—a man who could write masterpieces like *Die Frau ohne Schatten* and the *Metamorphosen*—but who chose at this point to put blinders on, not only in his personal life, but in his public life. He really sank to the lowest common denominator of behavior—greed, envy, and politi-cal collaboration." Quoted in John Tibbetts, "Richard Strauss Re-Examined," *American Record Guide* 55, no. 6 (November–December 1992), 13. See also Michael Kater, *Composers of the Nazi Era: Eight Portraits* (New York, 2000), 211–63.

19. Looking back on his career, Russell has described his critics as "unspeakable reviewers," as a "bigoted lot" for whom attacks on his work has become a "blood sport." "Having been pursued for years by unspeakable reviewers," he noted, "perhaps I have developed a taste for blood myself." See *The Lion Roars*, p. 151.

20. Who knows if Russell really said this to the studio's "suits"? Certainly, he has quoted himself to this effect many times. See *Altered States*, p. 56.

21. Quoted in Baxter, p. 183.

22. Russell, *Altered States*, p. 135. Indeed, there are some striking parallels between Russell and Mahler: both men converted to Catholicism, both fervently believed in the programmatic implications of music, both have been preoccupied with themes of death, both have created works that are unstable blends of spiritual ecstasy and carnal banality, and both have endured hostile attacks on their work. Alex Ross's description of Mahler's music could well stand in for Russell's films: "Everyone knows his swooning intensity of emotion, not only the famous grandeurs and sufferings, but also the intermedi-ate states of waltz-time languor, kitsch-drenched sweetness and sadness, medieval revelation, military

rancor, dissonant delirium, adagio lament." See Alex Ross, "Mahlermania," *New Yorker*, September 4, 1995, 89–90.

23. Jack Kroll, "Russellmania," *Newsweek*, October 20, 1975, 99.

24. Richard Eder, "Screen: 'Lisztomania,'" *New York Times*, October 11, 1975, n.p.

25. Each location sequence is keyed either to the composer's nine symphonies or to several of his other well-known works (*The Fantasy on a Theme of Thomas Tallis*, "The Song of the Lark Ascending," etc.). Occasionally Russell and Ursula Vaughan Williams dispute the meanings behind the music. For example, when Ursula rebukes Russell's programmatic interpretations of the Second ("London") Symphony, Russell retorts, "But it's got a lot of naturalistic ingredients, like trams and a lavender girl crying her wares; and you can hear the beggars rattling the coins in their hats!" Ursula scoffs, "Maybe it's just a horse's harness!" Russell replies, rather lamely, "It's a very beautiful sound, anyway."

26. Bax is another of Russell's artists whose clumsy attempts to cling to impossible ideals, to sustain the fantasies of lost youth and love, are doomed to failure. Watching Russell act out this role cannot help but suggest that he is enacting similar struggles in his own life. The difference between Russell and Bax, of course, is that whereas Bax ceased his search, Russell continues. Bax is not "the last great Romantic artist," as Russell describes him in the film's prologue. Rather, Russell may well lay claim to that title.

27. *Bruckner* is also essentially a chamber drama, with only three characters, Bruckner (Peter MacKriel), a beautiful nurse named Gretel (Catherine Nielsen), and her male companion, Hans. Bruckner arrives at what seems to be a sanitarium tucked away in the forest, where his affliction of "numeromania," or the obsessive impulse to count things, is cured by the kindly, semierotic ministrations of the lovely Gretel. It is true that as a result of three nervous breakdowns, in 1867, 1887, and 1891, Bruckner appears to have sidestepped reality, falling into an obsession with numbers. He kept lists of the numbers of prayers said each day, the numbers of dances with girls, the number of statues in the park, etc. "He was obsessed with the need to discover the numbers, characteristics, and substance of inanimate objects," declares biographer Derek Watson, "such as the ornamental tops of the municipal towers in Vienna." See Derek Watson, *Bruckner* (New York: Simon and Schuster, 1996), x. Yet here, contends commentator Robin Holloway, was a man with an unflinching belief in God, who possessed a "colossal drive to create," and within whose textbook psychoses lay "one of the mightiest music-machines ever known." See Robin Holloway, "A Colossal Drive to Create," *Times Literary Supplement*, May 8, 1998, 19.

28. Quoted in Brian Large, *Martinu* (London: Gerald Duckworth, 1975), p. 101.

29. Subtitled "A Revelation by Ken Russell," *The Mystery of Dr. Martinu* is a psychological detective story about a man searching for clues to his lost identity, a breezy blend of the dime-store psychologizings of Hitchcock's *Spellbound* and the narcissistic fantasies of Jean Cocteau's *Blood of a Poet* (with a dash of Hitchcock's *Vertigo* thrown in). The first half assaults the unprepared viewer with a bewildering barrage of seemingly randomly connected images dominated by the recurring shots of a tower—a lighthouse—and a hand covered with crawling ants. The second half has the amnesia-suffering Martinu (Patrick Ryckart) and a psychiatrist, Professor Mirisch (Martin Friend), struggling to interpret these images. Music from Martinu's Sixth Symphony predominates throughout. Russell finds in this music

aural connotations of the church tower from which the boy Martinu gazed down at the villagers far below. "From my room in the tower, the whole of Politcka seemed to be populated with ants," Martinu tells Professor Mirisch, "all scurrying about their business. . . . It was always quite a shock to come down to earth." Such early impressions had a lasting impact on Martinu and his music, as Russell found out when he visited Politcka.

30. The work in question is probably Scriabin's *Le poeme de l'extase* ("Poem of Ecstasy"), his Fourth Symphony, first performed in 1908. Scriabin supplied sectional subtitles in French detailing the intermediate states leading to a final musical "orgasm," represented by fifty-three consecutive bars of C major.

Ken Russell Interview:
The Last Fires of Film's Old Devil

Stuart Jeffries / 2011

From *The Guardian*, April 29, 2011. Reprinted with permission.

Ken Russell is leaning on his stick outside the Pebble Beach restaurant in Barton-on-Sea, Hampshire, while his fourth wife parks the car. "Thanks for recognizing me," he says as I shake his hand. It would be hard not to. Russell is wearing open-toed sandals, red trousers pulled up so far over his waist they're bearing down on his nipples, and stripy shirt, while his big florid face is topped by a rage of gray hair.

But today, Russell, now eighty-four, has the air of a last-act Lear, or Tigger unbounced. Two weeks ago he suffered a stroke; this is only his second outing from the New Forest hospital where he's been recuperating. After greeting me, he looks rheumily out into the middle distance, forestalling conversation. Lisi Tribble, that fourth wife, helps him shuffle to our table. Diners furtively view our procession. Tribble carries a star-spangled wizard's robe that Russell recently wore in a film about Aleister Crowley, the occultist nicknamed the Great Beast. She's a determinedly upbeat and chatty foil to the wounded beast. The photographer and I trail in their wake like minor officiants.

We're meeting because Russell's notorious film *The Devils* will be shown in a rare uncut screening on Sunday at the East End film festival. Filmgoers will be able to savor its so-called "rape of Christ" sequence in which seventeenth-century French Ursuline nuns defile a statue of Jesus during an orgy—not to mention the scene in which Sister Jeanne (Vanessa Redgrave) masturbates with a charred bone from a burned priest played by Oliver Reed. Plenty of other sequences kept censors the world over in business. *The Devils* had the singular fate of winning a silver ribbon for best foreign film from the Italian National Syndicate of Film Journalists in 1972, while being banned throughout Italy.

After Russell orders a bottle of Sauvignon blanc, I ask what he remembers about making *The Devils* forty years ago. "Nothing," he replies. "I have short-term memory loss." "You don't have long-term memory loss," says Tribble sensibly. Surely, I suggest, you must remember that after the *Evening Standard*'s Alexander Walker called *The Devils* "monstrously indecent," you hit him with a rolled-up copy of his newspaper? "I wish it had been an iron bar," he says.

"He usually thinks horrible thoughts about his critics," Tribble says.

"I thought him to death," Russell replies.

Certainly, Russell seems to outlive his foes. "Yeah—don't cross Ken," Tribble says. Russell jerks his chin in approval.

You directed another film the same year, I prompted him. *The Boy Friend*, starring Twiggy, a musical comedy that was cleansing sorbet to *The Devils*' main course of lust and gore. "Did I?" And this was the year after your adaptation of D. H. Lawrence's *Women in Love* triumphed at the Oscars. (Glenda Jackson won Best Actress award, and cinemagoers were transfixed by Oliver Reed and Alan Bates wrestling in the nude.) Was *Women in Love* your signature film? Russell waves away the question and orders fish-and-chips.

Perhaps more *Devils*-related questions will get more in the way of response. Russell's film was adapted from Aldous Huxley's 1952 nonfiction novel *The Devils of Loudun*, as well as John Whiting's follow-up 1960 play, *The Devils*. They were all inspired by the notorious case of supposed demonic possession in seventeenth-century France, in which a charismatic Catholic priest, Urbain Grandier, was accused of bewitching nuns. The accusation was trumped up by Richelieu as an excuse to destroy a Protestant stronghold.

Russell takes even more liberties with this material than Huxley. Why portray the king as a cross-dressing homosexual who shoots Protestants dressed as birds in his royal park for fun? "Because that's exactly as I saw him," says Russell.

In among *The Devils*' manifold Pythonesque moments, Oliver Reed is the standout as Grandier, turning in a performance both erotically charged and nobly restrained. Do you think Reed's restraint juxtaposes powerfully with other performances in the film? "He was very restrained, yes. He was such a presence," Russell says. "He was the most beautiful man on the Earth," says Tribble. "And in lots of films he was your alter ego," she tells her husband. "He had quite the barrel chest." Russell, gamely, puffs up his own by way of reply.

Russell mentions he was inspired by one particular line in Huxley's book. "The exorcism of sister Jeanne," wrote Huxley, "was equivalent to rape in a public lavatory." Hence the film's vision of Loudun as a pristine, white-stone city and the convent as clad in white tiles (Derek Jarman designed the sets). Russell recalls the film's final shot: "The girl goes up the hill of broken bricks." The girl (Grandier's recently widowed wife) walks over Loudun's ruins into a landscape in which the only objects are posts topped by carriage wheels, on which Protestant corpses turn in the wind. "Polanski is said to have been inspired by that shot for the last scene of *The Pianist*," Tribble says.

Russell then suggests *The Devils* is a religious film that takes inspiration from his own Catholic faith. "It's about the degradation of religious principles," he says. "And about a sinner who becomes a saint."

Appropriately, for a sinner who became a saint, Russell had to cut his own film to ensure it got even an "X" certificate. Out went the "rape of Christ." The pubic hair had to go for the US censor. Surely there was on-screen pubic hair when Reed and Bates went mano a mano in *Women in Love*? How could it be a problem in *The Devils*? "That was men's pubic hair, not women's," says Tribble.

Tribble and Russell met in Charlotte, North Carolina, in the early seventies. He came to town for a screening of his 1972 film *Savage Messiah*, and she was working at the box office. She already loved his work. Why? "The way he expresses the truth of emotional pain with such energy." Russell asked her to appear in his 1975 film *Lisztomania*, but her mum wouldn't let her. A quarter of a century and three wives later, he married her.

"He's always needed beautiful women," she says. "Haven't you, dear?" Russell nods and then winks at me. The old devil. "If you look at his films, there is regularly an afflicted man saved by a woman."

Where did this come from? "Southampton," Russell says, curtly. He's referring to his upbringing in the city of departures and arrivals, one to which he says he never really belonged. "What did you say when your mother found you dancing naked to Stravinsky in the living room?" prompts Tribble. "Like a nice cup of tea, Ken?" retorts Russell with what his mum said to him. But she wasn't the problem. "Your dad was brutal and undermining," says Tribble. "What was it he said when you told him you wanted to be a dancer?" Russell: "I don't know what they'll think about that in St. Mary's."

Russell says he spent much of his youth in the cinema with his mum, eluding his dad—but with a typical little-boy's disdain for her choice of romantic movies. "I used to say to her when we got to the cinema, 'It's not going to be love?' 'No, Ken.' But it always was," he says ruefully. "She'd say: 'So listen to the organ.'" Occasionally, he went on his own. "A man felt my leg during *Pinocchio*," he recalls. "I saw *Secret of the Loch* [the 1934 Nessie flick] on my own. They seemed to use a plucked chicken for the monster. Never in my life have I been so frightened. I ran out of the cinema."

As a teenager, he joined the Merchant Navy, ostensibly to find Dorothy Lamour (from the Crosby-Hope *Road* movies). "When he realized she wasn't in the South Seas, he had a breakdown," says Tribble. This sounds like a cock-and-bull story, but Russell adds: "I did have a breakdown. Listening to Tchaikovsky cured me." Which Tchaikovsky? "B-flat minor. Solomon." He means the Piano Concerto no 1.

Russell is exhausted and can only just be persuaded to pose for photos. We stand on the terrace, with its view of yachts on a silver sea and the Isle of Wight behind. This is Hampshire on Easter Saturday, but it looks like festival time at Cannes. Tribble drapes her husband in the Aleister Crowley robe. Russell leans on his cane, like a theosophical Fred Astaire.

We say our farewells. I tell Russell I hope he's well enough to attend the screening of *The Devils*. "I don't know what he's talking about," he says to Tribble. She goes off to get the car to drive him back to hospital. Did he really not understand, or was he just being cantankerous? Let's hope the latter. Better Ken Russell the old devil than anything less.

Index

About the Editor

Barry Keith Grant is professor emeritus of film studies at Brock University, Ontario, Canada. He is author or editor of many books, including *Fritz Lang: Interviews*, published by University Press of Mississippi, and his work has appeared in numerous anthologies and journals. An Elected Fellow of the Royal Society of Canada, he serves as the editor of the film and media studies list for Wayne State University Press.

Printed in the USA
CPSIA information can be obtained
at www.ICGtesting.com
CBHW030524150724
11209CB00015B/56

9 781496 851833